RE-VISIONING MYTH

Manchester University Press

Re-visioning myth

Modern and contemporary drama by women

Frances Babbage

Manchester University Press

Manchester and New York

*distributed in the United States exclusively
by Palgrave Macmillan*

Published by Manchester University Press
Oxford Road, Manchester M13 9NR, UK
and Room 400, 175 Fifth Avenue, New York, NY 10010, USA
www.manchesteruniversitypress.co.uk

Distributed in the United States exclusively by
Palgrave Macmillan, 175 Fifth Avenue, New York,
NY 10010, USA

Distributed in Canada exclusively by
UBC Press, University of British Columbia, 2029 West Mall,
Vancouver, BC, Canada V6T 1Z2

British Library Cataloguing-in-Publication Data
A catalogue record for this book is available from the British Library

Library of Congress Cataloging-in-Publication Data applied for

ISBN 978 0 7190 6752 5 hardback

First published 2011

The publisher has no responsibility for the persistence or accuracy of URLs for any external or third-party internet websites referred to in this book, and does not guarantee that any content on such websites is, or will remain, accurate or appropriate.

Typeset
by Carnegie Book Production, Lancaster
Printed and bound by
CPI Group (UK) Ltd, Croydon, CR0 4YY

In memory of my parents,
Stephana and Dennis

Contents

Acknowledgements ix
Introduction 1

1 The lie of the land 10

Theorising myth 10

Re-visioning myth 21

Staging myth: Hella Haasse's *A Thread in the Dark* 32

2 Political acts 48

Furiously funny: *The Same Old Story* and *Medea*
of Franca Rame and Dario Fo 56

'And she stopped the world': Sarah Daniels's
Neaptide 73

3 Out of character 93

Nothing sacred: Maureen Duffy's *Rites* 103

'I don't know what got into me': Caryl Churchill
and David Lan's *A Mouthful of Birds* 111

Making silence speak: Timberlake Wertenbaker's
The Love of the Nightingale 124

4 Stages of subjectivity 139

The voices within: Serena Sartori, Renata
Coluccini and *Demeter Beneath the Sand* 146

Hélène Cixous and the scene of the unconscious: *The Name of Oedipus: Song of the Forbidden Body*   162

The scene of history: Cixous's *The Perjured City, or The Awakening of the Furies*   174

5   Sites of experience: myth re-vision at the end of the century   187

Shock treatment: Sarah Kane and *Phaedra's Love*   196

'I've got the feeling we'll be eternal': Hrafnhildur Hagalín's *Easy Now, Electra*   210

Coda   Many Medeas: women alone   229

References   239

Index   258

Acknowledgements

First of all I thank the many playwrights and practitioners whose work has inspired me and which is featured in this study. I am especially grateful to Renata Coluccini, Serena Sartori, Gilla Cremer and Hrafnhildur Hagalín, all of whom responded in detail to my questions and in many cases allowed me access to unpublished material that has proved invaluable. Thanks also to Marya Mazor, Lena Simic, Fiona Templeton, Jill Greenhalgh and Julia Dobson for variously assisting my work. I am grateful for help given by the (former) Theatre Museum in London; the National Theatre of Iceland, Reykjavik; and King's College London, where the archive of Maureen Duffy is held. I am hugely indebted to those who have read parts of my work in draft form, especially Marcus Nevitt, Bill McDonnell, Bridget Escolme and Steve Bottoms; their astute comments and suggestions have greatly strengthened the end result. I am equally appreciative of the friends and colleagues who have supported me personally and professionally, especially Bridget Escolme, Jane Plastow, Angela Wright, Steve Nicholson, Sue Vice, Samantha Matthews, Terry O'Connor, Bob Godfrey, Margaret Llewellyn-Jones, George Savona, Franc Chamberlain and Samantha Beere. My thanks go too to Geraldine Cousin and Viv Gardner, both of whom encouraged me greatly in the very earliest stages of this research. I would also like to acknowledge the scholars, too numerous to single out as individuals, whose research continues to inform my own.

I would like to thank the Arts and Humanities Research Council (AHRC) for funding a period of research leave that contributed crucially to this book's research and writing. I am equally grateful to the School of English Literature, Language and Linguistics at the University of Sheffield for supporting me in completion of the final stages. Huge thanks too to Matthew Frost and Kim Walker and all at Manchester University Press for their work towards publication.

Finally, I thank my family. I acknowledge with deep gratitude all the love and support I received in their lifetimes from my parents. Above all, thanks to Marcus and Samuel, although neither precisely speeded the project to its conclusion: the former, as my severest critic; the latter, a source of endless happy distraction.

Introduction

In December 2004, Marina Carr's *By the Bog of Cats* opened at the Wyndham's Theatre in London, directed by Dominic Cooke. The first image was arresting: actress Holly Hunter, as Carr's 'Celtic Medea' Hester Swane, made her way across a white stage, suggestive of icy bog lands, tugging the heavy corpse of a black swan. Hunter, an established Hollywood star, was the main attraction for many in the audience. And she was hugely striking, tiny but wiry and muscular, dressed in ragged black, her face half-hidden by matted hair. Then she spoke: and it was impossible not to be equally startled by her voice or, more prosaically, her accent, a peculiar and inharmonious coupling of thick 'central Irish' with native Texan twang. The impression was extraordinary, Hunter the locus of so many meanings: in that moment, she seemed to drag behind her not just the swan's body but the legacy of classical drama, ancient myth, Carr's Irish heritage and her own professional career. Reviews of *By the Bog of Cats*' London premiere – which, though inevitably 'divided', tended on the whole more to criticism than praise – focused recurrently on the same two issues: first, how far short the play fell of Euripides' original; second, the curiosity that was Hunter's accent. Responses to the latter included an observation from the *Independent* that the actress appeared to be 'from Louisiana and struggling with false teeth', while another reviewer for the same paper noted a 'thick but approximate brogue that at times sounded like a contender for the Dick Van Dyke award' (Bassett 2004; Taylor 2004). The *Telegraph*'s critic had the most fun of all, finding Hunter's voice 'like absolutely nothing on earth, all strangulated vowels and improbable consonants, as if a visiting Martian were attempting to pass itself off as an Irishwoman' (Spencer 2004).

The journalists may have felt provoked to outdo each other's witticisms: immediately after the play's opening an excerpt from one of Hunter's speeches had been broadcast on Radio 4's *Today* programme, inspiring the presenter James Naughtie to invite listeners to nominate a worse example of an Irish stage accent.

In some ways, the 'mess' of Hunter's accent was presented as a side issue, the light relief in reviews ostensibly more concerned with the serious matter of Carr's method of reworking *Medea*. *By the Bog of Cats* is set in present-day rural Ireland, with Carr's Hester Swane a traveller – in the eyes of some characters, a 'tinker' marked by 'lazy shiftless blood' – and community outsider (Carr 1999: 312). The play begins, as does Euripides' *Medea,* with the protagonist contemplating the forthcoming wedding of her long-time lover to a younger woman. Like Medea and Jason, Hester and Carthage Kilbride are bound together through their complicity in a past murder that brought rewards, at least for the man involved; and, like Medea, Carr's protagonist ends by killing, here the couple's one daughter as opposed to the two sons of Euripides' version. These two issues – Hunter's accent and the nature of Carr's rewriting – are not unconnected. The *Independent*'s reviewer judged both elements fundamentally inauthentic: in place of the power of Greek drama, Carr had substituted 'high-class hokum hoping to gain some tragic glamour by association' (Taylor 2004). Charles Spencer was equally damning of 'this hubristic attempt to write a modern Medea set amongst the Irish bogs', an undertaking in which Carr had proved 'far more fanciful, and far less moving, than Euripides'; for him the play, like the accent, was 'manifestly a fake' (Spencer 2004). Michael Billington for the *Guardian* raised a different problem with Carr's updating in an article later that month, in which he compared the work unfavourably with David Eldridge's *Festen*, a stage adaptation of Thomas Vinterberg's film then playing at the Lyric Shaftesbury: 'Admittedly, dramatists have tried to adapt Greek tragic myths to modern times. But, with a few exceptions [...] such plays mostly come across as literary exercises. Even Marina Carr found herself in difficulties when transposing the Medea story to rural Ireland in *By the Bog of Cats*. A modern setting prompted questions such as why the local Garda and social services showed so little interest in a woman with a tendency to murder her relatives' (Billington 2004). Yet alongside such criticisms, virtually all the reviewers acknowledged something undeniably powerful about the work as well as the extraordinary impact of Hunter's performance, erratic accent and all. At its best, the production was 'enthralling', 'harrowing', 'gripping' or 'riveting', with Hunter's Hester Swane variously described as 'scalding', 'visceral', 'primal', 'feral' and 'unsettling' (Bassett 2004; De Jongh 2004; Spencer 2004; Taylor 2004; Wolf 2004). The broad consensus, with one or two exceptions, was that play and production both were deeply flawed and occasionally ludicrous *but also* bold, impassioned and occasionally sublime.

I choose to begin with the example of *By the Bog of Cats*, since this production and its critical reception together encapsulate a strong sense of the excitement and possibilities of reworking myths in contemporary drama but simultaneously indicate the accompanying difficulties. Clearly, the problems are many. Since myths are frequently best known in the form they have assumed within the canon of classical drama, today's playwrights immediately find their work measured against this regardless of the intentions of a new work or attitudes towards the old. The undertaking in itself invites, and regularly receives, charges of 'hubris' (as in Spencer's review), since merely to attempt such rewriting is considered arrogant overreaching; playwrights are setting themselves up for a potentially humiliating fall. And, while the tragedies of the Greek dramatists were themselves versions of narratives already in circulation, they are regularly regarded as if they were effectively originals, masterly realisations of which later playwrights can produce only weak imitations. At the same time, classical tragedies maintain their status in so far as they continue to be staged and studied and inherent in that engagement is the search for new resonances. Myths, similarly, only really achieve significance in the telling: in this sense they are open structures differently filled by each generation. Thus the existence of myths embodies the invitation to retell them; and, where myths have been crystallised in classical drama, writers, actors, directors and audiences are provoked to look for bridges that might connect ancient tragedy with contemporary experience. Sometimes, of course, those structures do not quite hold up; Billington's comment about the moments where Carr's analogy breaks down – at least, for the more literal-minded in the audience – is a case in point.

None the less, these narratives are revisited again and again, despite such challenges, because of their strength and power.

Myths deal with extreme situations and violent passions, yet they are not remote, since they are stories of human vulnerability and, very often, stories about the fragility of families. Medea's story, the inspiration for *By the Bog of Cats*, is by turns moving, gripping, appalling and cathartic: no wonder the contemporary stage has returned to it so regularly through adaptations, new directed productions, opera and dance.[1] Such a narrative makes extraordinary demands upon a writer and equally the performer; in Carr's play and the London production these are met without flinching. Even amidst the barrage of criticisms is the acknowledgement of qualities that enabled the material in a sense to exceed the frame: moments so undeniably powerful that they could puncture the 'blarney' that, for some, threatened to drag the whole piece down. I do not argue, of course, that all myth reworking of necessity achieves this; nevertheless, I propose that to accept the challenge in the first place indicates an ambition and perhaps a courage that are at the very least unlikely to produce an insipid result.

This book addresses reworkings of myths in contemporary drama and confines itself more or less exclusively to plays by women (two exceptions are made for plays with male co-authors). This choice in no way implies that such rewriting is only, or even predominantly, engaged in by women; indeed, the focus of this study seeks in part to offset the greater attention work of this kind by male playwrights has historically attracted. Early critical studies focused largely on notable myth reworkings by Anouilh, O'Neill, Sartre, Cocteau, Brecht, Eliot and Bond (Belli 1969; Dickinson 1969); subsequent assessments might include Hélène Cixous, Caryl Churchill, Timberlake Wertenbaker and perhaps Sarah Kane, alongside Heiner Müller, and might well involve consideration of directors such as Robert Wilson, Andrei Serban and Ariane Mnouchkine (see for example Green 1994; McDonald 2003; Reitz and Rothkirch eds 2001). Numerous articles deal with individual reworkings or compare plays that appropriate the same source; many of these discuss texts by female authors, but to date no full-length study exists that traces this practice through women's playwriting more generally. This book aims to fill that gap and in addition to show why and how rewriting myths has had – and, I argue, continues to have – distinctive meanings in women's drama. My focus is European and on plays produced between the early 1960s and the turn of the millennium. To examine women's writing in any genre across this period is inevitably also to consider the shifting arguments and preoccupations of feminism, although it does not follow from this that all the plays here admit a feminist agenda. I address the importance of rewriting or 're-visioning' myth in feminist theory as well as in women's creative work, equally acknowledging the tensions, and perhaps the contradictions, that are embedded in this practice. Myths are by definition stories we feel compelled to return to and retell, over and over; classical myths in particular have been integral to the development of western culture and have in fundamental ways shaped structures of thinking and perceiving. Recognition of the role and persistence of myths raises issues of manifest importance for feminist analysis. In what ways have myths defined 'woman' and to what ends and effects? How far have the embedded values and gender encodings in myths persisted in contemporary consciousness and by what means can these be resisted or unsettled? To what extent do women consider themselves *makers* of myth? Through the last decades of the twentieth century, western feminism has done much to question mythical paradigms and posit alternatives; through this, it has become entirely clear that the meanings uncovered in specific narratives, as well the attitudes towards myth discourses in general, are neither universal nor unchanging. This point almost 'goes without saying' but does in the end need to be said, since one of the critical challenges accompanying the territory hinges on the acknowledgement that myths self-evidently *do* cut across (some) cultures and time periods; they are narratives that inherently imply shared resonance and the potential for expansive application. One of the central purposes of this book, therefore, is to emphasise the precise resonances myth reworkings have sought to expose in discrete contexts and at particular cultural moments, but at the same time to explore ways in which myths and practices of rewriting can be a means of revealing shared attitudes and experience, as well as harnessing energies, through a rich and distinctive language that speaks to the imagination and to desire as much as to the intellect.

In electing to discuss myth re-vision in plays drawn from several decades and from a number of European countries, I have necessarily had to be selective rather than comprehensive. Alternative studies might opt to restrict focus to work produced in a single country, or to engage with diverse reinventions of a single myth narrative; such projects would be welcome. Here, however, I wanted a certain breadth of perspective as well as to widen my knowledge of theatrical practice to embrace contexts with which I was less familiar; to examine individual myths, but also to expose their intersection with others; and to bring to critical attention a number of plays that are relatively obscure, but which deserve to be better known, alongside others with which readers may already be acquainted. I also made the decision to limit the examination to plays rather than extend it to embrace devised theatre practice. This was not an easy choice, nor an instinctive one. It meant, for example, excluding the excellent work of the Magdalena Project, an international network of women artists many of whom have treated myths in their practice; fortunately, Magdalena's history and continuing activities are well documented elsewhere (see Bassnett 1992 and the network's own journal, *The Open Page*). Having said this, processes of devising are to an extent represented by two works that are included here: *Demeter Beneath the Sand*, by Serena Sartori and Renata Coluccini; and Gilla Cremer's *m.e.d.e.a.*, which features in my conclusion (and Cremer's work has in fact been supported by Magdalena). Both these texts are as much documentations of performance as scripts for subsequent re-enactment. Concentration on re-vision of myths in plays and playwriting make a number of things possible, however. First, the existence of published scripts in English in all but one case means that readers can readily turn, or return, to the works discussed, stimulated I hope by this analysis. Second, whilst the majority of cases refer to particular productions of plays and the implications of performance choices, I am equally alive to the knowledge of these as *scripts* that inherently imply the possibility of future stagings, perhaps in radically different contexts. Frequently, devised performances are in a sense 'owned' by their creators, and importantly so, although they may be recreated further down the line and will certainly influence other theatre makers. By contrast, this book deals with the perpetual transition of narratives from one place to another and the metamorphoses these have undergone in the process. This in turn raises the issue of translation.

Plays are included in this study that I would not have encountered had they not been translated into English. Hella Haasse's *A Thread in the Dark* is one such; Hrafnhildur Hagalín's *Easy Now, Electra* is another. For other works, by Franca Rame and Hélène Cixous,

I have relied upon English translations alongside the originals and used the former for referencing purposes. *Demeter Beneath the Sand* is published only in English; for *m.e.d.e.a.*, I have used Cremer's own unpublished translation from German. Had I been able to read these plays in their original languages, further insights would undoubtedly have become available that it has not been possible for me to access. However, I defend inclusion of drama in translation for several reasons. Through translation, texts can be drawn into discussion that I would otherwise be obliged to pass by; further, this study can offer and invite a perspective on women's re-vision of myths that is European, rather than simply national. Analysis of some of these works for an English readership will, I hope, result in their becoming better known and perhaps receiving future productions and further translations. But, more fundamentally, it is worth recalling that to study plays is in and of itself to accept the existence of gaps, of distance and profound unfixity. A play is an invitation to production, in the mind of the writer, perhaps, to multiple productions; it may also stand as record of an event passed. In this sense, the script is less the 'original' than a vital document that exists within a wider process of collaboration, production and transformation. Moreover, where playwrights begin, as here, with the aim of appropriating and reinventing a narrative that has already multiple previous lives, there is an acknowledgement of separation, of a leap of comprehension and imagination that the writers themselves must perform.

My first chapter sets out the theoretical terrain. In this, I examine changing conceptions of myths and their importance; I discuss particular ways in which women have been preoccupied by myth narratives and represent arguments that advocate the imperative to rewrite as well as others that contest the very possibility of doing so. The last section of this chapter considers the especial potential of theatre as medium for myth re-vision and includes a detailed analysis of one 'proto-feminist' drama from the early 1960s, the Dutch writer Hella Haasse's *A Thread in the Dark*. Chapter 2 deals with plays in which ideological issues predominate and where myths serve as literal 'pretexts' for contemporary sociopolitical debate: I begin with two solo plays by Franca Rame and Dario Fo, *The Same Old Story* and *Medea*, both first staged in Italy in the late 1970s; I turn then to Sarah Daniels's *Neaptide*, written and set in mid-1980s Britain. Chapter 3 considers a series of plays all first produced in Britain between 1969 and 1988: chronologically, these are Maureen Duffy's *Rites*; *A Mouthful of Birds*, by Caryl Churchill and David Lan; and *The Love of the Nightingale*, by Timberlake Wertenbaker. These three re-visions in different ways exploit tensions between daily experience and the mythical/fantastical, suggesting a permeable skin between them: here, ordinary lives are infiltrated by spirits, or alternatively a predominantly mythic frame cracks under the insistent pressure of a contemporary world. The plays are linked by their engagement with Euripides' *Bacchae*, a text itself preoccupied with the fragility of boundaries. The focus of Chapter 4 is first of all on re-visions that excavate and chart an almost wholly inner landscape: *Demeter Beneath the Sand* was created and performed in 1986 by Serena Sartori and Renata Coluccini, artists from Milan's Teatro del Sole; Cixous's *The Name of Oedipus* was originally performed in Avignon in 1978. Both works depict mythical worlds and adopt archetypal imagery in studies of identity and subjecthood that make no explicit reference to a social frame. In the same chapter I consider *The Perjured City*, also by Cixous, produced in 1994 by the Théâtre du Soleil; the piece echoes some of the concerns of Cixous's earlier play, but uses myth – embodied in the Furies of Aeschylus's *Eumenides* – to resituate the self and individual ethical choices within an overtly political realm. In this way, the discussions of Chapters 2 to 4 articulate and examine a shift of emphasis from re-visions whose target is the contemporary world and whose perspective is manifestly political; through 'hinge' plays showing leakage back and forward between the mundane and the mythical and with their gaze directed as much upon internal as external conflicts; to re-visions that appear, at least at first, to be fundamentally inward-looking. Chapter 5 examines two works of myth re-vision, from Britain and Iceland, written at the cusp of the millennium. Sarah Kane's *Phaedra's Love* and Hagalín's *Easy Now, Electra* are linked more immediately by their emergence from a particular historical moment than in the deployment of shared strategies or common purpose. My discussion does not attempt to play down the diversity, the very lack of consensus, that is in part what characterises a contemporary stage regularly and not always usefully described by that which it rejects, whether variously as post-structural, postmodern, postfeminist or postdramatic. Rather, I argue that Kane and Hagalín exploit myth re-vision productively to support two contrasting yet not wholly unconnected directions pursued on the late twentieth-century stage: of (so-called) in-yer-face theatre and contemporary postdramatic performance. Each of these chapters begins with an introduction contextualising the works selected and addressing larger issues of dramatic myth re-vision provoked by the texts and critical to each; individual plays are then considered discretely to accentuate their distinctive qualities and contexts.

A recurrent theme pursued throughout the book is what it means for playwrights to forge connections with myths and figures they seemingly desire to appropriate. In all chapters my discussion emphasises this sense of communication over distance, an attempt undertaken in full recognition of the structures – conceptual, ideological, fictional, theatrical – by which all participants are constrained. The effort to bridge a gap is an apposite image for a book like this one that invites conversation across so many gaps: of time and place; of national contexts; of languages; of feminisms past and present; of the texts themselves; and their actual and potential enactments.

Note

1 For some indication of the quantity and diversity of treatments of the Medea narrative see Hall, Macintosh and Taplin eds 2000.

1

The lie of the land

What's the use of stories that aren't even true? (Rushdie 1990: 20)

I'm interested in myths [...] just because they *are* extraordinary lies designed to make people unfree. (Carter 1998: 38)

Theorising myth

This is a book about myths: the forms myths take, their interaction with history and with individual lives, their significance and effects, and how far myths can be changed. It is about figures of women represented in myths and about women themselves as mythmakers. It is about strategies of writing and rewriting, and especially of playwriting and performing. It is about stories and ways of telling them. It is also, inevitably, a book about feminisms. This does not imply that all playwrights included here define their work in feminist terms; rather, it is to assert first that feminist thinking crucially shapes my own way of seeing and reading and secondly and more generally that it is scarcely possible to examine women's cultural contributions from the 1960s onwards without this strongly marking the frame of reference. Further, 'myth' has proved to be an especially potent concept, if never an untroubled one, for feminist analysis and within women's aesthetic practice: and if, as Angela Carter suggests, myths are 'lies designed to make people unfree', then interrogating, exposing and rewriting myths in a general sense must stand as key ambition of a wider feminist project. In this study, however, at least initially, I concentrate upon myths in the narrower sense of traditional narrative. Yet what might seem a relatively straightforward jumping-off point does not prove so in practice, since there is little real consensus on what constitutes myths, or mythic thinking, in western culture with studies of myth typically prefaced by an acknowledgement of the impossibility of satisfactorily defining their central term (see for example Honko 1972; Rogerson 1979). The breadth of perspective from which myth has historically been approached – through philosophy, theology, psychology, anthropology and the natural sciences, as well as the arts – has contributed much to our understanding of the subject but equally suggests that no single, universally acceptable definition is likely to be achievable; the very slipperiness of myth might also hint at the difficulties inherent in attempts to 'rewrite' it. The first section of this chapter provides a brief overview of diverse ways in which myth has been conceptualised.

At a fundamental level, to engage with myth is to engage with story. A myth implies a particular kind of story, a mythology a collection of stories that reveal family resemblances. Such stories will usually be set outside of historical time in 'primal or eschato-logical time', or in the supernatural world; they frequently feature anthropomorphic and theriomorphic divine figures, heroes or animals; they regularly deal with comings and goings between the supernatural world and a recognisable world of human history (Coupe 1997: 5; Larrington ed. 1992: xi; Leeming 1990: 3). But while such distinguishing features help to identify myths, they do not clearly exclude other, associated forms. The relationship of myth to folktale is close but contested. The religious historian Mircea Eliade argues that myth preceded the folktale or fairy tale and was sacred in function where the latter was determinedly secular; moreover, 'for archaic man, myth is a matter of primary importance, while tales and fables, however amusing they may be, are not' (Eliade 1976: 25). Such a view is not universally accepted; distinctions between myth, legend and folktale were made only when Jakob and Wilhelm Grimm began recording traditional tales in Germany in the early nineteenth century, and before this were not recognised in any European language (Zipes 1994: 1–3; Csapo 2005: 5). Evidently myths and folktales blend very early in oral and literary traditions and it can be difficult to tell them apart. Many myths incorporate the motifs of folktale; equally, a story may have a protagonist who happens to be a god. Once myths are separated from the context that might once have held them as sacred, there is little to distinguish them from more obviously secular stories.

Simply recognising myths is less problematic than establishing either their origins or their relationship with 'truth'. The dominant critical paradigm of the late nineteenth and early twentieth centuries was to interpret myths as imaginative, pre-scientific attempts to account for the origin of the world and explain natural phenomena. The studies of the American folklorist William Bascom, based on the records of anthropologists examining myths in so-called 'primitive' societies, concluded that myths were 'prose narratives which, in the society in which they are told, are considered to be truthful accounts of what happened in the remote past'; Bascom defined folktales by contrast as 'prose narratives which are regarded as fiction' and thus 'not to be taken seriously' (Bascom 1965: 8–9). Stories have always been used as a way of explaining those things that cannot otherwise easily be understood; the implication of Bascom's remark is that increased cultural sophistication renders myths obsolete, with mythic thinking effectively a stage human beings pass through on their way to more advanced levels of comprehension. The myth historian Alexander Eliot shares Bascom's view that myths are foundational stories but not his assumption that these are based in ignorance. For Eliot, myths 'are never factual, but seldom are [...] totally "untrue"'; they 'have to do with what we don't know and yet can't dismiss' (Eliot 1990: 1). Eliot's 'we' is crucial: no longer attached to 'other' cultures, carefully distanced (geographically or historically) from the modern western mind, myths are perceived as alive in contemporary consciousness, and calling on faith or intuition, rather than reason, for their validation. Beyond this, his words emphasise myth's distinctive double-voicedness: it speaks of truth, but in overtly fictitious or fantastical terms. Angela Carter similarly emphasised this duality, but from a political standpoint that led her to almost opposite conclusions.

Bascom's view of mythmaking as crude but creative thinking is characteristic of the comparatist method, of which his forerunner James Frazer is the best-known exponent. The contribution of Frazer and his fellow anthropologists was important not least in the scope of their research: before the twentieth century, references to 'myth' more or less always meant Greek myth, but the comparatists were able to collect and disseminate mythologies from all over the world. Frazer's monumental work *The Golden Bough*, abridged to a single volume in 1922 from its original twelve, provides an evolutionary account of human social organisation based on his study of myth and religion in ancient cults and folklore. Frazer's research, built on data freely gathered across cultures and epochs – collected remotely rather than through field work – led him to hypothesise a three-phase scheme of human cultural development: an age of magic, superseded first by an age of religion and ultimately by an age of science.[1] For Frazer, myths were associated with the 'error and folly' of the first two phases and contrasted with the supposed truth and superiority of the third (Frazer 1922: 711). Systems of magic and religion were both based, he proposed, on false premises: for the former, a belief in nature as an impersonal force that could be manipulated through ritual acts, such as shooting fire-tipped arrows into the air to rekindle the sun's rays; for the latter, the conviction that nature was ruled by the will of the gods (1922: 78). Science, by contrast, was founded on the 'true' premise that nature is governed by general principles of cause and effect. Once the flaws in early patterns of thinking are recognised, the culture is able to progress to the more 'advanced' level.

Of course, in both method and conclusions such an assessment raised problems. Frazer's insistence that myths and rituals had firmly pragmatic purposes was contradicted by their continued survival even once the belief systems with which they were said to be associated had been superseded; that they did survive implied a purpose beyond the directly functional. Furthermore, the universalism of Frazer's approach led him to assume that all cultures shared the same 'developmental' process and so obscured what might be vital distinctions between them; the identification of evolutionary stages common to all peoples invited the supposition that some cultures had simply 'progressed' more swiftly than others. Since at the time only Europeans had attained the fully rational 'age of science', Frazer's anthropological model provided a seemingly authoritative justification for belief in the intellectual superiority of the European mind. This argument fed the imperialist ideology that underpinned the colonial project. Frazer asserted, with supreme confidence, that 'there is more liberty in the best sense [...] under the most absolute despotism, the most grinding tyranny, than under the apparent freedom of savage life' (1922: 48). In time, all societies could rise to this level of 'higher thought', but, it was implied, this goal would be reached all the sooner with the help of the more 'advanced' nations. The principle of benevolent control could easily be extended to encompass 'semi-civilised' elements within European society as well, which is to say all those who did not belong to the (white, male) intelligentsia. Yet, while Frazer seems utterly assured of the rightness of this project, the conclusion to *The Golden Bough* acknowledges that its attainment is cast into doubt by a 'dark shadow' of superstition and 'regressive' thinking. He uses the striking image of a web of ideas, shot through with threads of black (magic), red (religion) and white (science): originally chequered black and white, 'a patchwork of true and false notions', it is subsequently stained with crimson which then itself 'shades off insensibly into a lighter tint as the white thread of science is woven more and more into the tissue'. It remained to be seen, he suggested, whether the 'great movement which for centuries has been altering the complexion of thought' would ultimately prevail (Frazer 1922: 713). The racist implications of such analogies are hard to avoid.

Aspects of Frazer's thought find echoes in Freud's view of myth, based in the then newly emergent 'science' of psychoanalysis. For Freud, mythmaking was to be understood as manifestation of the primitive in the human psyche rather than as an indicator of primitive cultures. 'Uncivilised' impulses and desires were not part of an earlier evolutionary stage but remained present, repressed by the conscious mind; such impulses found their expressive release above all in dreams, the analysis of which was for Freud the 'royal road' to comprehending the activities of the unconscious mind (Freud 1958: 608). The fact that dreams related to him by patients frequently displayed symbolism common to mythic traditions suggested myths were a language of which the unconscious mind made use and which could therefore be regarded as signposts towards that which could not be acknowledged in rational discourse. Freud believed that familiarity with mythology was indispensable to understanding the human psyche and equally that knowledge of (in particular) infant sexual development would illuminate myths in all the diverse forms through which they were perpetuated. Myths were examined for their latent as well as manifest content; for example, Freud interprets the tale of how the god Kronos swallowed his offspring as metaphoric expression of the child's fear of castration by the father (Freud 1959: 211–12). Freud's most notorious myth rereading is of course his analysis of *Oedipus Rex*. In Oedipus's transgressive rewriting of familial relations, claimed Freud, we see the fulfilment of our own childhood impulses;

recognising instinctively that in reality to act on these desires would result in neurosis, we 'shrink back from [Oedipus] with the whole force of the repression by which those wishes have since that time been held down within us' (Freud 1958: 263).

Freud's theories have been thoroughly challenged, not least for their reliance on phallocentric principles: the male child is adopted by him as the universal model, the female essentially regarded as inferior variant (see for example De Beauvoir's attack on Freud in *The Second Sex*). In 'Some Psychical Consequences of the Anatomical Differences Between the Sexes' (1925), Freud argued that the boy's Oedipal complex is destroyed by the onset of the castration complex which supports development of the superego, and that the girl, whom he perceives as in a sense *already* castrated, lacks the same motive to transcend the Oedipal phase. He concluded that females were more inclined to remain at the libidinal stage; they would not develop strong superegos and would be less repressed and ultimately less civilised than males (Freud 1961: 248–58). One can see here that Freud's theory begins to resemble Frazer's, only this time it is women who are the savages, the 'dark continent' that must necessarily be mastered and subdued. In this way, psychoanalysis provided new justification for the subordination of women by reviving ancient beliefs in the supposed weaker moral sense, more limited sense of justice and lesser capacity for sublimating instinct of the female sex. Such authorisation proved timely, viewed within the context of the growth of women's movements throughout Europe and their implied threat to male domination (see Anderson and Zinsser 1990: 216–19). Freud's theories of female development have since been widely rejected; it does not follow that the attitudes that underpinned them ceased to exist. In the mid-1970s, Hélène Cixous argued that women had for centuries been 'riveted [...] between two horrifying myths: between the Medusa and the abyss. That would be enough to set half the world laughing, except that it's still going on' (Cixous 1976: 885).

An appreciation of mythology is perhaps still more central to Jungian psychoanalysis. Jung claimed that beyond the individual unconscious, which was susceptible to 'Freudian' analysis, lay the collective unconscious: this contained patterns of psychic perception common to all humanity. Jung argued that the fantasy-images, or archetypes, found in dreams were not conscious and thus could not have been repressed. For Jung, the unconscious was crucially 'an *impersonal* psyche', even though it articulated itself through an individual consciousness:

> When anyone breathes, his breathing is not a phenomenon to be interpreted personally. The mythological images belong to the structure of the unconscious and are an impersonal possession; in fact, the great majority of men are far more *possessed by* them than possessing them. (Jung 1968: 186–7)

Archetypes were understood as patterns of instinctive behaviour, with archetypal images the manifestations of these in myth, literature and art. Studying such imagery in dreams was considered the key both to understanding the unconscious mind of the patient but also, more importantly, to gaining knowledge of 'essential' human experience and perception (Jung 1968: 42–53). Jung's archetypal psychology, or analytical psychology, as he termed it, contains much that theorists in many disciplines have found appealing; it is clear too that popular interest in myths owes a great deal to Jung and others influenced by his writings (see for example Pinkola Estés 1992; Bly 1992). In privileging myths, Jung's approach challenged the Enlightenment faith in the power of reason; myths were not to be explained away as relics of an inferior understanding but cherished as revelations of the pre-conscious mind. This notion of revelation has been important to many artists who have been inspired by Jung, directly and indirectly, to use myth and dream as a stimulus in creative work. Jung's emphasis upon imagery and symbols over and above narrative has meant that his impact on the visual arts has been particularly marked. Jung's theories of myth and the psyche are potentially applicable to theatrical practice also; his writings emphasise identity as something flexible and improvised, and show mythic life as a matter of role-playing rather than authenticity. In addition, he does not propose abandonment to the forces of the unconscious (or to any single 'role'), but advocates a condition of equilibrium. For these reasons, as well as for the greater value he attaches to the female role, Jung has on the whole been more gently treated by feminist critics than has Freud. For example, some thinkers, such as Bettina Knapp, have sought to adopt and adapt Jung's concepts of *anima* and *animus* to offer a model of the psyche which balances masculine and feminine principles; others, however, like

Diane Purkiss, contend that Jung's notions of 'masculine' and 'feminine' are themselves based on traditional and unhelpfully limited perceptions of gender; still others, Cixous amongst them, have drawn on Jung's work in proposing a radical bisexuality with the potential to disrupt gender norms (Knapp 1989; Purkiss 1992; Cixous 1986). I revisit these arguments in Chapter 4.

Confident belief in the superior reasoning power of the European mind underpinned the research of nineteenth-century anthropologists like Frazer and informed their conclusions that 'savage' thinking could be characterised as chaotic and irrational by contrast. The psychologists' 'discovery' of the unconscious, together with the wider social and cultural upheavals that marked the *fin-de-siècle* period and early years of the new century – the threats to empire, the growth of feminism, the beginnings of trade unionism, the development of consumer capitalism – all served to mount an ongoing challenge in the face of previously upheld ideological certainties. The disruption of stabilities and perceived fragmentation of experience found expression in the modernist period's shift from representation towards abstraction, with subjects increasingly examined less for individuality than for structure and interrelationship. This radically changing framework of ideas helps contextualise Saussure's model of linguistics, developed early in the century, which in its turn informed the emergence of structuralism. Structuralism contributed an important and largely new dimension to the study of myth, most fully elaborated in the work of anthropologist Claude Lévi-Strauss. Like Freud and Jung, Lévi-Strauss was concerned to expose 'connectedness' within and between myths, but his analyses of recurrent patterns and motifs, conducted through a series of field-based investigations, led him to propose not a common origin for the myths themselves (as with Jung's notion of the 'collective psyche') but rather a commonality in the mental structures that had created them. His work built on principles earlier established by Saussure to articulate a 'grammar' of myth, made up of smaller units or 'mythemes'. For Saussure, language was a system in which terms acquired meaning only by their relationship to other terms; Lévi-Strauss drew on this model to demonstrate that myths too formed a language similarly based on notions of opposition and relatedness. That such 'rules' could be identified stood for Lévi-Strauss as evidence of 'a basic need for order in the human mind', a view reinforced by his proposition that myth's deep structures revealed the persistent attempt to reconcile oppositions: between order and chaos, abundance and dearth, life and death (Lévi-Strauss 1995: 13). Where these tensions were not ultimately resolvable, as would generally be the case, the function of myth was to effect a form of mediation that served to relieve anxiety (Lévi-Strauss 1963: 229; and 1985: 162). Lévi-Strauss's view, in marked contrast with Frazer's, was that mythical thought employed a logic 'as rigorous as that of modern science', the difference simply in the nature of those things to which it was applied (Lévi-Strauss 1963: 230).

As a means of understanding myth, the structuralist model evidently has its limits. Numerous critics have raised objections to, for example, its repetitive formulae that in effect make each myth like every other myth; to a perceived 'coldness' in the method, which seems in tension with the violence and sensuosity of content that is surely what, in part, makes mythic narratives interesting; to the impression sometimes given of the method's disconnectedness from history (Clarke 1972; Geertz 1993; Lapointe and Lapointe 1977). The religious historian Wendy Doniger argues persuasively that, while structuralist models usefully identify broad patterns, they are less helpful in exploring the shades of meaning that are apparent in myths and which render them always more complex than a straightforward articulation of dualisms. The final result of the reading will often be anticlimactic, she suggests, a 'formula [that] bleeds the myth of all its meanings' (Doniger 1998: 149). We can see something of this in Lévi-Strauss's analysis of the Oedipus myth which, although considering multiple versions, eventually reduces the whole to two sets of binarisms: one, the 'overrating' or 'underrating' of blood relations; two, the tension between competing theories of human origin: autochthony versus bisexual reproduction. Whilst interesting in its conclusions – and certainly addressing the narrative from a very different perspective than does Freud – the method has the disadvantage of forcing together what seem vastly different *kinds* of action, driven by the necessity of its own rules (Lévi-Strauss 1963: 213–17). Doniger does not reject the structuralist approach outright; she rather proposes that we 'jump off Lévi-Strauss's bus one stop before he does. In order to remain truly engaged with our texts, we must wallow in the mess for a while before the structuralists clean it up for us' (Doniger 1998: 149).

For Doniger, dealing with 'mess' requires combining structuralism with a broad spectrum of other approaches – political, psychological, theological – and the methodological eclecticism that her position represents is characteristic of approaches to myth analysis later in the century. In *Mythologies* (1957), Roland Barthes expanded the concept of myth decisively beyond its conventional sense of a traditional tale to include the operations of contemporary communication systems and the media, his discussions dealing with subjects ranging from soap powder advertisements to wrestling matches. For Barthes, as for Lévi-Strauss, myth was a type of language or speech; what made it distinctive was the particular way it communicated its message. Barthes claimed that myth was constructed as a '*second-order semiological system*' beneath language's manifest meaning, functioning at a largely subconscious connotative rather than denotative level (1973: 123). In the essay 'Myth Today', Barthes describes a *Paris-Match* magazine cover depicting a black soldier in French uniform saluting the French flag: explicitly, the image of willing allegiance endorsed the French empire by communicating the absence of colour discrimination; but, at the level of latent meaning, it violently erased the history of French colonialism, presenting the soldier as an empty form deprived of memory, 'at once stubborn, silently rooted there, and garrulous, a speech wholly at the service of the concept' (1973: 132). Throughout *Mythologies* Barthes is concerned to expose the duplicitous workings of a mass media that disguised what was cultural as natural, represented its loaded messages as transparent truths; his deconstructive method sought 'to track down, in the decorative display of *what-goes-without-saying*, the ideological abuse which [...] is hidden there' (1973: 11). Far from being simply the necessary activity of the human mind that Lévi-Strauss had considered it, the attempt to reconcile oppositions was interpreted by Barthes as a mechanism of bourgeois domination, effective precisely because depoliticised.

Barthes's use of the term 'myth' is broad. That breadth has important implications, not least for attempts at rewriting. In his 1971 essay 'Change the Object Itself', Barthes clarified the distinctive quality of this new conception of myth. In contemporary society, myth 'is discontinuous. It is no longer expressed in long fixed narratives but only in "discourse" [...]; myth disappears, but leaving – so much the more insidious – the *mythical*' (Barthes

1977: 165). The recognition that anything can become 'mythical' should help to keep us alert to the filtering of ideological interests through what might otherwise seem 'innocent' signs. However, the reframing of language as 'discourse', a process constitutive of subjectivity and identity (and of which, therefore, we are not in control), implies the difficulty – although not, in Barthes's view, the impossibility – of demystifying or dismantling power structures. The amplification of 'myth' also raises the question of how far Barthes's methods (which combine structuralist and Marxist principles) can usefully be applied to myths understood in a more conventional sense. Contemporary myth may well be dispersed, in the way Barthes described it, but traditional myth narratives also persist, both 'whole' and in fragments. That these might appear to be relics, or 'heritage', separable from more evidently contemporary production, could itself be – to use Barthes's terms – a subtle effect of naturalisation.

Since *Mythologies*, the concept of myth as ideological text has been widely absorbed within contemporary cultural criticism. Both in its earlier sense (as traditional narrative) and in its subsequent interpretation as manifestation of discourse, myth has come to be studied far more in terms of structures, operations and effects than from an interest in origins. Yet ideological analysis of myths is far from simple to implement, given the elusive and pervasive character of ideology in contemporary societies. This difficulty has in its turn inspired the borrowing of techniques from a plurality of contexts rather than selection or invention of any single approach, seen for example in the self-conscious eclecticism of Doniger's methods. Within this widened frame, structuralist and psychoanalytic methodologies have proved especially popular sources for plundering. From the former, the emphasis on uncovering systems of binaries within the myth/text can be deployed not to effect a reconciliation of 'opposites', or arrive at any 'truth', but to expose the artificiality of such constructions and make space for the tensions produced: the equivalent, perhaps, of Barthes's wish to 'hold [the text's] *signifiance* fully open' (Barthes 1977: 141). The notion of repression, fundamental to Freudian psychoanalysis, is similarly utilised and reinvented to explore and release latent ideological content. Lacanian theory builds on structuralist and psychoanalytic methods and has in its turn provided a potent framework for, especially, feminist and postcolonial myth rereadings (see for example Sellers 2001; Uskalis 2000).

Barthes's disgust at the seemingly 'transparent' image on the front of *Paris-Match* that disguised its act of imperialist erasure spoke of an urgent need to reinscribe myths within their historical context. This imperative is forcefully pursued by Marina Warner, the novelist, historian and cultural critic whose work is pertinent here since her perspective on myths incorporates both its traditional and its Barthesian senses: Warner's 1994 Reith Lectures, 'Managing Monsters: Six Myths of Our Time', precisely addressed the ways in which stories from mythology persist, filtered through and reinvented by the contemporary imagination (Warner 1994a). In the same year Warner published *From the Beast to the Blonde*, a compendious study of fairy tales and tale-tellers that rejects notions of folklore as 'archetypal' language and provides instead a genealogical view (re)claiming a 'secret history' of matriarchal storytelling. The story of fairy tales, she argues, has been a story of struggle to control the processes of their transmission; in terms that recall Barthes, Warner demonstrates how voices – principally, women's voices – have become all but lost as '[t]he historical context of the stories has been sheared away' (Warner 1994b: 416–17). The attempt to recover such voices, and to invite new ones, is central to Warner's practice of re-vision, as it is to this study.

Re-visioning myth

> Children's books, mythology, stories, tales, all reflect the myths born of the pride and the desires of men; thus it is that through the eyes of men the little girl discovers the world and reads therein her destiny. (De Beauvoir 1960: 30)

The role of myths in the formation of consciousness has proved an attractive locus for feminist investigation from both academic and artistic standpoints (see for instance Cavallaro 2002; Gamble ed. 2001; Lauter 1984; Ostriker 1986; Purkiss 1992; Sellers 2001). The majority of dramatic interventions considered in subsequent chapters of this book are situated within feminism's so-called 'second wave', but concern with myths manifestly persists in a 'postfeminist' era. Furthermore, and as studies like Warner's demonstrate, women's role in myth's mediation is as old as the stories themselves. Unsurprisingly, given the current trend towards critical pluralism and the reality that feminism is not monolithic, there has been no uniformity of approach. However, it is possible to identify recurrent concerns that build on the debates summarised above. Feminist thinking has recognised the vital function of myth in transmitting and shaping cultural beliefs, often in forms that make these accessible to the minds of the youngest children, and has repeatedly argued that any claims made for myths as embodiment of unchanging or universal truths must be treated with profound suspicion. A central project of feminist analysis has thus been to re-examine the narratives of mythologies sacred and secular, and especially to deconstruct supposedly archetypal images of the feminine to reveal how these – far from being 'timeless' entities outside the processes of human development – are reflections of the symbolic order through which cultures are produced. Classical myth inevitably holds special interest for European feminism since the art, philosophy and science of western civilisation developed with reference to its terms. But approaching the task of deconstruction provokes engagement with a fundamental problem: how can women *see through* myths if, as De Beauvoir suggested, they must *look through* the lens they provide?

In her seminal essay 'When We Dead Awaken: Writing as Re-Vision' (1971), the poet and theorist Adrienne Rich urged the necessity of feminist rewriting: 'the act of looking back, of seeing with fresh eyes, of entering an old text from a new critical direction'. It was necessary that women should come to terms with 'old' texts, and old myths, in order to explore the possibilities of creating new ones. She emphasised: 'We need to know the writing of the past, and know it differently than we have ever known it; not to pass on a tradition but to break its hold over us' (Rich 1979: 35). Since myths and fairy tales depend for their continuance on being retold, this would suggest that they provide fertile ground for feminist intervention. The term 'revision' – minus the hyphen Rich had introduced to emphasise a female gaze – has also been taken up by Jack Zipes. Zipes is primarily a critic and collector of fairy tales but, as the title of his 1994 study *Fairy Tale as Myth: Myth as Fairy Tale* implies, he makes few fundamental distinctions between these and myths. In this discussion of fairy

tales and their metamorphoses throughout history, Zipes distinguishes between 'duplication' and 'revision', categorical terms he
adopts that refer to processes as well as their products. The former
implies the attempted reproduction or recreation of an original,
the latter the re-examination of this. Since 'originals' cannot by
definition be recreated, the work of duplication is to testify to the
existence of an original by offering a faithful homage. Where no
original exists, as in the case of the classic fairy tale, duplication
implies reproduction of a set pattern of ideas and images that
reinforce a fundamentally conservative way of seeing and believing
(an act which, he considers, requires little imagination or skill). By
contrast, revision implies creation of a new work that incorporates
the critical and creative thinking of the new author, perhaps as
reflection of a society's altered tastes and demands (Zipes 1994:
9). It does not follow that all revisions are aesthetically satisfying
or politically progressive. In the nineteenth century, fairy tales for
children were carefully regulated and in many cases expurgated,
sanitised and domesticated to make them more 'appropriate' for
young minds; this too was a process of revision, by Zipes's
definition, but one which later critics of the genre sought to
challenge (Carter ed. 1991; Tatar 1987 and 1992; Waelti-Walters
1982; Warner 1994a; Zipes ed. 1986). Zipes's 'duplication or
revision' model is somewhat lacking in flexibility, although it might
be fairer to say that the brevity of summary makes it appear so.
After all, retelling a specific story at a particular historical moment
would in some contexts constitute a radical act, even if so little is
altered of the prior text that such a retelling should technically be
classed as 'duplication' and thus, supposedly, an unimaginative and
conservative cultural contribution. To be useful, both terms of the
equation must be more subtly nuanced if the creative and critical
impulse could be located in the timing of telling – or, indeed, in the
identification of the teller or selected audience who receive it – as
much as in the content and structuring of the narrative told.

Re-visioning, reclaiming, rewriting: Rich and Zipes, speaking
from different political identifications, similarly urge radical
intervention so that literary traditions are not closed conversations but actively dialogic. But how is this to be achieved? Rich's
words are a rallying cry, yet also hint at fundamental tension in
the re-visionary project: women are themselves already shaped
by the discourse they hope to challenge. Dissociation from this

is thus exceptionally problematic, as comically expressed in a
Ros Asquith cartoon of the mid-1990s in which a mother reads
a feminist fairy tale to her small daughter – 'And so the princess
killed the dragon and rescued the prince' – only to be interrupted
by the eager question: 'What was she wearing?' The implication
is that ideological programming is deeply embedded, effectively
instinctual: how far, then, is rewriting possible or productive?
Asquith's sketch hints that literal role reversals, at least, will not
be sufficient: numerous 'feminist fairy tales' have been written that
employ this strategy, but these fail to satisfy when the reader senses
that a story's deepest challenges have been sidestepped rather than
confronted (see for example Binchy et al. 1992; Walker 1996).

The historian Diane Purkiss has examined the issue of feminist
rewriting at some length through an analysis of classical myth in
the work of contemporary women poets. Since historically the
dissemination of myths in literary form has occurred through
processes that severely limited women's participation, Purkiss
argues, rewriting myths necessitates engagement with 'gender
asymmetries agreed upon for centuries' (1992: 441). This implies
not just the magnitude of the task but the inescapability of
adopting at least some of the terms by which women have been
excluded. Purkiss considers a wide range of rewriting strategies
but emerges frustrated at the 'failure and difficulty and doubt'
her research uncovers; many attempts stand as little more than
empty gestures, remaining ultimately entrapped within myth's
restrictive framework (*ibid.*: 455). Her conclusions recall Barthes's
observation, two decades earlier, that 'demystification (or demyth-
ification) has itself become discourse [...], in the face of which,
the science of the signifier can only shift its place and stop
(provisionally) further on'; the task as Barthes saw it was rather
'to fissure the very representation of meaning' (1977: 166–7). But
the problem remains: how can one combat the discourse that is at
once the object of struggle and the means by which that struggle
is conducted?

Feminist assessments of the virtue and feasibility of 'mythic
re-visionism' as critical strategy have ranged from valorisation,
to cautious or selective support, through to extreme scepticism
or outright rejection. My discussion thus far has emphasised
the difficulties of such a project but feminist debates have been
equally coloured by more optimistic assessments. One argument,

frequently (if not always fairly) associated with radical and 'cultural' strands of second-wave feminism, has been to celebrate myth as a potentially feminine sphere and site of 'authentic' female experience; to reach this sphere, however, it is necessary to peel away layers of false – by which is meant patriarchal, or 'institutionalised' – myth. This position is frequently justified through assertion of an ancient woman-centred culture, long buried, that could be (at least partially) recovered through a process akin to archaeological excavation. The view that matriarchy preceded patriarchy continues to be debated, and was certainly believed by Freud and Frazer, as well as numerous other commentators (Bachofen 1992; Campbell 1991; Frazer 1922; Freud 1964; Graves 1961b; Neumann 1955). It has been claimed that the 'goddess religions' upon which early matriarchal societies are thought to have been based were gradually overtaken by Christianity which, for its own purposes of empire, distorted tales and transformed symbols into a new mythology stripped of female power (Diamond and Orenstein eds 1990; Göttner-Abendroth 1995; Whitmont 1983). The appeal of this analysis from a feminist standpoint is self-evident, not least in demonstrating that women can hardly be subordinate by nature if they were not so in the past. Elinor Gadon's *The Once and Future Goddess*, a study of women's prehistory along these lines, provides a cross-cultural analysis both diachronic and synchronic. Gadon asserts that goddess worship was 'of this world not other-worldly, body-affirming not body denying, holistic not dualistic' and aligns these values with the feminine (1990: xii). The subsequent ascendancy of the male God is both effect and symbol of the rise of patriarchy, with the suppression of goddess religion and the feminine a necessary part of this reversal. Especially significant within this process is the abandonment of an underlying principle of unity, founded on the inseparability of unborn child from the maternal body, to be replaced by a dualistic order that privileged the masculine (see also Cavarero 1995: 57–90; Irigaray 1993: 15–22). Gadon's project is the reclaiming of the Goddess, on behalf of men as well as women, not in order to idealise or idolise women but to embrace values that the Goddess is felt to symbolise: principally, a spirituality that is earth-centred and ecologically aware; and a sexuality enriched by the resacralising of women's bodies and wider transformation of social relations.

Despite the quantity of documentation they provide, such studies as Gadon's have not been widely accepted as the uncovering of historical truth. There are good grounds for this scepticism. Once late nineteenth- and early twentieth-century scholarship had established the idea that prehistoric peoples had at one stage worshipped a feminine deity it was not difficult to find evidence to substantiate this, for example through identification of Neolithic figurines that appeared to represent the female form. Serious doubt has been cast on the status of such evidence, however. A study that predates Gadon's, by comparative archaeologist Peter Ucko, argues that most such figurines suggest asexuality as much as femaleness; that no obvious 'majesty' attaches to them, so there is no reason to suppose they represented deities; that they might, indeed, simply be dolls (Ucko 1968). There is no space here to examine the archaeo-logical debate; more pertinent to my discussion is how 'Goddess' claims have functioned in some feminist contexts as resonant and persuasive counter-myth.[2] Gadon's study is at its best, I suggest, when inviting readers to reflect on the value choices a society makes and to consider what a holistic culture might look like. Far more problematic is the assumption, not unique to Gadon, that a matriarchal society would of necessity be one that is nurturing, 'peaceful, and egalitarian' (Gadon 1990: xiii). To make this leap is to see historical analysis risk distortion into what Judith Antonelli justifiably terms 'the feminist fairy tale' (Antonelli 1997).

Gadon's study was largely based on visual evidence such as wall-painting, sculpture and tapestry. A contrasting and profoundly combative approach is that of the philosopher and theologian Mary Daly, forcefully articulated in her groundbreaking work *Gyn/Ecology* (first published in 1978). Daly's emphasis here was on 'man-made language', which in this text and elsewhere she radically reworks as a step towards creation of a female-centred future culture. Recognition of the interrelatedness of myth and language is fundamental to her method, since for Daly patriarchy 'perpetuates its deception' through both. Daly argued that mythical characters are normally represented as symbols that, 'it is said, open up depths of reality otherwise closed to "us." It is not usually suggested that they close off depths of reality that would otherwise be open to us' (Daly 1991: 44). The strategy Daly advocated was twofold: on the one hand, the deconstruction or destruction of 'patriarchal' myths; on the other, the discovery and creation of gynocentric alternatives, 'stories arising from the experiences of Crones' which articulate female-identified power (Daly and Caputi 1988: 114). Daly was not concerned to prove that every patriarchal myth had its antecedent in a gynocentric one; her perspective was not chronological but 'Crone-logical', aiming to create a women-centred mythology that could interweave pasts, presents and imagined futures (Daly 1991: 47). *Gyn/Ecology* is a dazzlingly inventive work: on every page linguistic structures are wittily and scathingly dissected, not through superficial reversals but more by a process that Daly, paraphrasing Andrea Dworkin, describes as 'double-double unthink' (*ibid.*: 60). Thus, she insists, for women merely to make claims of 'womb envy' and fixate upon female biological fertility is no solution, but rather keeps them 'boxed into the fathers' house of mirrors, merely responding to the images projected/reflected by the Possessors', when the task is to break through the glass (*ibid.*: 46–7).

Daly's work attracted charges of essentialism, as have many of the productions of 'Goddess' feminism (from which Daly's arguments should, however, be distinguished). Daly herself did her cause little service by an unwillingness publicly to defend her most controversial arguments. The most damaging instance of this was her failure to respond to an influential 1979 open letter from the writer and activist Audre Lorde that criticised the homogenising tendencies of *Gyn/Ecology* and the inattention of its author to the perspectives of non-white women (Lorde 1984: 66–71). Despite these difficulties, I will comment on Daly's method a little further since I consider she contributes something valuable and distinctive to the re-visioning project; at the same time, such challenges to her work provide a useful reminder of the dangers that beset attempts to appropriate myths for ideological purposes. Critical resistance to Daly's particular brand of feminism is often preoccupied with the very play of language that forms her chief strategy: what Daly offers as empowering metaphor can too easily, in dissemination and imitation, become hardened into literalism. For example, some might well consider injunctions to 'release the Wild Woman within' at best off-putting and at worst essentialist, but a more generous reading of *Gyn/Ecology* could treat such formulations more as a bid to cultivate resistance than as a laying claim to an innate female self that is somehow immune to patriarchal manipulation. To some extent, accusations of essentialism seem to go with the territory where reworking myths is concerned. But to turn to myth is not of itself to disconnect from history; to invoke mythic metaphor in exploring femininity is not to assert an unchanging or universal female self. Diane Richardson, by no means a defender of Daly, highlights the problem of labelling work 'essentialist' when it fails to fit a favoured (here usually post-structuralist) critical paradigm: and if whole bodies of work – which will inevitably encompass considerable diversity – are described in this way in dismissive shorthand, then a 'dominant' feminist model effectively enforces its own version of discourse control (Richardson 2000: 53–6).

The argument that women must break and remake language is fundamental to feminist theory. The proposal of *écriture féminine* was a key response to this challenge and one with particular appeal for many theatre-makers. The now notorious argument for 'feminine writing' drew on deconstruction and aspects of Lacanian theory in the search for a form of writing or discourse closer to the body and the emotions, elements considered to be repressed within the symbolic order. In 'The Laugh of the Medusa' and 'Sorties' (both 1975), Cixous proposed that because women are similarly marginalised they potentially had intimate access to this form of writing and through it might reveal what is normally kept secret and simultaneously find a space for *jouissance*: a totality of pleasure. Although generally associated with literary and autobiographical practices, *écriture féminine* has offered a way for some women to think about making and unmaking specifically theatrical language (Goodman and De Gay eds 2003; Moss 1987). There are many reasons why this should be so. The medium of drama inherently invites exploration of multiple voices and competing subjectivities, and, since performance demands that temporal and spatial dimensions also be confronted, their conventions may be exposed and challenged through stage action. For Cixous's own practice of *écriture féminine* a journey into myth was essential and inevitable: on a formal level, the associative intertextual patterning of stories, memories and images provided an alternative to the linear logic of patriarchal discourse; equally, since in her view myths reinforced the repressive dualistic structures of western thought, they could not be left unchallenged; finally, undermining these conceptual foundations was the necessary first step towards releasing an alternative, 'feminine' voice.

From the beginning, the claims of *écriture féminine* seemed to bear troubling implications. If the 'repressed feminine' were considered the site of an authentic voice, did this not reinforce, even celebrate, women's inferior position within the social contract? Moreover, *écriture féminine*'s emphasis on writing the body appeared to locate that difference anatomically and to uphold a singular aesthetic that threatened to obscure or overrule women's heterogeneity. One might choose to defend *écriture féminine* as primarily strategic, a subject-position that was not in the end uniquely female but could rather be assumed by men and women alike; that Cixous's earliest examples were male writers, such as Jean Genet, would seem to bear this out. None the less, concerns about the assumptions underlying *écriture féminine* remained. Toril Moi feared an underlying biologism in Cixous's approach, highlighting moments of elision in her writing where 'feminine' became 'female'; Ann Rosalind Jones suggested that proponents of *écriture féminine* failed to acknowledge how far our relationships with our bodies might be damaged by the effects of acculturation (Moi 1985; Jones 1985). A later article by Anu Aneja usefully revisits the main arguments on both sides of the debate. Aneja emphasises that 'The Laugh of the Medusa' and 'Sorties' are in a sense works of utopic fiction, and, crucially, reminds the reader that they were written in the mid-1970s: they are not representative of Cixous's work more generally – and certainly not since then, as I discuss in Chapter 4 – and it is unhelpful to continue to use them 'to flog the back of "*écriture feminine*"' (1999: 67). In similar vein, Anne-Marie Picard suggests that both as name and as concept *écriture féminine* has become thoroughly 'deformed and overused'; if potent once, it is inadequate now as a way to conceive of women's relationship to the symbolic order (1999: 28–9).

One of the most thoughtful and distinctive contributions to feminist re-vision of myth is offered by the Italian philosopher Adriana Cavarero. Like Cixous, Cavarero bases her arguments on the premise that western philosophy has taken 'Man' (rather than men) as prototype for the universal human being, and that from this distortion others follow: the maternal role is devalued so that Man may become giver, as well as taker, of life, and the biological realities of birth that would necessarily problematise this are evaded by asserting the superiority of the intellectual and philosophical sphere. The inferiority of women to men is thus deeply inscribed at every level of classical thought and so has powerfully affected the subsequent history of western cultural production. Cavarero's *In Spite of Plato* (1990), subtitled 'a feminist rewriting of ancient philosophy', seeks to 'free' four Greek female figures from the discourses that have entrapped them. Cavarero's rereadings of Penelope, Demeter, Diotima and the Maidservant from Thrace (this last a character only briefly mentioned by Plato) do not glorify these figures as archetypes who express an authentic female voice. Indeed, fundamental to Cavarero's strategy is the acknowledgement that they are the inventions of male authors and she herself equally caught in a masculine conceptual universe (Cavarero 1995: xiii). There is no nostalgic longing here for a maternal order; Cavarero's perspective is politically engaged and rooted in the here and now, drawing on immediate experience. Her method is provocative and productive and has influenced the ways in which I 'read' plays featured in this book. I briefly discuss one of Cavarero's rereadings now to illustrate the practical operation of her approach.

Cavarero's first subject is Penelope, famously the 'perfect' wife of Odysseus. Ever patient in his absence, Penelope weaves and then unravels her cloth so that it will never be finished and she will not have to accept a new husband from amongst the suitors. It is this act of un/weaving upon which Cavarero builds her analysis, inviting us to see in this not wifely stratagem but the creation of resistant symbolic space. Penelope's story *is* this act, Cavarero suggests; Odysseus's return would mean the end not just of the task but of Penelope herself (Cavarero 1995: 12). Weaving and unravelling constitute a motion without progress, a halting of time that marks her own separation from the great history of Odysseus's adventures, the Homeric epic. In this sense, Cavarero argues, Penelope's un/weaving keeps all men at a distance, including her husband: that Penelope, unlike others in the household, does not recognise Odysseus when he returns is read by Cavarero as a small, final gesture of holding herself back. At the centre of this resistance is the exercise of un/weaving, a performance that creates a seemingly impenetrable space: 'Antinous simply waits. In the weaving room something illogical is happening in the face of whose logic he can only keep away. He has to remain in that patriarchal society which the tireless industry of the loom keeps at a distance' (*ibid.*: 17). Cavarero interprets Penelope's act as frustration not simply of the desires of the men around her but implicitly of the masculine symbolic order, explaining this through reference to Plato's *Phaedo*. Here Plato remarks that the task of a true philosopher is to untie the soul from the body, and that men who are preoccupied with the pleasures and pains of life and with the body's eventual end in death are misguidedly seeking to retie the two together: in so doing, he suggests, they mimic Penelope in her endless task. To make this comparison requires a kind of inversion. Plato's 'bad' philosopher is one who illogically reweaves what philosophy has untied. One would expect the 'illogicality' in Penelope's act to lie in the unravelling of material she has previously woven, but Plato's example turns this around: here *re*weaving signals foolishness. Pursuing this idea, Cavarero argues that Penelope's task is not the untying (to keep suitors at bay) but the *retying*: she 'simply weaves together what the philosophers have undone' (*ibid.*: 28). She is not the only woman Plato implies to be 'at fault' in this regard.[3] Evidently, women are bad philosophers: where the ideal is to separate soul and body, they insist upon tying the two together; like Penelope, they hold on to the materiality of the present moment, to a world of living resistant to a masculine order that glorifies death as the perfect, definitive untying.

While each of Cavarero's four rereadings can be studied discretely, adopting this approach would miss the patterns that emerge through *In Spite of Plato*. Cavarero works *with* women's exclusion from and devaluation within the western philosophic tradition, seeking to locate in its discourse those tensions that threaten to destabilise its order. There is no concept of a female 'essence' or 'authenticity' here. Rather, Cavarero re-activates (her word) her figures to show how they might unsettle the dominant order by revealing its internal contradictions: they represent starting-points that direct her to a reassessment and reimagining of gender relations in contemporary society and its institutions.[4] For Cavarero, re-vision is not about searching either for truth or lies in philosophical texts and myth narratives but for loose threads to pull. In exposing the double-voicedness of discourse her work is dialogical in the Bakhtinian sense; her re-readings make meaning by exploiting the conflict – actual or potential – of competing voices. The principle of sexual difference serves, as Rosi Braidotti observes, as the 'grid' through which Cavarero examines her material; it is this principle that she aims to inscribe at the heart of the phallogocentric code underpinning the symbolic order (Cavarero 1995: ix–xii). The philosophy of sexual difference (*pensiero della differenza sessuale*) has been a major school of thought within Italian feminism, one symbolically 'launched' with the formation in 1983 of the Verona-based Diotima group, a 'philosophical community of women' of which Cavarero was a founding member (Re 2002: 50; Cavarero 1986). Sexual difference as understood here implies neither a strictly biological nor a sociological category, but exists at the intersection of these two levels with the symbolic dimension. As Bono and Kemp explain, this is feminist theory that runs the risk of essentialism, but 'by taking that risk "seriously", it may seem to speak essentialism, but enacts a new kind of empiricism' (Bono and Kemp eds 1991: 17). That this is a risk feminism *must* run has been powerfully argued in a study by Vikki Bell, one suggesting that the manoeuvres of 'constructionist' arguments may constitute a deferral of the encounter with essentialism rather than its avoidance altogether (Bell 1999: 115). However, Diotima's publications, under the leadership of Luisa Muraro, do speak unmistakably of valorisation of the feminine and the necessity of female separatism; it was this shift of Diotima's collective stance that eventually led Cavarero to break away from the group (Re 2002). As I have argued, Cavarero asserts the actuality of difference but without glorification – no substitute theology is posited – or insistence upon female sameness; as such, her practice of revision provides a stimulating model that has helped shape this study.

Staging myth: Hella Haasse's *A Thread in the Dark* (*Een draad in het donker*)

> The point is not to bring myth to life, nor to kill the stories, but to highlight the uneasy distinction between the two. (Goodman ed. 2000: xvii)

In the preceding section I examined the practice of feminist re-vision from a predominantly theoretical perspective; I turn now to the particular challenges women playwrights face when they attempt to re-vision myths for stage production. Jane de Gay has noted the longstanding popularity of myths as creative source for women theatre-makers but cautions that, since mythologies have enshrined ways of seeing the world and seeing women that are problematic and deeply rooted, the challenge is finding ways 'to play with fire without getting burned' (De Gay 2003: 11). This is effectively the argument Purkiss made with reference to women poets: that there is a danger of finding oneself unable to evade or dismantle the ideological snares set by the source material (Purkiss 1992). But in re-visioning myths for performance the risk of 'burning' runs especially high. The theatre provides an immediate and very public form of exposure, and the writer will rarely put only herself on the line: typically she draws a crowd of others with her who, as co-creators, necessarily share the heat. The example with which I began this study – Hunter as a modern-day Medea in *By the Bog of Cats* – illustrates this point: she, and by extension the whole cast, must anticipate a degree of critical mockery for their part in Carr's (to some) hubristic attempt at myth transposition. Yet, despite such risks, the attractions of the material evidently remain strong: classical myths would not reappear with such frequency in contemporary plays if their authors' sole motivation was a sense of duty. The counter-side is surely what myths *offer*: by this I mean not so much the outdated notion of uncovering 'positive images' – let alone 'role models' – but rather a vivid territory of action, transformation, language and metaphor that can stretch and enrich the creative imagination.

What substance does a playwright grasp hold of in the attempt to re-vision myth? This must depend in part on the depth of familiarity an audience has with the narrative and, equally, whether that knowledge comes already filtered through specifically dramatic form. The myth of Medea, for instance, Carr's inspiration, has proved enduringly popular across cultures and generations as a vehicle through which to interrogate changing expectations of the maternal. In tackling Medea 'the character', the playwright meets a figure whose name stands for a crime: infanticide. But simultaneously, that name evokes a theatrical image, one marked by the structures of Greek tragedy. The playwright finds she must tackle not just Medea, but *Medea*. Before she so much as opens her mouth, Medea – like Clytemnestra, Electra, Antigone, Phaedra – speaks of the classical stage. The associations are many and weighty, formal and ideological: dignity and stature; the 'grand scale' that tragedy seemingly demands; a striving for the 'universal', through a stage picture stark and uncluttered by local or domestic detail; a protagonist who overturns 'order', counter-balanced by a chorus who reason and mediate but will not intervene; pride, clash, catastrophe; ultimately, the retribution or resolution that might create 'catharsis'. A contemporary dramatist might not want all or any of this – might very well prefer intimacy, informality, irresolution – but in a sense it comes along anyway; how writer and audience read the myth is shaped by a complex of intertextual relations that can never be fully known but of which these form at least a part. A challenge for re-vision becomes what to 'do with' this cumbersome frame. If not adopted, can it wholly be rejected? Or is to do this to provoke its spectre to haunt the 'new' text all the more?

Sometimes such hauntings can be turned to advantage. A 1986 staging of Franca Rame's *Medea*, in Canterbury, offered this play as afterpiece to the main event that was Euripides' *Medea*.[5] I recall only the haziest shape of the Euripides production (more reflection on the selectivity of memory than comment on the work itself), but vividly remember the shock when a solitary actress burst on to the stage, running through the set the earlier cast had deserted. Deliberately, too little time had been allowed for the first play to 'settle': its after-image still hovered there, and this new Medea darted in and out of it, at times echoing its shapes but elsewhere resisting, almost literally kicking up its traces as if to dislodge its legacy and implant an alternative.[6] Her isolation onstage underlined her equivalent position in the narrative: she seemed painfully cast off, an outsider left with nothing but her rage. The decision to present the plays in tandem drew out the double-voicedness already present in the Euripides play. It was not that Euripides' *Medea* represented the problem and Rame's the solution; the latter took on more the character of a retort, an answer back that did not resolve the argument but at least refused to let it lie. The form of the one-woman play helped to release the character from the apparatus that conventionally surrounds her, if not from the myth's ideological structures; yet at the same time, the ghosts of that framing remained, proving their strength almost by their visual absence, so that at times it was as if Medea was running into invisible walls. Thus this 'double-bill' consciously exploited tensions the myth already implied, but beyond this drew on qualities peculiar to live performance, as Marvin Carlson examines in his book *The Haunted Stage*:

> The retelling of stories already told, the reenactment of events already enacted, the reexperience of emotions already experienced, these are and have always been central concerns of the theatre in all times and places, but closely allied to these concerns are the particular production dynamics of theatre: the stories it chooses to tell, the bodies and other physical materials it utilizes to tell them, and the places in which they are told. (Carlson 2001: 3)

The experience of performance is always palimpsestic, with stages and bodies, as well as minds, carrying with them the traces of what has gone before. When that layering is exposed, the operations of what Carlson calls theatre's 'memory machine' are made unusually visible: momentarily, we can glimpse an expanded horizon that reveals not so much what might have been, or even what might yet be, but a more truly multidimensional and multivocal present.

Many figures of classical myth are not primarily known to us through theatre and as such might travel a little lighter, although they never arrive empty-handed. Philomela and Demeter are among these, and both feature in re-visionings I examine later. Their stories are theatrically challenging for other reasons, not least in the quality they share of moving through multiple realms, or worlds. These characters journey, or their narratives do; where typically classical drama fixes its action to a single space – 'before the palace/temple/house' – these are myths that speak of displacement, dislocation and alienation. Philomela departs Athens with Tereus to join her sister, but suffers rape, mutilation and imprisonment at his hands before she and Procne are reunited; Demeter, devastated at the loss of Persephone, wanders the earth which turns sterile beneath her feet. Such worlds have form in the imagination, simultaneously vivid and transparent, and as such might resist translation into the concreteness of theatrical space and action. We do not want or need a pantomimic change transporting us to 'Hades' palace' to tell us where Demeter's daughter has been taken. However, when myths do not come dramatically pre-shaped, arguably the playwright can the more freely explore the capabilities of stage language and perhaps extend this in new directions. The Teatro Cooperativo del Sole's revisioning of the Demeter myth is founded on a theatrical landscape that draws its energy directly from the solidity – the awkwardness, even – of bodies and things (see Chapter 4). In markedly different style, Timberlake Wertenbaker adopts the forms of classical tragedy for her Philomela retelling but in order to parody, critique and subvert these (see Chapter 3).

What of those figures of myth we know not through classical drama but in dramatic form none the less? Ariadne's story has inspired writers and artists throughout history and has frequently been told through music, with Monteverdi's *Lamento d'Arianna* (1608), Handel's *Arianna in Creta* (1734), Strauss's *Ariadne auf Naxos* (1912) and Martinu's *Ariane* (1961) amongst numerous operas based upon the myth.[7] Typically these operas hinge upon Ariadne's emotions of loneliness and suffering, born of desertion by Theseus, for which music is perhaps the ideal vehicle. It is less apparent, however, what might constitute Ariadne's *drama*: what are her actions, her arguments? As a woman abandoned, she seems 'done to' rather than doing. The desertion of women is a recurrent motif in myth: it is in effect one of the means by which the epic hero defines himself, and is a theme played out in the tales of Ulysses and Penelope, and Jason and Medea (although with seemingly divergent 'femininities' produced as a result). Traditional perceptions of all three women might suggest that Ariadne has faith like Penelope's, but no eventual reward; equally, she receives punishment like Medea's, but for no obvious crime. For Cixous, Ariadne is almost the inversion of a male hero: 'Ariadne, without calculating, without hesitating, but believing, taking everything as far as it goes, giving everything, renouncing all security – spending without a return – the anti-Ulysses – never looking back, knowing how to break off, how to leave, advancing into emptiness, into the unknown.' Cixous locates Ariadne amidst a procession of mistreated, devastated women of literature, but, whilst acknowledging the courage of this character, she ultimately rejects her: 'I could not have been Ariadne' (1986: 75–6).

How far might a myth like Ariadne's be re-visioned: one familiar, dramatically, but arguably predefined by its protagonist's inaction? I have argued that direct reversals or refusals of known myth narratives are typically unsatisfying, since they avoid rather than address the real tensions these contain and are thus ineffectual in combating the weight of predominant canonised versions. Ariadne is left behind on Naxos; Medea kills her children; Penelope waits at home for Ulysses' return: these invariants shape the myths' deep structures, elements that in a sense cannot be changed. If Ariadne is widely perceived as 'victim', the playwright's challenge might be, as De Gay puts it, 'how to present a suffering female figure – physically, on stage – without rendering her a powerless object of pity' (De Gay 2003: 16). Penelope, conventionally the very model of idealised passivity, is I suggest successfully 'reactivated' by Cavarero, both within the terms of Plato's philosophical frame and as force that bears on the contemporary context. Yet it is less apparent how such a purpose might be realised through drama, for all that this medium offers: in particular, how live action – whose momentum necessarily limits spectators' opportunities for reflective pauses, let alone rereadings – might tease apart meanings layer by layer, subtly tuning into the forms of resistance already present in the text to uncover an agency for such a figure that proves resonant and relevant. In conclusion to this chapter, and as chronological and conceptual preface to those that follow, I examine one striking attempt to (re)write Ariadne's drama.

First staged in the Netherlands at the beginning of the 1960s, *A Thread in the Dark* by Hella Haasse (1918–) is the earliest play examined in this book, poised on the brink of feminism's second wave.[8] Haasse is a major literary figure in Holland; she is best known as a novelist, but her formally experimental writings span several genres including travel essays, literary criticism and autobiography as well as drama. Her work has been translated into around a dozen languages; *A Thread in the Dark* has been staged in Bahasa-Indonesian and French and an English translation published in 1997. The play is still regularly produced in the Netherlands and Flanders and premiered in New York in 2001.[9] As Mieke Kolk suggests, *A Thread in the Dark* follows the predominantly French tradition of the 1930s and 1940s established by Giradoux, Sartre, Anouilh and Yourcenar of rewriting classical tragedy from a modern existential viewpoint (Robson ed. 1997). Other sources similarly emphasise the influence of the French prewar theatrical philosophers on mid-century Dutch theatre, whose contemporary plays tended to focus heavily on debates on the morality of war and associated issues of individual and collective responsibility (Van Deursen and Eggermont 1994: 596). This aptly describes *A Thread in the Dark*, which examines the role myth can play in the operation of political power.

Haasse's writings consistently deal with the role of women in society and the constraints placed upon them. She does not describe herself as a feminist author, however, despite the fact that her work

is largely received in this spirit; in particular, her part-autobi-
ographical, part-philosophical text *Zelfportret als legkaart*
(Self-portrait as jigsaw puzzle), published in 1954, has been widely
considered 'a feminist document *avant la lettre*' (Breedt Bruyn
1992: 13). Haasse claims distance from the 'hard-line' feminism
that takes shape as 'an anti-attitude to a man's world', a stance
she finds unappealing and unproductive (Michielsen 1990: 46).
Nevertheless, female characters are central to her writings, their
desires and choices presented from a perspective both political
and transhistorical. Haasse observes: '[w]hen you are young you
perceive everything as being personal. Later you find out that there
are patterns to do with everyone's life, throughout time' (Breedt
Bruyn 1992: 11). Haasse's obsession with patterns and connections
is played out in her work in two principal ways: the selection of
source materials from diverse periods and genres, in the creation of
deeply layered textual worlds which deliberately blur the boundary
lines between 'fiction' and 'history'; and a recurrent use of the
puzzle or enigma, influenced in part by her interest in crime
writing.[10] Both these strategies are evident in *A Thread in the
Dark*, her re-visioning of the classical myth of Ariadne, Theseus
and the Minotaur. Like Cavarero, Haasse bypasses the familiar
'heroic' centre of the narrative to focus instead on a secondary,
even a homely motif: here, Ariadne's gift of the ball of thread that
will enable Theseus to escape the labyrinth. For both writers, it
seems, such small beginnings might nevertheless cause a whole
structure to unravel.

In Ovid's account of this myth, the Minotaur was the monstrous
offspring of Pasiphaë – wife of King Minos of Crete – and a white
bull sent from the sea by Poseidon. When grown, the hybrid
creature, which ate human flesh, was shut away by Minos in a
labyrinth. From then on at regular intervals Athens provided seven
youths and seven maidens for sacrifice as a 'tribute' that would
protect the country from invasion by Minos's armies. Eventually
the Athenian prince Theseus ended the practice by going into the
labyrinth himself and killing the monster, afterwards escaping
from the maze with the aid of Ariadne's thread. The Athenians
departed from Crete, Theseus taking Ariadne with him as his
bride-to-be; inexplicably, he then left her on the island of Naxos.
Ovid describes the abandonment as 'cruel', but can provide no
explanation for it. Robert Graves suggests that Ariadne could

have been deserted for a new mistress, or that Dionysos appeared to Theseus in a dream and claimed Ariadne for himself (Ovid 1955: 183–4; Graves 1961a: 339–40). In *A Thread in the Dark*, Haasse retains the narrative outline, but ingeniously subverts its conventional emphases by posing her own answer to the puzzle of why Ariadne is ultimately abandoned. Haasse's protagonist discovers a secret, that no Minotaur exists, or has indeed ever existed: it is itself a myth, a fiction created by her father as a means of generating fear and obedience, and maintaining belief at home and abroad in Crete's invincibility. Haasse's Minos explains that the people have inflated his idea of a Minotaur 'with their own imagination. He stamps and snorts and roars and spreads death and destruction, driven by what lives in every Cretan of secret hatred and resentment and black thoughts and suppressed appetites' (Haasse 1997: 109). What kills the sacrificial victims is not a monster but their own terror and the labyrinth itself, since the latter's complexity frustrates all bids to escape. Guided by Ariadne's thread, Haasse's Theseus emerges safely to proclaim not the deception, as she confidently expects, but rather that he has slaughtered the beast and won Athens's freedom. Ariadne comes to realise that Theseus's 'heroism', like Minos's authority, depends on a lie to sustain itself. She presses him to publish the truth: 'I don't want you to be famous for a deed you did not perform. I would start to doubt the truth of your other heroic deeds' (*ibid*.: 126). To preserve the secret, and with it his reputation, Theseus leaves Ariadne on Naxos and thereby severs her decisively from the rest of humanity.

In some respects *A Thread in the Dark* recalls the better-known *Antigone* (1942) of Jean Anouilh, although Haasse's work contains none of the anachronistic references that helped make explicit the earlier play's reference to its immediate context of anti-fascist resistance. There are marked similarities of style: the plays share formal elegance, heightened sense of structure and self-conscious patterning; there is in both a playful blending of the ordinary and the fantastical that aims to create something 'more real than real life' (Anouilh 1997: 23). Thematically the connections are stronger still. In both, the dynamics of idealism and cynicism are skilfully played off against each other: Anouilh and Haasse examine the behaviour of societies in times of war, and the imperative for individual acts of resistance against tyranny; each also poses the counter-argument that repressing such acts in the name of 'order' is a necessary but inevitably dirty business (Anouilh 1960). *A Thread in the Dark* was written some time after the Second World War, but it is still useful to read it with this in mind as a play about oppression, opposition and collusion. As late as 1995, Blom insists that the legacy of that war remains 'a more important topic and a more painful memory in the Netherlands than perhaps in any other country' (Blom 1995: 65). Haasse herself has remarked that the years between 1940 and 1945, during which her parents were put in Japanese concentration camps in the Dutch East Indies, were the most important of her life (Taylor 1994: 426; 433). At the time of the war, Haasse was working in the Netherlands as an actress. German troops in the Netherlands, as elsewhere, identified the arts as potentially a valuable source for the dissemination of Nazi ideology. Somehow Haasse managed to evade the requirement, formalised in 1942, for practising artists to sign up to the Nederlandse Kultuurkamer (Chamber of Culture) organisation, an act that would have brought generous subsidy but at the cost of swearing Nazi affiliation (*ibid.*: 426). Such small gestures form part of the wider picture of widespread Dutch resistance during the occupation, a history which left a modest legacy of patriotic pride (Moogk 1995). However, the broad national consensus about Dutch determination to oppose the enemy was seriously undermined in the 1960s, when a revival of interest in the war, one aspect of the wider anti-militarist fervour of the period, readdressed the issue of collaboration from a more complex perspective than hitherto. Rather than reserving this term for those who had overtly betrayed their country, by joining the Dutch National Socialist Movement or the SS, scrutiny turned on the behaviour of the economic and administrative elite of the day: 'Had not this elite actually been guilty of large-scale collaboration, and how democratic were its actions now?' (Blom 1995: 67). Read with this knowledge, *A Thread in the Dark* asks questions that are recognisably those of a country trying to come to terms with its own history: what choices are available to the individual in times of war, and what principles might a community be prepared to give up in the name of order?

The motif of the labyrinth is at the heart of Haasse's play and, as with 'puzzles' in her writings elsewhere, this comes to take on multiple meanings. At the physical level, the labyrinth is the trap by which Crete's victims perish even without the presence of a devouring Minotaur. Metaphorically, it represents the web of deception which maintains the myth, as Minos explains:

> MINOS: It is the power of Crete that's at stake. That is of interest for all Cretans.
>
> ARIADNE: Oh, a labyrinth of cunning and lies.
>
> MINOS: The labyrinth is the national symbol. *(Ariadne buries her face in her hands.)*
>
> Prove your intelligence. Accept things as they are
>
> (Haasse 1997: 109).

At the metaphoric level, Ariadne's determination to expose the truth seems to imply a desire to blast open the labyrinth and throw light into its darkest recesses. But, as the play proceeds, the labyrinth takes on an additional, psychological meaning. Literally, it is a complex of pathways that runs beneath the perceptible surface of the real: to enter the labyrinth is to go deeper than the everyday, to make that descent into the self that necessarily precedes the birth of new awareness. This journey represents a profound passage to self-recognition. Van Buuren has observed that Haasse's works consistently imply a universe that is itself labyrinthine; human beings constitute no stable centre, but exist rather as an integral part of this ever-fluctuating, web-like world. As Haasse sees it: 'Everything turns, myself as well, a fragment of this whole, I turn' (Van Buuren 1986: 12, my translation). Theseus's greater failing is not, finally, that he will not admit the secret that there is no monster at the labyrinth centre: it is that he dares not enter the labyrinth at all. Ariadne is comically surprised by the promptness of his reappearance from the maze: 'He can't have gone far, nor have descended very deep' (Haasse 1997: 118). In *A Thread in the Dark* it is not Theseus who truly enters the labyrinth, but Ariadne. It is she who draws the thread down into the darkness, whilst he uses the line only to pull himself higher. Cixous remarks of Plutarch's *Life of Theseus* that '[a]ll the figures of a rise to power are inscribed in the route Theseus takes'; for Haasse it seems that Ariadne's descent makes Theseus's elevation possible (Cixous 1986: 75–6).

Theseus's reluctance to encounter the depths of the labyrinth signals his inability to confront both the complexity of his motives and his own ultimate inconsequentiality. His tale of battle with a monster rings false: he has no wound to display, no dent in his sword, no blood. Entirely unscathed, he is no more than the sign of a champion. Demanding that Ariadne cease to challenge his authority, he warns that it is 'a virtue of civilisation to know when to desist from fighting' (Haasse 1997: 124). But Ariadne's vision has become too clear to close down again. She was always 'strange', as her sister Phaedra tells Theseus: 'She hears and sees things that aren't there. And she doesn't believe what is there' (*ibid.*: 127). The labyrinth, occulted from the everyday, comes to stand additionally for the myth of which Ariadne discovers herself to be a part, knowledge previously only accessible to her, fleetingly, in dreams. The play opens with her cry, whilst still half-asleep: 'No! Don't go! Don't sail away without me! Don't leave me alone!' (*ibid.*: 94). Van Buuren notes that revelations in Haasse's works produce a vision of life that is heavily layered, yet at the same time 'astonishingly clear, to such a point that the characters [...] become aware of the multiplicity of realities, each one concealing itself behind another that itself reflects yet another reality. The everyday thus becomes ambivalent, it acquires a fresh meaning of all being the sign of something else' (Van Buuren 1986: 13, my translation). Haasse's Ariadne becomes an abandoned figure in a double sense: she has been given up on, by Theseus, and has given herself up, to an altered vision that places her outside society. This is a position which, paradoxically, allows her a kind of freedom of speech. As the critic Lawrence Lipking has argued, '[a]n abandoned woman has nothing left to lose. She reminds us that even the ground we stand on can shift like sand' (Lipking 1988: 1).

The metaphor of shifting sands is literally theatricalised in the closing minutes of Haasse's play. Deserted, Ariadne wakes on the shores of Naxos. Suddenly cymbals, singing and dancing footsteps herald the arrival of Dionysos: 'young and radiant, crowned with vines, wrapped in a leopardskin'. The language changes to verse, signalling the status and 'otherness' of the god. He has come, he says, to grant Ariadne the happiness available to all his followers through divine intoxication that will free her from a human consciousness enslaved to false dichotomies of truth and lies, good and evil: 'There is a Minotaur, Ariadne, and there is none' (Haasse 1997: 146). As Dionysos's bride she would be a goddess, inhabiting a realm beyond light and dark. But for Ariadne, who has lived always in the shadow of the Minotaur, this course cannot be contemplated. She prefers to remain an abandoned, mortal woman, even though that decision forces her on to a 'razor's edge' as 'a human, alone, and without other humans' (*ibid.*: 147–8). Doubting her resolution, Dionysos gives Ariadne another chance: the opportunity to rewrite her own mythology. As she lies there, the light changes and the sands of the beach disperse, transporting her back to the couch where she lay at the play's beginning. Again she wakes from her dream; again she watches from her window the victims arrive for sacrifice; again she determines that the ritual must stop. But her righteous determination is now replaced by a calmer knowledge. Previously she exited the room to confront her father; when this time the Nurse demands where she is going, she simply replies: 'To Naxos' (*ibid.*: 150). Ariadne thus reaffirms her original act, in full knowledge that it condemns her to absolute exile.

For Haasse, Ariadne's decision appears to be the moral imperative although simultaneously one that the social order cannot sustain. To an extent, then, her Ariadne's actions could be judged futile. Arguably, *A Thread in the Dark* protests against corruption but remains ultimately pessimistic about reform: the truth-seeker should expect, even volunteer, to be expelled from the community. Politically, therefore, the stance of the play becomes ambiguous, especially within its original context, in its implied invitation to an audience to reflect on their own individual and collective choices past and present. Since Ariadne will not renounce the human world yet accepts banishment to its borders her choice seems to confirm the inevitability of the myth's outcome. Alternatively, this might evidence a decision, of Ariadne and Haasse, to accept the mythic frame in order to explore the viability of erosion from within. An enlightening comparison can briefly be drawn here with Haasse's 1976 novel *Een gevaarlijke verhouding of Daal-en-Bergse breiven* (A dangerous liaison or letters from Daal-and-Berg), which takes the conclusion of Laclos's *Les liaisons dangereuses* (1782) as its starting point. *Een gevaarlijke verhouding* is based upon an imagined correspondence between Haasse herself and Laclos's fictional Marquise de Meurteuil, the latter now living in exile in the Netherlands following her very public humiliation in Paris. In adopting a pre-existing character it is allowable, Haasse suggests, for an author 'to continue interrupted contours, colour those white spaces that stimulate the imagination, [and] make intriguing shadows transparent'; nevertheless, she reaffirms that 'fictitious characters never escape through breaks in reality out of their world of fiction. They have no other existence than what has been given to them' (Michielsen 1990: 47; 50). The Marquise and Ariadne are each condemned to solitude and neither character, fictional or mythical, can alter fundamentally the path that led them there. All that *is* possible is for another writer, another reader, to attempt to reach them in that place. Like Cavarero, Haasse addresses her characters and tries to uncover new meanings in their actions. What drove such women to be outcasts? What would it have cost to stay 'in'? It is this contact, of writer and character, that becomes the truly dangerous liaison, since the attempt to find a shared ground of understanding exposes the values of each in the encounter.

Ariadne may not break out of her reality but neither, Haasse suggests, is she forced to play it out in interminable and unchanging repetition. Her words and actions at the drama's close do not precisely mirror those of its beginning. *A Thread in the Dark* seems 'haunted', to use Carlson's term, by its own re-enactment: but crucially it is an echo with difference. It is not just Ariadne but other characters who appear subtly changed, as when the Nurse, who formerly merely urged her not to disturb her father, now clings to her to try and prevent her going. The play's conclusion thus envisions a perpetual replaying of the myth in which Ariadne's 'abandonment' becomes, increasingly, a conscious resolution inscribed from the very start. And, in that implied replaying, the self-awareness already exhibited by other figures in the drama might steadily increase, under the pressure exerted by Ariadne's action: Theseus's embarrassment when pressed to relate the story of his victory; Phaedra's distaste for the role of complaisant ingénue that masks covert practices of manipulation. Perceptibly, the cracks in the frame begin to widen. This, I think, is what Haasse's re-vision effects: less outright attack than gentle teasing open of her subject, as if pulling a thread to see where it could lead.

Haasse's appropriation of historical and legendary characters has been criticised by compatriot and fellow writer Monika Van Paemel. In Von Paemel's view, this method serves Haasse as 'a way out, as camouflage', to be contrasted with the 'totally honest' self-exposure of her earlier *Zelfportret als legkaart*. This challenge can be readily refuted: autobiographical writing, far from transparent, might offer no more reliable an account of the self than is produced through a manifestly literary device. However, Haasse would probably agree that re-vision *does* offer a 'way out'. She has commented that going deeply into other narratives and periods 'has something to do with a need for more time and space. It extends your life. Going deeply into the past allows you to place many associations and dimensions that do not fit the here and now' (Breedt Bruyn 1992: 13). This journey attempts not to uncover 'truth' as such but to read the past, in whatever guise, from the perspective of the present and in turn see the narrative of one's present as a story that could be told in multiple ways. A way out does not equal a retreat. In this play, Ariadne is the medium through which the author – perhaps indeed, 'camouflaged' – can penetrate the surface of the everyday; in so doing she pulls submerged meanings back up to the surface, in a project of psychological and wider cultural reconnection.

The plays I consider in Chapters 2 to 5 were written some time after *A Thread in the Dark* and as such sit more comfortably within the broad frame of second-wave feminism. Haasse's play is less explicitly concerned with gender than are most of these others, although one can hardly read it without recognising how fundamentally her characters' power positions and opportunities for action are constrained by their sex. *A Thread in the Dark* is also less formally experimental than the majority of works I discuss later. This is not to say that the text does not allow for innovative staging. That it is still regularly performed suggests it remains eminently usable, with some indication of the text's accessibility to imaginative interpretation demonstrated by its 2001 New York premiere: this production, by Lost Tribe Theatre Company, took place on the *Yankee Ferry*, the oldest ferryboat in the US, a suitable setting for a play whose action occurs on two islands and the voyage between them. In its treatment of myth, *A Thread in the Dark* seems to me to travel in two seemingly opposite directions: the first, towards a recognisably contemporary reality; the second, to the inner landscape of the self. The labyrinth acts as underlying symbol for both, at once representing the complex machinations of politicians that strive to maintain the social order and simultaneously serving as metaphor for the deeper fragmentation of a universe in flux, perpetually splitting and reforming, and a human self within this that is equally unstable and divided. Re-visioning myth, I propose, expressly requires authors to pursue multiple and in a sense divergent routes. The conditions are not unlike those that pertain when explicitly historical material is used: a playwright necessarily steps away from the immediate context to investigate an 'other' reality, whilst still retaining the connection to familiar ground. Both directions or applications are evident in re-visionings of myth, always braided together even though one strand may dominate. Subsequent chapters explore how these emphases are pursued in practice.

Notes

1 According to Lévi-Strauss, Frazer responded 'Heaven Forbid!' to the notion of carrying out research in the field (Lévi-Strauss 1963: 372). He was by no means unique in adopting an 'armchair' approach to anthropological investigation since this was generally endorsed by the comparative method.
2 Goddess worship has found specifically theatrical expression in some contexts. One example is the work of Kathy Jones's company, Ariadne Productions, which in the 1980s and 1990s staged a series of ritual dramas in Glastonbury. I have not included these in my discussion, finding them on the whole too straightforwardly celebratory to be of profound interest. Texts of some of these events are included in Kathy Jones ed. 1996.
3 According to Plato, when Socrates is in his cell with his male friends, waiting for death, his wife Xanthippe has to be thrown out; inappropriately, she weeps and screams at his fate, not understanding that, as a true philosopher, death is the end he has lived for. Cavarero 1995: 28–9.
4 As *In Spite of Plato* progresses, Cavarero turns increasingly to contemporary issues, although always with Penelope, Demeter, Diotima and the Maidservant as reference points. Within a wider discussion of bioethics she focuses on the legislative and juridical structures that attempt to control maternity and reproduction, and through her 'reactivation' of female figures suggests ways in which these processes might be fundamentally reconceived. See especially Cavarero 1995: 64–90.
5 The *Medea* double-bill was presented at the University of Kent's Gulbenkian Theatre in 1986.
6 Rame has commented that the *Medea* she and Fo created was 'una Medea popolare, che ricalca la tragedia scritta da Euripide'; her use

of the verb *ricalcare* suggests a self-conscious tracing, or following, of Euripides' drama (Cottino-Jones 2000: 21).

7 Famous paintings inspired by the myth of Theseus and Ariadne include Titian's *Bacchus and Ariadne* (c. 1522) and Tintoretto's *Ariadne, Venus and Bacchus* (1580). Ariadne is written about by Homer in the *Iliad* (c. 720 BCE), by Catullus (c. 84–54 BCE) in poem 64, by Ovid in the *Heroides* and *Metamorphoses* (both 1 CE) and is referred to in Chaucer's *The Legend of Good Women* (c. 1385–86) and Shakespeare's *A Midsummer Night's Dream* (c. 1595–96); later versions of the story include Marguérite Yourcenar's *Ariane et l'aventurier* (1939), André Gide's *Thésée* (1946) and Mary Renault's *The King Must Die* (1958). Yourcenar also wrote a short play based on the myth, *Qui n'a pas son minotaure?* (1943).

8 According to Nederland Theater Institut records, *A Thread in the Dark* was first staged in 1960–61 in Amsterdam by the Puck Toneelgroep, and was awarded the Visser Neerlandia Prize in 1962. It was published in the Netherlands the following year and has since been reprinted many times.

9 Twenty-first century productions of Haasse's play in the Netherlands include stagings by the Theatergroep Zout (2000) and Verteltheater van Pagée (2004).

10 Hannah Van Buuren notes that Haasse's father, a Dutch government official, wrote crime novels in his spare time and that Haasse inherited from him her passion for the genre. Her mother was a concert pianist, and Haasse herself has emphasised the significance of music as a key formative influence that directly informs the structural principles of her writing. Van Buuren 1986: 13; Breedt Bruyn 1992: 12.

2

Political acts

> To keep on making theatre is in itself a political choice: opting for
> human relationships rather than mechanical, for intimacy rather
> than mass media, for memory and resistance rather than neglect
> and success. Politics has very different meanings across time and
> geography, and the meaning is constantly changing. Politics can
> quickly be related to power: a way to keep in power, or a way to
> criticise, overthrow, counterbalance and take power; a way to live,
> survive and deal with power or a way of separating from power and
> of refusing. (Julia Varley, in Varley ed. 1998: 3)

In this chapter I discuss three plays born of second-wave feminism
which examine the political potential of re-visioning myths: the
monologues *The Same Old Story* and *Medea*, co-authored by
Franca Rame and Dario Fo (1977), and Sarah Daniels's realist
drama *Neaptide* (1986). Yet if theatre-making is inherently
political, as Varley suggests, any such selection may be challenged:
why these texts rather than others? First, the discussions of this
chapter aim to facilitate analysis of the political beyond Varley's
claim that theatre is already, of itself, resistant. I have chosen plays
where engagement with political subjects is self-conscious and
systematic rather than, in a sense, a coincidence of their theme.
Further, these plays manifestly assume a partisan position: they are
left-wing in viewpoint, voicing the concerns of those whom society
makes vulnerable; they aim to expose and fight injustices and to
provoke in their audiences a heightened recognition of the necessity
for social change. Yet whatever analysis such plays offer, a politics
of content alone is insufficient to address questions of efficacy.
The communication of ideas is mediated through the means of
theatrical production: the question of where plays are performed,
how and to whom is self-evidently as vital to this process as
their internal dramaturgy. My selection of texts addresses such

questions by considering plays presented in 'mainstream' as well as 'alternative' contexts and that adopt sharply contrasting aesthetic forms.

The underlying enquiry of this chapter is to ask how far re-visoning of myth in drama can assume a political shape. The degree of abstraction from the immediate that attention to myths demands might seem at best to entail some weakening of a play's political import and at worst point to the indulgence of escapism (as with Von Paemel's accusation, discussed in the previous chapter, that Haasse's use of this strategy constituted a 'way out'). However, I argue that the practice of rewriting myth leads playwrights simultaneously in (at least) two directions: away from their contemporary reality, in pursuit of a narrative that is 'other' to it; and back towards it, in order to understand both the motivations behind the journey and the implications of its discoveries. It is through this dual trajectory, I suggest, that political application becomes possible. The engagement with stories not one's own requires temporary detachment from proximate concerns, but this is itself a political act since it necessitates a widening of perspective that invites us to think globally, cross-culturally: the events of our lives are regarded not narrowly but in their intersection with the lives – including lives historical and mythical – of others. Ideally such re-visionings will forge meaningful connections that keep this encounter alive, precise and provocative; the risk is that artificial or reductive 'parallels' may be drawn that fail to illuminate in either context. This problem is one of which I have been acutely aware in writing this book. By commenting, in different chapters, on 'Medeas' originating from 1970s Italy, 1990s Ireland and twenty-first-century Germany, I do not suggest that this narrative or archetype is a uniformly serviceable tool for any place or period, or that, since each play is able to turn the myth to its purpose, there must be little fundamental difference between their contexts. Far from it: by studying myths in the drama of diverse cultures I seek to highlight dissimilarity as much as points of affinity.

Yet, as the preceding statement acknowledges, I do consciously look for connectedness, if not 'parallels', across texts and contexts and between playwrights, despite the difficulties this brings. The impact of postmodern and postcolonial analyses, in particular, has been such that assertions for correspondence of this kind may be viewed with suspicion; in the contemporary academic climate, to propose that phenomena from different cultures are in any significant way 'the same' may be felt to undermine the individualism of each. This recognition of difference has powerfully shaped the development of modern feminism; while tensions and repressions – along lines of class, race, ethnicity and sexuality – were apparent within Anglo-American and continental feminist 'movements' virtually from their inception, the reluctance of (perhaps predominantly white, middle-class and heterosexual) activists to face up to the implications of internal divisions arguably hastened the fracturing of feminism as meaningful political identity. But it is surely possible to explore ideas of women's subordination through patriarchal gender relations, for example, without claiming universalism of experience; an identity position may be adopted strategically with full awareness of its limits. One cannot assume commonalities of knowledge and experience, cannot take the characteristic features of a group as true for, and sufficient to define, its adherents: to bypass the specificity of individuals through exclusive focus on their existence as 'social category', from whatever ideological perspective, is to dehumanise. What the practice of re-vision must not do, therefore, is to use myths as shortcut through a supposition of sameness. Yet the fact that myths do persist and are continually recycled, cross-culturally, suggests they are available as significantly, if not infinitely, malleable texts; moreover, the degree of recognition that attaches to myths hints at their unusual potentiality as vehicles for the proposition of mutually shared experience. However, each act of (re)telling will be ideologically marked, whether more or less consciously.

The plays I discuss in this chapter investigate the ideological function of myth-making and attempt to direct this to radical ends. *The Same Old Story* and *Medea* are drawn from the vast repertoire of Dario Fo and Franca Rame, renowned actor-playwrights whose personal and professional partnership has lasted more than half a century. My commentary deals more with Rame than Fo, since it was importantly her frustration with the limited roles then available to her that provided the stimulus for the plays to be created; both, however, had become increasingly aware that the oppressions facing women in contemporary Italian society merited specific attention in their theatre. The two texts form part of the now extensive body of one-woman plays for which Rame has since become famous, but it is evident that these plays and the majority of their output emerged from a process that has remained profoundly collaborative. *The Same Old Story* (the Italian title, *Abbiamo tutti la stessa storia*) and *Medea* employ elements of fairy tale and Greek tragedy respectively to deconstruct pervasive myths, in the Barthesian sense, of feminine sexuality, marriage and motherhood that seemingly raise women's status whilst in practice limiting their rights as individuals. Similar themes are contrastingly addressed in *Neaptide*, by the British playwright Sarah Daniels, a play that uses the myth of Demeter and Persephone to explore and ultimately to assert the power of female affiliations. The concerns of Daniels's play, its central character a lesbian mother struggling to retain custody of her young daughter, were highly topical in 1980s Britain, when the very notion of a 'lesbian mother' was widely viewed as a contradiction in terms. The same year *Neaptide* was produced saw the attempt to pass a Private Member's Bill in the UK that would prevent local authorities from 'promoting' homosexuality in schools; whilst this first move failed, the initiative resurfaced the following year as the infamous Clause 28 within a Local Government Bill, becoming law in 1988 as Section 28.[1] It is important to read *Neaptide* with knowledge of this context; not least, the perceived imperative to counter popular prejudice helps explain Daniels's decision to present, in the character of Claire, so emphatically 'positive' a protagonist.

To set plays by Rame and Fo alongside another by Daniels is not to imply parallels between what are evidently contrasting styles of drama, presented in very different theatrical contexts and at distinct cultural moments. My intention is rather to highlight a shared strategy whereby myth is adopted as 'pretext' for political debate. Whilst myths serve principally here as form of social commentary, the plays simultaneously interrogate the processes by which myths are constructed and exploited. This strategy of double deconstruction is especially apparent in Rame's work, through protagonists able to comment, with ironic detachment, on their own position within dramatic and mythic frames; this critical edge is heightened through an event structure that typically juxtaposes several monologues against each other, connecting all of these through direct audience address by Rame 'out of character'. The two monologues discussed explore myth in both classical and more domesticated forms. Rame's *The Same Old Story* takes no single narrative but creates an anarchic concoction blended from bits of every fairy story a 'sweet little girl' would know and some she certainly would not (Rame and Fo 1991: 55). Like Haasse's *A Thread in the Dark*, Rame's *Medea* adheres to the familiar narrative of its source myth but invites us to view the protagonist's motivation in a new light; *The Same Old Story*, freed from the strictures of a single narrative, offers a radical 'breaking apart' of the terrain of fairy tale that transforms this virtually beyond recognition. The two monologues also diverge formally. *Medea* draws the audience into the world of the myth; although Rame as performer repeatedly shifts representation of the protagonist and a female Chorus, that world itself remains intact. *The Same Old Story*, on the other hand, has two distinct parts. The first gives a comic representation of a reality that is recognisably contemporary (regardless of its elements of farcical distortion), again with Rame switching perspectives to demonstrate interactions with other characters. In the second part, which begins with the protagonist telling a story to her daughter, Rame establishes surreal fairy tale as the new 'reality': the audience does not return, except by implication, to the dramatic context with which the monologue began. Stylistically diverse, *The Same Old Story* and *Medea* are connected in presenting myth as ideological text adopted by those who profit most from an unequal system and perpetuated by almost everyone within it. In this too the plays recall *A Thread in the Dark*, but unlike the earlier play focus directly on the complicity of women in maintaining their own oppression through subscribing to supposedly feminine ideals of patience and self-sacrifice.

The function of myth in *Neaptide* is more complicated to define. The narrative of Demeter and Persephone underpins the play's contemporary action, its most concrete appearance channelled naturalistically through the device of a mother reading to her daughter. The depiction of storytelling as means of female bonding links Daniels's play with Rame's, but here the construction does not take over. In *Neaptide* the relationship of myth to present-day action remains analogous rather than direct, serving a variety of symbolic functions. As an overtly female-centred 'bedtime story', the Demeter myth is used to underline the loving relationship which exists between mother and daughter, but since narratively the tale hinges on Persephone's abduction this prepares the audience to anticipate disruption of what seems the idyllic *status quo* through intervention of a male outsider. However, the ending of the myth, with its compromise that Persephone will spend part of the year with Demeter and part underground with Hades, is not mirrored in the play. In this sense *Neaptide* is more than reinterpretation, since Daniels proposes an alternative outcome that denies the masculine principle right of ownership; the play's emphasis on the transformative potential of love between women invites an audience to consider whether a normative 'balance' of male with female need be the only possible conclusion.

Selection of these very different plays also allows us to examine the fitness of contrasting dramatic styles for politicised myth re-vision. In his 2003 study of left-wing playwrights in postwar Britain, Michael Patterson highlights two distinct theatrical models: the reflectionist and interventionist. The first approach is broadly realistic, if not necessarily fully naturalistic, its aim to provide an accurate representation of the contemporary world that exposes its tensions and oppressions. The second, Brecht-influenced approach may employ a variety of theatrical elements within a fragmented and open-ended text that seeks not just to analyse and challenge the world 'as it is' but to interrogate our modes of perception. As Patterson is quick to point out, these approaches may be best regarded as the two ends of a spectrum, an indication of divergent tendencies rather than either/ or options of dramatic strategy (Patterson 2003: 11–24). For the plays examined in this chapter, we can usefully see *Neaptide* as broadly illustrative of the reflectionist tendency and Rame's monologues, by contrast, as interventionist. From this basis one can begin to consider how appropriate the two modes prove for myth re-vision. One difficulty of the realist/reflectionist approach will immediately be apparent: myths do not deal overtly in the real but are conceived as heightened departures from this; furthermore, myths in the sense discussed here emerged not from the contemporary present but from an ancient past, although they are evidently revived and reshaped by succeeding generations. The most obvious option for reflectionist myth rewriting is to choose, as Daniels does, to relocate the narrative in the modern world through analogy. This can prove problematic in practice, since it is difficult to find meaningful realistic equivalents for the extreme characters and conflicts depicted in myths: not because the contemporary world lacks strong passions or violent oppositions but because the translation risks seeming forced or bathetic. Another difficulty for an audience is that recognition, gradual or immediate, of a mythic subtext can serve to distract attention from the play's realistic 'surface': paradoxically, knowledge of the myth may distort spectators' reception of the conflicts presented and their sense of the playwright's intentions. Finally, the strategy of reflectionist analogy leaves the author especially vulnerable to charges of 'hubris', as we saw in some of the responses to *By the Bog of Cats*. (You think you can write a *Medea*? Best to leave that to Euripides.) I am emphasising here qualities that make the reflectionist model a difficult one for myth rewriting – particularly for expressly political ends – and my discussion of *Neaptide* will show how these problems are confronted in practice; at the same time one should credit the political-realist approach for its determination to voice arguments and represent sides of 'reality' that dominant ideologies normally overlook or actively seek to suppress. It will also be relevant for the reader to recall the example of Haasse's *A Thread in the Dark*, which treats its source myth in largely realistic *style* although it does not resituate the action; Haasse does however allow herself a significant 'non-realist' departure by opting to replay the first scene at the end of her drama, this time with the benefit of hindsight for protagonist and audience.

The interventionist model, here exemplified in the two monologues of Rame and Fo, is potentially at considerable advantage in the appropriation of myths for the purpose of ideological critique. First, a theatrical strategy that endorses fragmentation and montage is better suited to the simultaneous representation of multiple alternatives; in this way, one of the inherent problems of a rewriting project – the difficulties attached, for instance, to deviation from a narrative's prescribed outcome – is partially surmounted. The interventionist model more easily allows the playwright to adhere to and depart from the myth in the same moment: this would seem crucial if the intention is to depict an oppressive situation authentically and plausibly yet to avoid closing down the possibility of alternative choices. In addition, although I began this chapter by pointing out the risk that the abstraction of myth may appear to divorce the action from contemporary experience, one can equally argue the reverse: for many political playwrights, critical analysis is positively facilitated by the introduction of distance. As Brecht proposed, a historically removed or fabulous setting aids the defamiliarisation needed to help spectators recognise ideological contradictions that had become invisible or normalised. It is also arguable that the 'predetermined' character of myths may be used to advantage rather than prove a stumbling block: for if the narrative and its conclusion are already known quantities, spectators should focus – one hopes critically – on the steps that lead to the denouement, rather than be preoccupied by suspense. Furthermore, the interventionist model readily permits juxtaposition of contemporary and mythic worlds, whereas the reflectionist approach must find a plausible excuse to introduce mythic references (for instance through a realistically framed moment of storytelling, or a play-within-a-play); such layering of different realities could also prompt audiences to make the connection between mythic text(s) and modern experience. Yet while an undoubted strength of interventionist drama is its ability to be 'coolly critical' and correspondingly to encourage this attitude in spectators, this very quality may sit uncomfortably with the myth or myths that have inspired it. Myths typically deal in extreme passions: how will contemporary interventionist re-visions negotiate the balance between expression of feeling and its analysis? The reflectionist model clearly has its limitations, but a strengths is its ability to make a powerful emotional case – although, arguably, at the risk of distorting spectators' judgements in the process.

It is one matter to examine these plays, interventionist or reflectionist, for their resistant content; it is altogether another to attempt retrospective judgement of their efficacy as socio-political acts. Any attempt to assess the latter will be fraught with problems, since aside from discontinuities in time and place there is the yet more fundamental difficulty of how the relationship between theatrical event and spectator response can conceivably be evaluated with any accuracy. It is obvious that a play which is confrontational in one context can be conservative in another; equally obviously, no audience's experience is unified (however strong might be the impression of consensus) and what is unchallenging for a majority may still prove profoundly so for some spectators. In my discussion, then, I draw attention to the plays' original contexts but make no attempt to fix them there. The fact that all three plays are still performed, and in many parts of the world, suggests that political impact can hardly be defined by and confined to the occasion of first production.[2] And in what follows, as throughout this book, I am also concerned to engage with each play as *text*: to value reading as well as watching of this work, and to anticipate and invite future stagings.

Furiously funny: *The Same Old Story* and *Medea* of Franca Rame and Dario Fo

> Why did I continue? Because through my work I can talk to many people every day and I can deal with political issues, I can fight for the causes I believe in, like an occupied factory, a house for a homeless person, a job for an immigrant family, a bed in a hospital for someone who is HIV positive. (Rame 2004: 19)

The two monologues I discuss here were first produced in the late 1970s, but Franca Rame's career in the Italian theatre began much earlier. Born in 1929 into a family company of touring actor-puppeteers, she famously made her first stage appearance just eight days old (Farrell 2001: 30). Rame became an actress without making a conscious decision to do so; she has often remarked that she has no great love for the theatre and stated a few years ago that if she could turn back the clock she 'would have done anything in my life, apart from this job' (Rame 2004: 21). Rame's training-by-experience and natural aptitude – together with physical attractions that few reviewers let pass without comment – brought her considerable success in the traditional theatre.[3] However, it is for her long association with the comic actor and playwright Dario Fo that she is best known. The couple met and married in the early 1950s, and in 1959 formed their own company with Fo as writer, director and actor and Rame as leading actress, developing a performance style influenced by commedia, storytelling, clowning and puppetry. They specialised in political satire, an emphasis that brought them regularly and increasingly into conflict with the Italian government, censors, police and Vatican (this last through Fo's play *Mistero Buffo*, 1969). In the early stages of their joint career the satire was relatively gentle, in shows staged predominantly in 'bourgeois' contexts: that is, to largely middle-class audiences in commercial theatre venues.

They became a popular celebrity couple: Farrell notes that Fo adopted the role of 'scoffing but jovial bohemian rather than [...] enraged iconoclast', while for a long time Rame played the part of fashionable actress 'happy to be photographed encased in furs, tight skirts [or] staged *déshabillé*, seducing the camera and the reader with a girlish pout' (Farrell 2001: 51). Rame's offstage persona was not dissimilar to the *svampita* role type for which she had become known, a combination of the Hollywoodesque 'dumb blonde' and the 'chattering housewife' figure of popular Italian theatre (Cottino-Jones 2000: 11).

By the late 1960s, escalating political unrest and increased labour militancy prompted the couple to make the move they had already been contemplating: finally to leave their 'gilded ghetto' and place themselves at the service of the workers, the class to which they felt they belonged (Rame and Fo 1991: x). In 1968 they formed Nuova Scena, a theatre collective linked to the Communist Party that sought to be structurally egalitarian and popularly accessible, touring to factories, market places, clubs and street demonstrations. Frustrated by political infighting and Party bureaucracy – and criticised by the Party itself as well as by the Italian state – the company lasted only two years, but many of its principles took root. In 1970 Fo and Rame founded La Commune, a company allied to the political left but not specifically to the Communists. La Commune was flexible, improvisatory and responsive to the changing social situation and throughout the 1970s staged hundreds of performances on topical issues to large popular audiences. Within the company's organisational structure, Rame's role in particular was expanding and changing in profound ways: now far more than simply its lead actress, she had become chief administrator and principal political spokesperson and campaigner (Farrell 2001: 105–11). Onstage, however, the characters she portrayed – written for her by Fo – had not evolved radically from those with which she had originally been associated. Fo's plays represented women as part of the wider 'oppressed', his female characters active in criticising and at times subverting the abuses of authority, but thus far they had exhibited little consciousness of exclusions from power specific to their status as women.

By the mid-1970s, feminism in Italy was a force difficult to ignore. An autonomous women's movement had emerged publically at the start of the decade, born from the wider atmosphere of disruption that marked the late 1960s, drawing energy in particular from the protests of workers and students and swiftly expanding from its middle-class base to establish an extensive network of activists throughout the organised labour movement. There were some early and significant achievements: fundamental was the legalisation of divorce in Italy in 1970, a ruling that a referendum instigated by the Vatican, four years later, failed to overturn. Women's educational opportunities had also increased; following the general elevation of higher education in the country in the 1960s, women's access rose proportionately more than men's, starting a trend that continued steadily through the 1970s and 1980s (Beccalli 1994: 92–3). However, there was a widespread sense that, whilst women might be better off in material terms than before, their oppression continued on a subjective and 'symbolic' level. As early as 1970 Carla Lonzi, one of the movement's founders, had argued in a pamphlet titled 'Let's Spit on Hegel' that campaigns for 'equality' failed to recognise the depth of the problem: 'Culture, ideology, institutions, rituals, codes and mores are all surrounded by male superstitions about women. This background pollutes any private situation: from this background man keeps gathering his presumptions and arrogance' (Lonzi 1970: 51). Rame and Fo acknowledged the justice of criticisms levelled by feminist collectives that their jointly produced work for theatre and television had, in its primary focus on class analysis, largely failed to address such questions. In an interview at this period, Rame remarked that, for a theatre like theirs, *not* to connect with women's issues 'would be really serious' (Wood 2000: 163). Their initial attempt to redress this perceived deficiency was *Parliamo di donne* (Let's talk about women), a collection of co-authored sketches on women's lives, acted by Rame and broadcast on Italian television in 1977; this was the first time in her partnership with Fo that Rame had had an explicit and acknowledged input as writer. The play won her an IDI prize as Best Television Actress, but in political terms *Parliamo di donne* was less successful. Whilst the piece certainly put female experience into the foreground, it was severely challenged by women's groups for representing this without providing the feminist analysis necessary to make sense of it (Piccolo 2000: 127). A significantly revised version of

Parliamo di donne was presented later the same year as *Tutta casa, letto e chiesa* ('All home, bed and church'), the title a play on the colloquial Italian phrase 'tutta casa, lavoro e chiesa' ('all home, work and church') used to describe the supposed preoccupations of the petit-bourgeois Italian (Hirst 1989: 140). It is from *Tutta casa ...* that the monologues *The Same Old Story* and *Medea* are taken.

Interviewed in Italy's Marxist newspaper *Il manifesto* in 1977, Rame acknowledged the influence of feminism on her own thinking but at the same time was careful to assert a degree of distance from its more extreme positions:

> One must take one's hat off to what the feminist movement has achieved. Feminists have made so many people understand so many things, and, thanks to their efforts, I too have a different relationship with my family. I, however, believe that the new condition of women depends on the transformation of society. First we have to change class relationships: I believe women's liberation is tied to the class struggle. And, as well, we need to change men, make them learn and discover and respect our dignity. Then finally women will be really free. (Hirst 1989: 146)

Rame stops short of Lonzi's more radical conclusion that since women's oppression preceded the birth of capitalism their liberation could not be anticipated as consequence of the revolution. For Rame, a Marxist analysis remained crucial. Male social privilege was to be seen as product not of 'patriarchy' as such but of unequal class relations. From this perspective, capitalist principles of labour and profit, ownership and exploitation are thought to infiltrate and distort relations within the domestic sphere; as Sue-Ellen Case outlines it, the wife-mother provided a form of unpaid labour, through housework and by reproduction, that created leisure and privileges for the male worker-homeowner that she did not herself enjoy (Case 1988: 84). Each of the monologues of *Tutta casa, letto e chiesa* illustrates this system at work; but, as their protagonists struggle within and try to change that system, inevitably they find themselves wrestling as much with 'rituals, codes and mores' as with more material inequities. Thus all of these plays tackle myths in the wider Barthesian sense of ideological narrative, but *The Same Old Story* and *Medea* show further how the discourses of storytelling and mythmaking in the traditional sense might be appropriated for radical ends.

'They got married and lived happily ever, ever after. The very next day ...'

The Same Old Story is constructed in two parts. In the first, the audience witness a succession of events that culminate in the protagonist giving birth; the second takes the shape of a fairy tale, supposedly related by the new mother to her daughter but in fact enacted so fully that spectators might well lose sight of the context by which it was introduced. Distinct as they initially appear, these two parts are integrally linked. Each implicitly comments on the other: both deal directly with themes of gender relations, sexuality and sexual responsibility, but where the first does this semi-realistically the second escapes into a subversive fantasy world where utopian alternatives are playfully explored. The placing of fairy tale within this encourages the audience to keep in mind both the fictional, and thus alterable, character of all stories – especially those that present themselves as the way things happen in 'real life' – and the necessarily manipulative role of all storytellers.

In common with the majority of the Rame–Fo monologues, *The Same Old Story* requires only minimal *mise-en-scène*. At first we simply see the performer, an anonymous 'young woman', stretched out on a rostrum in dim light. We discover she is engaged in (evidently unsatisfactory) lovemaking with a male partner, unseen:

> No, no, please ... please ... keep still ... not like that, I can't breathe. Wait ... Yes of course I like making love, but I'd like a bit more ... well I don't know how to put it ... you're squashing me flat ... Get off me ... Stop that! You're slobbering all over my face ... (Rame and Fo 1991: 49)

The scene paints a comical picture of sexual frustration, to some degree gender-stereotypical: the woman longs for 'a bit of feeling' while the man, we are told, treats her like 'a bloody pinball machine ... just slap 50p in the slot and all the lights start flashing' (*ibid*.: 49). This impression that the woman is emotional and talkative, her partner 'strong and silent', is heightened by a monologue structure that does not allow any comments from the man except by mediation. Self-evidently the form privileges the woman's perspective (reflecting the co-authors' decision that this should at last be prioritised), yet the more Rame's character speaks, the more we become aware of the struggle to articulate inequities in the couple's relations. While she may not 'know how to put it', there *is* nevertheless something the woman demands more of: 'feeling' is one attempt to define it, but the word is thrown back at her as part of the sentimental discourse of romantic fiction.

Struggling to communicate with her partner, Rame's protagonist adapts the language of the class struggle. The couple's sexual relations reflect the oppressive class system which both are actively engaged in fighting within the public sphere. When their lovemaking is at its most mutually responsive and reciprocal she finds him 'almost a comrade'; ultimately, however, he shows little solidarity with her position since he refuses to use contraception – since to do so diminishes his pleasure – leaving her to face the risk and, as it transpires, the reality of pregnancy as if this were a problem exclusively her own. She is forced to conclude that his 'dick is [his] real true comrade': he has signally failed to extend critical analysis from the workplace to address the exploitation inherent in his sexual and other relationships with women. A young woman, forced to cope on her own with an accidental pregnancy: this could be the 'same old story' hinted at in the play's title. Disempowered in her relations with her lover, the protagonist is next exploited by the medical profession when she tries to obtain an abortion; the two equally unacceptable choices before her are an agonisingly painful and humiliating back-street operation or one performed privately by professional gynaecologists more than willing to set aside 'conscientious objections' for patients able to stump up the extortionate fee.[4] Rame and Fo used this section of the monologue to criticise the deeply repressive abortion laws, powerfully defended by the Catholic Church and for many years a central issue for the Italian feminist movement (and one which cuts across, although is not unaffected by, class divisions).[5] The culturally influential group Rivolta Femminile made this statement in its 1970 manifesto, in support of the widespread national campaign to decriminalise abortion:

> Woman's first reason for resentment against society lies in being forced to face maternity as a dilemma. We denounce the unnatural nature of a maternity paid for at a cost of exclusion. The refusal of the freedom of abortion is part of the global denial of women's autonomy. We do not wish to think about motherhood all our lives or to continue to be unwitting instruments of patriarchal power. (Bono and Kemp eds 1991: 38)

Rivolta Femminile produced statistics indicating that between one and three million women in Italy were having clandestine abortions every year, risking their lives as well as the likelihood of civil and religious ostracism (Bono and Kemp eds 1991: 214). Rame herself was known to be sympathetic to the campaign and indeed had been suspected of involvement in the practice of illegal abortion.[6] Following years of demonstrations – which had the positive side-effect of bringing together women with politically diverse affiliations – a law was passed in 1978 that legalised abortion, yet which in practice still proved severely restrictive.[7] Groups continued to campaign vigorously for deeper reforms, using slogans such as 'Aborto si, ma non finisce qui' (Bassnett 1986: 95). In *The Same Old Story*, Rame's protagonist refuses the intolerable position in which the Italian legal and medical systems conspire to place her and takes the only other available course: she keeps the baby. There follows a farcical, fast-forward tour of a pregnancy that within a matter of moments leads to the birth – 'Is it a boy? … (*Disappointed.*) No? … (*Gobsmacked.*) Well what is it then?' – of a girl impatiently urged by her mother to 'Grow up, come on', as if there is no time to be lost in imparting the lessons her own experiences have taught her (Rame and Fo 1991: 55). This is where the more explicitly framed 'storytelling' begins.

It is clear that the tale at the heart of this monologue is a story *about* fairy stories, a deconstruction of the genre to which it might initially be thought to subscribe. The playwrights adopt the ritualised language of storytelling precisely in order to subvert this: 'once upon a time there was a dear sweet little girl who had a beautiful dolly. Well, to tell you the truth the dolly wasn't beautiful at all; she was filthy dirty [and] used the most terrible bad swear words' (*ibid.*: 55). The juxtaposition of girl and doll 'characters' provides an image of conformity to an approved feminine type and simultaneously rebellion against it. Discussing Cixous's writing, Morag Shiach has argued that 'the putting-in-place of patriarchy […] generates anger, excess, a voice that seems to escape control and instead goes underground' (Shiach 1991: 14). *The Same Old Story* stages this principle in action, as a form of unconscious displacement: the 'foul-mouthed' doll can speak that which the 'sweet' little girl knows she must repress, or else risk rejection; this is indeed the initial fate of the doll, thrown out by the girl's mother on to a rubbish heap. The sheer

violence of this policing triggers the beginnings of resistance in
the girl who, in her turn, escapes the confines of the home and
embarks on a journey of discovery. The audience find themselves
plunged into an unfolding adventure that seems partially familiar
– little girls, dark woods, wolves – but reveals itself quickly as
an amalgam of fragments and ultimately as anti-fairy tale, Red
Riding Hood turned inside out. The ahistorical, placeless quality
that the genre typically reinforces, for example through formal
phraseology such as 'Once upon a time …', is invoked yet set into
sharp relief by a generous sprinkling of contemporary reference
points: Rame's female protagonists may meet a dwarf and a wolf,
but the former is denounced by the doll as a 'fucking bastard …
shitface … arsehole!' and the latter insists he is no 'dickhead wolf'
but actually a computer programmer transformed by a spell (Rame
and Fo 1991: 56–7). Thus although the consistently entertaining
story unfolds at breathless speed it is perpetually and intentionally
jarring. Rame's prowess as endlessly inventive teller will engage us
but we are not permitted to become spellbound; this is a story with
political application and the strategies employed are designed to
remind us of this. There are huge leaps of time, such that when the
doll is found, only moments after being thrown out of the house,
we learn she has undergone a whole, exhausting relationship with
a red cat – a reference back to the leftist man of the first part,
perhaps – who abused and exploited her but with whom she claims
she could at least have 'a decent political argy-bargy' (*ibid.*: 58).
Equally, the tale's 'little girl' has matured at comical speed and is
now united with the computer programmer: Rame wants to cut to
the chase, as if urging all participants to 'grow up, come on' and
confront the reality of adult men and women's relations.

The girl's 'blissful' marriage is immediately demonstrated to be
as unequal in its own terms as the alternative and more overtly
exploitative partnership of doll and cat. A nagging voice, ascribed
to the doll, suggests the woman has with complicity become a
domestic and sexual slave, lulled into a state of false consciousness.
Furiously, the husband attempts to silence this critic; in what is
perhaps the most bizarre turn in a consistently surreal story, the
doll disappears up his bottom. Now 'pregnant', he is forced to
give birth to the rebellious, 'dirty' femininity for whose existence
he bears partial responsibility. In so doing he explodes, a moment
signalling, I suggest – in reflection of the Marxism-plus-anarchy

that characterises the co-authors' approach – that the internal contradictions of the system have proved a force sufficient to blow it apart. From a performance viewpoint, also, it illustrates the liberating freedoms of (especially solo) storytelling: in a fantasy, objectionable characters may be simply zapped, poisoned or blasted out of existence. There is, after all, no necessity to tell the same old story, and the play is as much gleeful celebration of an endlessly transformative creativity as it is communication of materialist-feminist analysis.

Reunited with her doll, the girl hugs her until 'little by little she vanishes into her heart': the fracture which had forced these supposedly irreconcilable identities apart has been healed, and although now 'all alone' she is actually more complete than when married. This image of wholeness, of a newly unified self, is arguably simplistic; concern that this is the case might increase with the final sequence, which sees the heroine come upon other 'grown-up little girls' sitting under a tree whose sharing of experiences leads to the conclusion that 'every single one' has 'exactly the same story to tell' (*ibid.*: 60). It is a scene directly suggestive of feminist consciousness-raising, an activity that in Italy at the time took the form of the *autocoscienza*: perhaps more so than the Anglo-American term, the word stresses the self-directed quality of the process of developing personal and political awareness (Bono and Kemp eds 1991: 8–9). The play offers a democratic, inclusive vision of sisterhood, with the exchanging of individual 'confessions' the necessary first step in the formation of a collective political identity and common language; it is also a utopian vision, in that it bypasses those differences which would – and, in the reality of feminist practice, did – produce tensions that no singular account could satisfactorily contain. As Judith Butler explains, the 'premature insistence on a stable subject of feminism, understood as a seamless category of women, inevitably generates multiple refusals to accept the category' (Butler 1990: 4). Does the play then deny such 'refusals'? The story of feminist consciousness-raising is admittedly more positive than that of social and sexual disempowerment; nevertheless, it carries the risk that it, too, constitutes an officially sanctioned 'master-narrative' that individual accounts must be distorted to fit. This in turn raises a question I posed at the start of this chapter: whether myths are themselves sufficiently adaptable to serve as useful political tools in specific situations, or if the degree of displacement from the immediate that the abstraction entails renders them ultimately blunt and ineffectual.

We should remember, however, that the utopian consciousness-raising scene is firmly located in the *fairy tale* half of the play. It relates an experience of female solidarity that is unavailable to the protagonist of the monologue's 'realistic' section, and since it is she who is framed as the fairy tale's narrator, the audience are invited to receive this as a story she invents for her daughter and not an account of life as it is. Moreover, the impression that the 'feminist tale' enforces its own set of strictures and repetitions is heavily undercut by the way that the monologue as a whole has been presented. Both Italian and English titles of the piece may assert that we all have the same story, but the experience of reading or watching the play implies precisely the reverse: this story never unfolds in a way that is predictable, and just as Rame seems to be treading a familiar route she forges a new one, and in a direction we might not have realised that a path could run. Much of the pleasure of *The Same Old Story*, for spectator or reader, resides in its simultaneous closeness to and divergence from the tales we already know; in feminist terms, the play as a whole becomes a complex act of storytelling that speaks of a gender alikeness (rather than literal 'sameness') able to accommodate difference. *The Same Old Story* works overwhelmingly to suggest not unity and stability but unfixity: we may choose to tell a counter-narrative of togetherness, but this is a self-conscious and always temporary move. The reminder that all stories may be pulled apart and refashioned stands as a stronger and more radical message than any pre-formulated narrative could provide.

'Non più madri, no più figlie, distruggiamo le famiglie ...'[8]

Rame and Fo may choose to end *The Same Old Story* on a note of harmony and female solidarity, but this is not the conclusion of *Tutta casa, letto e chiesa* as a whole. *Medea* is usually presented last, and its stark picture of individual isolation provides the antidote to any hint of complacency. *Medea* is perhaps the hardest-hitting of the four monologues; a review of the period considered it the most striking piece of the evening, one in which Rame's performance achieved moments of 'absolute power' through 'intense and burning' authenticity (Poesio 1979, my translation). The role it affords could hardly be further from the *bellona* (dumb blonde) characters that Rame had throughout her early career been expected to portray; while the parts Fo had written for her thus far had been at least 'precise [and] human', she was rarely asked to play a strong woman 'who just might have been able to speak and think for herself' (Farrell 2001: 196–7). Both perceived Medea as a figure with authority and autonomy. Fo's original drawings and poster designs for the monologue emphasise the grotesque, the majority showing a roughly sketched female figure that is all energy and harsh, distorted angles. The photographs of Rame in performance show something rather different: swathed in black from head to toe, the figure captured by the camera conveys dignity and contained, rather than unleashed, emotion.[9] The medium of representation shapes the reception somewhat, but none the less we might read in the distinction between these sets of images some hint of the occasionally divergent preoccupations and stylistic preferences of the co-authors. The situation of Medea, abandoned by her husband, opens up multiple interpretative possibilities: Farrell comments that, while Fo saw Medea's response to Jason's treatment of her as grotesquely funny, Rame's performance by contrast emphasised the protagonist's pain and deep sense of injustice (Farrell 2000: 218–19) On a broader point of theatricalities, Anderlini-D'Onofrio observes that Fo's general tendency is towards farcical comedy and (physical and verbal) excess while Rame leans more to the succinct and dramatic (Anderlini-D'Onofrio 2000: 194). If the totality of pieces that make up *Tutta casa* … exploits the whole of this range, Rame's powerful Medea stands at its darkest, starkest point.

Tutta casa … called for 'respect for women everywhere: at home, in the street, in the family and in bed' (Rame and Fo 1991: xv). While *The Same Old Story* pursues this through satirical deconstruction of gender 'fairy tales', *Medea* accepts the more difficult challenge of tackling an especially notorious classical myth head on. Where mythographers typically provide a complex account of Medea as a character famous equally for her skill as healer as for the murders committed through her 'ill-starred' marriage to Jason, it is undoubtedly the latter that defines her in the popular imagination (Walker 1995: 628–9). She is a figure endlessly rewritten: whether as ultimate 'bad mother' or proto-feminist icon, Medea is 'recreated by each new generation, each looking through the lens of a culture and a period with all its attendant expectations for "motherly behaviour"' (Goodman ed. 2000: xv). Echoing the pattern of Euripides' tragedy, Rame and Fo chose to concentrate on the episode when Medea, learning that her husband is to take a new bride and that she herself will be exiled, kills the children born from their marriage. But where the Greek play sides with Medea to the extent of acknowledging the justice of her cause – although condemning the injustice of her actions – Rame stresses that the point of their version is 'not jealousy or rage but a new awareness, the taking of a moral stand' (Hirst 1989: 151). Their Medea's act – intended as 'an allegory not a call for mass infanticide', as Rame reassured a 1980s Edinburgh audience – signals defiance of the supposedly natural law that insists a woman should sacrifice her own needs for her children's sake.[10] Medea's uncompromising severance of self from children symbolises her claim to an autonomous 'personhood' that necessarily exceeds the purely relational category of 'mother'; in other words, she refuses the kind of self-effacement that prevailing discourses of motherhood strenuously promoted.

Medea is composed as multi-voiced monologue centring on a debate between protagonist and women of the chorus. As in Euripides' play, this confrontation contrasts the 'excessive' passion of Medea with the conventional wisdom and emphasis upon moderation espoused by the chorus. Classical tragedy is not the authors' chief source, however; significantly they draw inspiration from a popular Italian version of the myth originating from Magna Grecia, a region in southern Italy formerly colonised by the Greeks (Mitchell ed. 1989: 81) When performing the monologue, originally and in subsequent stagings, Rame adopts an invented dialect which creates the effect, as Gillian Hanna notes, of 'a woman rooted in the earth, in reality'; it also emphasises Medea's position as cultural outsider and thus in Greek terms a 'barbarian' (Rame and Fo 1991: 4; Euripides 1981: 44). The authors' decision to locate the play thus specifically reflects their persistent identification with the counter-hegemonic popular tradition. The speech idiom grants ordinariness to Medea that the conventions of classical tragic drama do not permit; in this way the audience are encouraged to see the human situation behind the 'infamous' mask.

The Fo–Rame *Medea* opens not with Medea herself but with popular prejudice about her. The actress launches the action in role as Chorus. Jason is taking a new bride, we learn, and Medea 'won't listen to reason'. The social ethos is succinctly expressed: it is men's right and women's expectation that the status of 'wife' be temporary, a privilege that may be conferred or withdrawn; when she has outstayed her welcome at the master's house she must go quietly 'for the sake of the children' (Rame and Fo 1991: 61). In the Chorus's estimation Medea's children will be better off if the proposed alliance goes ahead, since Jason's status, and therefore theirs, would rise. Medea's anger at being pensioned off, already inappropriate simply because immoderate, is doubly condemned since it indicates selfishness incompatible with 'good' mothering.

When finally Medea is persuaded to emerge from the house, we are told she is hoarse from screaming. Rame as Chorus member mimes handing her a glass of water, then uses this gesture to change role. Medea's first words show a woman unlike the virago we were warned to expect: 'Friends ... my dear women friends ... what does my husband's new girlfriend look like? I've only seen her once, and that was in the distance. I thought she looked ... so beautiful ... so young ...' (ibid.: 62). The tone suggests despair. As Medea nostalgically recalls her own youthful beauty – a pre-pregnancy ideal of slender, firm-fleshed, virgin fragility – the Chorus attempt to join her for a moment of sisterly commiseration. All of them have been through that stage, all traded in for 'new models': it is, they sigh, 'the law of nature'. The phrase revives Medea's anger. She counters the seemingly originary 'nature' with the violence of culture: whose interests does that 'law' serve? But the Chorus, relentlessly satirised, have plenty of answers ready to justify the *status quo*: 'Men get older slower than us. They ripen as they get older, we wither ... we swell up and then we fade away ... they get wiser and more mature. We lose our power and they grow more powerful ... that's the rule that makes the world go round' (ibid.: 63). The play's central section is based on a series of exchanges whereby the Chorus's increasingly vacuous arguments are demonstrated by Medea to be derived from false premises. Rame, switching back and forth between perspectives, reveals the mechanisms of ideological control: that for a system fundamentally rooted in inequality to continue and prosper, it is vital that the belief is fostered, in those whom it benefits least, that this system is both necessary and fair. *Medea* offers no equivalent for the *autocoscienza* represented in *The Same Old Story*. The

Chorus's support for the protagonist has no radical edge but derives from the belief that women should help each other accept their lot. The reward for submission is promise of a peaceful life; rebellion risks losing even that. For Medea, however, a life bought by bowing one's head is no life at all. Indeed, to those who desire her removal she is already 'like a corpse' (*ibid*.: 64). Her terms recall those of Haasse's Ariadne, for whom acquiescence implies 'non-being, death'; but whilst in *A Thread in the Dark* Ariadne is exiled by force (at least initially), Medea is expected to embrace this as a duty (Haasse 1997: 139).

Medea's recognition that her erasure has effectively occurred *before* the official banishment is highly significant. It is not, then, that her 'rights' are being removed; in reality, the status she believed she held was always illusory, no more than a temporary privilege that, in the very fact of being granted, only reaffirms the inequity of systemic power relations. Medea embodies the position of the outsider, her presence tolerated but never less than vulnerable. She reminds the audience: 'I'm a foreigner and don't really belong here', yet her 'not belonging' runs even deeper than this (Rame and Fo 1991: 64). By virtue of her sex, she is decentred by the social order; as 'woman', she is inessential to the discourse that takes 'man' as its foundational term. As mother she is marginalised still further, since motherhood according to patriarchy requires the suppression of 'self-centred' desire. Medea's experience of alienation is compounded by the knowledge that women, as much as men, are complicit in sustaining this; more profoundly disorienting even than Jason's rejection of her is the language the Chorus employ to justify this act. In her influential essay 'Towards a Theory of Sexual Difference', Cavarero writes:

> The mother tongue in which we have learned to speak and to think is, in effect, the father tongue. There is no mother tongue, since there is no language of women. Our language is a foreign language which we have not learned by translation from our own tongue. And yet, it is not ours, it is foreign, suspended in a faraway place that rests upon the missing language. That which we perceive in this foreign tongue [...] is thus the distance which separates us from it; the tongue in which we speak ourselves but do not recognize ourselves. (Cavarero 1993: 197)

Rame's Chorus characters speak in the 'father tongue', but without sensing that it is 'foreign'. Medea, by contrast, is painfully aware of its inadequacy; none the less, she has no other language with which to speak herself into being. Her only recourse for self-assertion, less for herself as individual than for woman as sex, lies in action. Thus she strikes at the place where man's hold is weakest and woman has at least the grounds of power: at maternity itself.

The last section of the monologue dramatises Medea's struggle for selfhood using the only means at her disposal. The Chorus's panic at her announcement that she will kill her children is momentarily calmed by the arrival of Jason. But this character is entirely silenced by the playwrights; indeed, depending on the strategies employed by different productions, he might not even be seen.[11] Instead, we see Medea's ironic self-transformation *for* him: 'it's all right ... [...] I'm quite lucid now.' Initially, sweetly, she adopts the father tongue, but in an act of deliberate mimicry that signals to the audience – if not yet to Jason – her alienation from that language: 'I can't think what got into me'; 'What was I thinking of [...]?' Then, as abruptly as she assumes the submissive mask, she lets it fall: 'That's how crazy I was, Jason, I actually believed all that ... and I still do!!' (Rame and Fo 1991: 65–6) For the final passages of the play Medea speaks uninterrupted. As she talks of her children's death it is as if that murder is yet to come and as if it had already taken place: linear time seems to disappear as she projects her action beyond this and into the dimension of myth. And although (as Rame patiently emphasised) we are expected to read the killing as symbolic rather than literal, this moment nevertheless remains highly visceral. The children are Medea's own flesh; cutting theirs, she rips into her own. Medea's anguish at her own action reveals this to be rational and premeditated, yet not cold-blooded. The murder stands as the ultimate rejection of motherhood, as oppressively defined, whilst at the same time asserting the lived reality of maternal love.

Rame's Medea is no role model, nor does the play present her as such. Murdering, bloodstained, denounced by the world, she is not herself the female subject that she urges into being. Medea, the sorceress, whispers to her children at the play's close:

> Die, die, so your blood and bones can give birth to a new woman!
> (*At the top of her voice*) Die! You must give birth to a new w-o-o-ma-a-a-n!!
> *The last syllable turns into a musical note which dies as the light fades.* (Rame and Fo 1991: 67)

To recognise woman as a truly equal and autonomous being demands a conceptual leap that is, as Cavarero argues, logically impossible since western *logos* is rooted in the definition of man, with woman included only as his 'other' (1993: 199). Perhaps this is why the final words of the play assume the quality of a spell: only an extraordinary act can rock the foundations of beliefs so deeply embedded. This moment when Rame's Medea turns sorceress – or rather, when she invokes the occult power that has always been part of Medea's mythical identity – seems to me to catch the creativity and urgency that characterised women's liberation demonstrations in Italy at the time the play was written. Susan Bassnett records that 'almost emblematic of Italian feminism' was the popular slogan of 1970s protesters: '*Tremate, tremate, le streghe sono tornate*' (Tremble, tremble, the witches are back). Women dressed as witches marched at 'Reclaim the Night' rallies; the brooms they carried with them suggested further an inversion of their role in traditional homemaking and the readiness to sweep a political system clean. In seizing this motif for their cause, they were referencing the persecution and marginalisation of women in historical reality and simultaneously exploiting the transformative power that attaches to the witch as mythical symbol. As Bassnett remarks, the witch was also a particularly apt metaphor for the 'oppositional woman' in a context where much of the movement's antagonism was directed against the Vatican (Bassnett 1986: 95–6). The Catholic Church has always exercised very real influence on the lives of Italian women, both directly, through political intervention (as when vigorously opposing campaigns to legalise abortion and to defend women's rights within marriage), and indirectly, by shaping prevailing images of femininity within the culture. In this context, the authors' deployment of the compelling and unavoidably confrontational Medea archetype can be read as a strategic manoeuvre, the audacious proposal of counter-myth.

The very starkness of the Medea myth seems to lead the play's authors to an expression of feminist opposition arguably more radical than that found elsewhere in *Tutta casa, letto e chiesa*. Medea's is a story that demands a strong response. Rame has performed this monologue countless times, across decades during which her own political activism has steadily increased, and undoubtedly its resonances have altered for her as for her audiences. In the late 1970s Rame emphasised the non-militancy of her personal stance, agreeing that she was a feminist 'if that means walking hand in hand' with men (Farrell 2001: 209). That sentiment is largely reflected in the project of *Tutta casa* ... in its entirety, yet the tone of *Medea* – especially the rebellious cry with which the play concludes – voices a passion that seems significantly more hard-edged. By the mid-1980s, Rame's perspective on her own life, particularly in terms of her relations with Fo, had radically changed and on this subject she became increasingly outspoken. Interviewed as part of her Edinburgh tour (where she performed *Medea* in tandem with a later play, *The Open Couple*) she was harshly critical of the institution of marriage: 'If I could go back I wouldn't get married even if the alternative was death.'[12] A decade later, when Fo was awarded the Nobel Prize for literature, Rame commented somewhat sardonically: 'Dario is a monument, but monuments can't stand by themselves ... they have a pedestal, and I am that pedestal. It is 45 years that I am bent over, carrying this monument on my back, and once in a while it weighs on me' (Piccolo 2000: 115). If *Medea* demands respect for women within a partnership, such statements as these suggest that, for Rame, its pertinence has only increased over time.

By selecting just two of Rame's monologues – and to date, she has created more than twenty-five of these – I am taking the plays 'out of context' (Rame and Fo 1989). Yet to do so is justifiable not simply in order to facilitate discussion of myth but because Rame's monologues are regularly treated by directors as stand-alone texts (as illustrated by my earlier example of a *Medea* double-bill); moreover, they have been so widely performed and by so many different actresses that they have taken on a life of their own.[13] Nevertheless, *Tutta casa* ... was designed as an event at which a series of female characters would be presented, with *The Same Old Story* and *Medea* typically preceded by *Waking Up* (*Il risveglio*) and *A Woman Alone* (*Una donna sola*). The overall style of this event is perhaps comic-grotesque, but individual pieces within this draw out shades of the farcical and tragic. Ugo Volli in an early review likened Rame's fluid and shifting characterisations to 'a stream of consciousness, an interior monologue, a chatty confession' (Volli 1977, my translation). Undoubtedly, the impact of *Tutta casa* ..., played as originally conceived, is significantly shaped by the juxtaposition and ordering of monologues as well as the charisma and presence of Rame herself as the locus in which all the characters meet. The importance of this last point is emphasised by Hanna:

> When Franca Rame performs the plays in Italy she is already well known in her own right. Her audience is aware of her history as a political being as well as an actress. She appears on the stage bringing with her the ghost of three decades of political activity, and everyone in the audience, be it in a theatre or sports stadium or factory is familiar with that. So whichever character she is playing, her audience recognises her within all her characters. (Rame and Fo 1991: xvi)

There can be no separation of 'personal' from 'political' when Rame presents these monologues. Walter Valeri makes the same point, insisting that '[w]omen identify with Franca's characters because they know that Franca herself identifies with them' (Valeri ed. 2000: 4). Whether built from myth and fairy tale, or from contemporary testimony, these figures are always necessarily fictions; Rame's performance – intimate, colourful, direct – invites spectators to find in these the shades of their own lived experience.

'And she stopped the world': Sarah Daniels' *Neaptide*

> People said [*Masterpieces*] was like a sledgehammer, but it was more like a scream really. If it had been more subtle, I don't think it would have had the impact that it did. (Daniels, in Stephenson and Langridge 1997: 5)

Masterpieces (1983) brought Sarah Daniels forcefully to the attention of the British critical establishment and theatregoing public. The play's passionate indictment of the porn industry, and argument that this was upheld by and inseparable from the masculinist hegemony, drew outraged reactions from the press. It was labelled 'vitriolic', 'melodramatic' and 'man-hating', and, together with the earlier *Ripen Our Darkness*, and *The Devil's Gateway* (also produced in 1983), was used as evidence of Daniels's extremism, prejudice and simply 'weak' playwriting. Mary Remnant records that the most damning assessments came from male reviewers; whilst some women 'reacted to Daniels' work with warmth and shocked recognition, much of criticdom had taken up arms against her: conceding that she could, at times, muster a certain surreal humour, many dozens of column inches were dedicated to her annihilation as a playwright' (Remnant ed. 1987: 8). Daniels's battles with the press have been well documented (Aston 1995; Dymkowksi 1997). Yet despite this controversial reputation, her work has generally been produced at 'mainstream' rather than 'alternative' venues: at Manchester Royal Exchange, Sheffield Crucible, London's Albany Empire, the Royal Court and others.[14] When *Neaptide* was presented at the Royal National Theatre in 1986 (on the Cottesloe stage), it earned a place in history both as that theatre's first full production of a new play written by a woman and as its first openly to address lesbian themes. But for some women commentators, especially, this establishment context – together with the perception that her plays veer towards escapism or utopianism – confirmed her problematically as 'the "acceptable" face of radical feminism' (Griffiths 1993: 47). As Dimple Godiwala notes, Daniels has tended to occupy (at least) a dual position: as extremist from the perspective of the mainstream press, yet conservative or assimila- tionist from the 'western radical-lesbian margins' (2003: 118–19).

Neaptide was written in 1982 when it won Daniels the George Devine award for new playwriting; it thus predates *Masterpieces,* although it was professionally produced only some years later. It was a relatively daring choice for an elite venue such as the National to stage what the reviewer John Barber disparagingly termed 'a tract so earnestly determined to air the grievances of lesbians' (Barber 1986). By the mid-1980s, public fervour over the AIDS epidemic had sparked a resurgence of hostility towards gay men and lesbians that was to an extent undermining the progress that had been made by the gay liberation movement in the previous decade.[15] Surveys in British social attitudes suggested that the percentage of individuals who disapproved of homosexuality rose dramatically between the early and late 1980s, approximately to the level of three people out of four; at the same time, the percentage that supported the legalisation of homosexual relationships fell sharply (Engel 2001: 90). The landslide victory of the Conservative Party in 1979 under Margaret Thatcher's leadership had heralded a general rightward shift in public policy. The Labour Party was beginning actively to promote gay equality through institutional practices of positive discrimination, particularly through the work of the Labour-controlled Greater London Council (GLC); by contrast, the official Conservative position towards homosexuals became increasingly antipathetic whilst traditional 'family values' were ever more heavily promoted. But the most repressive of the government's moves – culminating in the introduction of Section 28 – in their turn stimulated further resistance and collective mobilisation on the part of the gay and lesbian community.[16] That 'community' was by no means cohesive. As Jill Davis noted, the preoccupation of the gay liberation movement with campaigns around AIDS added to an awareness amongst lesbians that their interests were not being adequately represented; however, the heterosexist bias of the women's movement frequently conflicted with these also (Davis ed. 1987: 9–10). But besides their marginalisation within oppositional groups, lesbians had always been less 'visible' than gay men to the general public. One anonymous woman, quoted in a 1980 study, conveyed an acute sense of this: 'We are female outcasts or outcast identities in society. [...] Because women aren't given a separate identity in society, women together aren't given any either' (Ettore 1980: 7).

The issue of lesbian child custody, with which *Neaptide* is principally concerned, had come to public notice in 1975 after three high-profile cases in which the court ruled against the mother. These gave impetus for the formation that same year of the pressure group Action for Lesbian Parents (ALP). ALP provided support for lesbian mothers, through meetings, talks and a telephone link, but channelled much of its energy into the task of collating 'evidence' – at the demand of solicitors and barristers – to demonstrate the psychological health of children raised by lesbians. This increased campaigning had the additional effect of making lesbian mothers more prominent within the wider women's movement, yet the issue proved almost as contentious and divisive there as for a general public. From the perspective of some homosexual women 'you were not a real lesbian if you had children'; equally, many heterosexual feminists were then attacking motherhood as a role imposed on women, one that seemingly stood 'in the way of everything liberation would mean' (Allen and Harne 1988: 187–9). In this way lesbian mothers remained a marginalised and vulnerable group in progressive as well as reactionary contexts.

By the mid-1980s lesbian mothers had at least become significantly less isolated than previously, but there had been little in the way of concrete change. A report published in 1984 by the

Lesbian Custody Project (an offshoot of the feminist legal organisation Rights of Women) showed that, despite lobbying, there had
been no fundamental shift in the attitudes of the courts since the
mid-1970s. In addition, as the report demonstrated, other kinds of
institutional discrimination against lesbian mothers – for example
by schools, or the medical profession – remained extremely
common (*ibid.* 192–3). Daniels's *Neaptide* reflects this sense of a
disappointing lack of progress and strives to reignite the debate.
The play is passionately concerned to show that being a lesbian is
not incompatible with motherhood and that radical alternatives
to the nuclear family are both possible and positive. Daniels's
protagonist seems designed as much to reassure as to challenge:
she is nurturing, responsive, endlessly patient, fair-minded in all
her dealings with her daughter. *Neaptide* also comically discredits
numerous popular prejudices about lesbians more generally: that
they wear men's clothes and favour stereotypically masculine
pursuits; that lesbianism is the choice of women who cannot 'get'
men; that it is a kind of deformity produced by 'bent genes'; that
it is catching. Like *Masterpieces*, *Neaptide* is often comic; at the
same time, both plays seem powerfully fuelled by anger. Daniels's
work attacks the arguments of the right and equally refuses to
concede liberal 'grey areas'. But, whilst her critique of (then)
present conditions is uncompromising in both plays, *Neaptide*
feels the more optimistic of the two: its hopeful spirit does not
spring from a belief in reform of existing structures, however, but
from imagining alternatives to these.

Daniels has emphasised: 'A play, to me, should be relevant to
today's society; that's part of why I think you should write plays.
It should tell a story and it should also challenge' (Stephenson and
Langridge 1997: 4). Through *Neaptide* Daniels tells not one but
several stories. The play is set in contemporary Britain, its action
centred on the efforts of Claire, a lesbian mother, to defeat her
ex-husband's attempt to gain sole custody of their seven-year-old
daughter Poppy. When the play begins Claire has not 'come out'
except to her family but feels compelled to do so when two girls
at the school where she teaches are threatened with expulsion
for 'deviant' sexual behaviour. Going public costs Claire her job,
prejudicing still further her chance of success in the imminent
court case. Interwoven with this story is that of Claire's married
sister Val: deeply depressed and increasingly alienated from her

concerned husband and young sons, Val is hospitalised following a nervous breakdown. Joyce, mother to Claire, Val and Sybil – a third daughter living in America whom the audience do not meet – finds her children's lives incomprehensible and disturbing: 'I wanted three daughters like the Brontës and I ended up with a family fit for a Channel Four documentary' (Daniels 1991: 247). *Neaptide* is dense with plot and has a large cast (of nineteen, plus a number of doublings) that, unusually, includes five children under the age of seven. *Neaptide*'s focus on lesbian rights in general, and the principle of maternal child custody in particular, is thus set within a broad frame of reference that seeks to present this not as a minority issue but one whose implications touch society as a whole.

The narratives of *Neaptide*'s contemporary characters inevitably intertwine with and inform one another, but Daniels adds a further, symbolic framework to the action with the myth of Demeter and Persephone. The introduction of mythic reference is necessarily mediated through and to an extent constrained by the play's realist aesthetic. The myth is introduced explicitly, as Poppy's bedtime reading; the audience is reminded of it when mother and daughter pick up the story where they left off, mid-way through the second half. These moments apart, the myth acts as an allegorical subtext. In the version Claire tells Poppy – itself a 1972 revisionist telling by Phyllis Chesler with a strong feminist slant – Demeter has four daughters (Chesler 1997). Poppy promptly 'reads' herself and her family into the myth, making plain Daniels's intent to draw the parallel: grandmother Joyce is Demeter, with Claire, Sybil and Val as Artemis, Athena and Psyche respectively; Poppy is 'Pepsi-phone'; Joyce's husband Sid stands in for Zeus (Daniels 1991: 248–9). The myth's relevance for the contemporary action is clear and the application ingenious. More than any narrative in classical mythology, this one speaks of the love of mother for daughter and at the same time of violence to the maternal principle. Claire knows that Lawrence, backed by the law, seeks to drag Poppy away from the life she has known and from her own protective care; to win her he will contest Claire's 'fitness' and by extension the legitimacy of lesbian motherhood itself. The chasm by which the adults are separated – of distrust, resentment and, most fundamentally, of the difference signed by Claire's 'betrayal' of heterosexual marriage – finds apt reflection in the myth's divided world.

Claire is the protagonist and it is she who stands with most to lose, yet it is Joyce, the grandmother, whom Poppy casts as Demeter. Daniels sets more at stake thereby than simply the legitimacy of Claire's claim; the play's female characters are *all* in a sense 'Demeter's daughters', the re-vision underlining the importance of women's interrelationships and the power that might come from their reinforcement. Such inclusive interpretation of the myth's central motif is not new, for as Christine Downing explains, '[t]he love between Demeter and Persephone has been felt by many to symbolize not only the mother–daughter bond but more generally the intense, intimate connections among women whose loyalty to one another takes precedence over their relationships with men' (Downing ed. 1994: 136). This theme of connectedness is emphasised many times over: in Claire's nurturing of Poppy; in her close friendship with her heterosexual flatmate Jean; in Claire's decision to stand by the schoolgirls Diane and Terri, despite the cost to herself; and in the belated support she receives from the headmistress, Bea (who turns out to be a closet lesbian). But it is above all through Joyce that Daniels most forcefully asserts this. Joyce is the primary channel for the play's comedy and at first the laughter comes at her expense. She is drawn as thoroughly old-fashioned, interfering and narrow-minded, given to pronouncements on sex and marriage derived from clichés: she reminds the near-suicidal Val, 'You have a marvellous husband and a lovely family, sometimes I think you don't realise how lucky you are' (Daniels 1991: 248). Her relationships with her daughters are highly fraught, Val barely speaking to her and Claire, hypersensitive to her mother's criticisms, treating the latter with brittle politeness. Joyce's terms with Sybil, she who 'flounced off' to New York, are unclear; but the pairing of Sybil with Athena, the goddess born of Zeus who upholds 'the father's claim / And male supremacy in all things', invites us to see discord there also (Aeschylus 1959: 172). Set against this fragmentation, Claire's own thoroughly exemplary parenting of Poppy is further highlighted by contrast; theirs is a stable and loving environment that the play's 'nuclear families' have not managed to provide.

Initially, then, Joyce seems an unlikely Demeter. But ultimately the play demonstrates that the bond between mother and daughter is stronger for Joyce than the necessity of approving or even understanding Claire's sexuality:

JOYCE: [...] But when all's said and done, I'm still your mother and nothing is going to be able to change that for either of us.

CLAIRE: (*smiles*) No.

JOYCE: And sleepless nights won't change anything, so I said to myself, Joyce, I said, worrying won't make it go away, get off your behind and do something, so I went to the top set of chambers they call them to find a solicitor.

(Daniels 1991: 317–18)

Recognising at last how close Claire is to losing Poppy, Joyce provides a radical solution and the money to realise it: that daughter and granddaughter should skip the country to join Sybil in America. Claire initially refuses, determined to fight for justice in the courts; but, as her mother predicts, all the evidence in her favour is as nothing when set against 'the other thing'. Daniels makes clear that to play by the rules is to lose and in this she accurately reflects the likely outcome of lesbian mothers' custody cases in 1980s Britain.[17] But the playwright does not let the two be parted. The final moment – a notable departure from realism – shows us two 'worlds' at once: Lawrence beats furiously at the door of the house from which ex-wife and daughter have now escaped, while at the hospital Joyce has arrived to take Val home. The men and women of the play are most starkly opposed at this end point. Surreally, the male doctor can *hear* the noise Lawrence is making, although the women cannot: it sounds, he says, 'like someone is pulling the whole place apart' (*ibid.*: 327).

Daniels's decision to resolve Claire's predicament in this way has attracted criticism from various perspectives. A number of contemporary reviewers challenged the denouement on grounds of dramatic credibility. For Irving Wardle of *The Times* Joyce's offer implied 'unbelievable transformation' of personality; equally, Milton Shulman of the *London Standard* found it ludicrous that the 'harridan turns out to have a heart of gold' (Wardle 1986; Shulman 1986). The general consensus was that Joyce was essentially a stock character, the 'ever-so-ornery shocked mother', comical or tiresome according to the view of each (Barber 1986). However, that edge of cliché – the sense, quickly received, that audience and characters alike know all too well what they can expect from Joyce – is arguably part of the play's point. Daniels shows that her daughters have effectively dismissed her: with that in mind, Joyce's diatribes read like battles against their attempts at suppression. Her constant subject is her children's lives, and their attempts to divert her energies towards more conventional outlets of 'cookery classes' and 'brass-rubbing', or to silence her outright – 'For Christ's sake don't start all that up now!' – fail to deflect her. Their relationship worsens as the play goes on: increasingly Claire addresses her mother 'aggressively', 'sarcastically', 'flippantly' (Daniels 1991: 315–16). However, whilst Joyce's eventual decision to side so emphatically with Claire might stand as a *coup de théâtre*, we need not interpret this as a 'change of heart'. Joyce *cares* for her daughters. That she does so is rarely expressed overtly, but Daniels lets us glimpse it, as in a telling moment towards the end of the first half. Joyce boards up the window that Val in her misery has smashed, and in a long – and, again, largely comic – monologue, part to herself and part to the offstage Claire, confesses: 'You were always special to me.' Failing to make out her words, Claire's only response is to urge her mother, impatiently, to 'keep the noise down' (*ibid.*: 284–5).

Claire's fondness for the Demeter story and promotion of it to Poppy hint at some idealisation of the mother's role on her part. The archetypal myth of maternal loyalty and love, it suggests the antithesis of Claire's own relationship with Joyce. Next to that, Claire's (single) parenting of Poppy is almost artificially perfect. Daniels has commented that the depiction is dramaturgically flawed: 'I was so aware of the prejudice which exists against lesbians that I made Claire a bit too good and/or "right on" to be true. I was determined not to provide anyone with an excuse for thinking "Perhaps her ex-husband should have got custody anyway"' (*ibid.*: xi). But if Claire serves as spokeswoman for a political cause, one might equally read Claire the character as striving for an unrealistically high mothering 'standard', as if by her efforts she might make up the shortfall in Joyce's support for herself; thus, where Joyce is hypercritical and rule-bound, Claire is encouraging and democratic. The divergence is comically marked when Joyce discovers that Poppy calls her mother 'Claire': 'honestly, [...] if children grow up using their parents' names it's no wonder they end up rioting' (*ibid.*: 241). The two models of parenting are to an extent socially constructed. Mother and daughter have come to be divided by class, education and politics, as well as by generation and sexuality. Joyce has directly worked for (aspects of) this difference:

as she reminds Claire, 'if I hadn't made those sacrifices to get you the education that I never had, at least I wouldn't be made to feel small now, by you and your clever talk' (*ibid.*: 317). In her turn, Claire seems determined to reinforce what the sociologist Steph Lawler terms the 'self/(m)other distinction', whereby her own maternal identity is in part defined by 'the expulsion and exclusion' of Joyce (Lawler 2000: 107). Their behaviour towards each other suggests a fracturing of relations extending beyond the merely personal. In the unsettled spaces between mother and daughter – signed by Claire's 'clenched teeth' and faint condescension, and Joyce's angry defensiveness – we can read insecurities around difference on several levels, and in the wider socio-political perspective. But through *Neaptide*'s referencing of the Demeter myth we are invited to re-examine precisely these disconnections. The relations of mother and daughter are in crisis *before* Lawrence's violent intervention; paradoxically, it is his attempt at further rupture that brings the women back together.

The theme of female dividedness is explored further through the subplot of Val's depression. This character has been little discussed in analyses of *Neaptide*, perhaps a reflection of the reviewer Carol Rumens's criticism that Daniels herself does not give Val's narrative 'the development it might have deserved' (Rumens 1986).[18] Val's scenes are few and starkly drawn; we have only hints of the circumstances that led to her collapse and the life she will have once she has left the hospital. However, the under-development of Val's narrative could be read as purposeful abstraction: like the inclusion of the myth, Val's breakdown implies retreat from the 'normal' and through this the possibility of thinking outside its structures. This departure from the known is symbolised by Val's withdrawal from the conventional family circle, and relocation of herself within a history of female outsiders. This is most obvious in the play's first scene, where by her opening lines she identifies as witch, on trial for gender nonconformity, at the hands of a 'male Doctor-Inquisitor' (Daniels 1991: 235). Later in the same scene she makes another, somewhat different, connection:

VAL: (*quietly*) Here I sit, mad as a hatter with nothing to do but either become madder and madder or else recover enough of my sanity to be allowed back to the world that drove me mad.

JOYCE: (*shocked*) [...] What on earth possessed you to come out with a mouthful like that?

VAL: I didn't say it.

JOYCE: (*gently, slightly patronisingly*) Oh, Val, who did then? The washstand?

VAL: Some woman years ago. I don't think there are any original states of mind left to reclaim.

(*Ibid.*: 237)

The 'woman years ago' whose words Val/Daniels borrows is the American writer Lara Jefferson, diagnosed as schizophrenic and committed to a mental hospital shortly before the Second World War. Jefferson's record of her experience, later published as *These Are My Sisters*, describes the mental journey she made, not from a state of insanity back to the rational but deeper into madness to 'find a sound mind on the other side' (Jefferson 1975: 22). Jefferson is no parallel to Daniels's character, but nevertheless voices a sense of the world – and her own displacement within it – that reflects the ambiguity surrounding Val's breakdown: 'We are here because we couldn't take it, whatever it was' (*ibid.*: 44). The quotation from Jefferson that occurs in *Neaptide* is included in Chesler's *Women and Madness*, the source Daniels draws upon for her Demeter myth. For Chesler, as for Daniels, the myth is a narrative of loss: of the mother's loss of her daughter, but equally of loss of 'self' through mental illness. Yet, as Chesler acknowledges, for women the concept of a 'lost self' is especially problematic (Chesler 1997: 82). Val seems to feel this too; while her family long for her to get 'back to [her] old self', she knows that no such coherence is, or ever was, available to her: 'I haven't got an old self. I haven't got a new self' (Daniels 1991: 237; 325). It is the social system – termed by Jefferson 'a regular Hades' – that has instilled in her a permanent experience of estrangement.

Within *Neaptide*'s mythic framework Val stands for Psyche. In classical myth Psyche's partner is Eros, god of love; becoming separated from him, Psyche is forced to undergo trials – which include descent to the underworld – in order for them to be reunited. In *Neaptide*, Val has become distanced from her (evidently loving) husband Colin, but he is not the object of her search. Val is a Persephone, as well as a Psyche: life within her 'lovely family' has proved itself hell and her severance from her mother has been of long duration. The line that connects her with Jefferson is something, albeit frail, to hold on to. In the following scene, another such connection is made. To Joyce's breezy recommendation, 'Laugh and the world laughs with you, weep and you weep alone', Val responds: 'One by one we all file on down the narrow aisles of pain alone' (Daniels 1991: 245).[19] It is again a quotation, this time from the American poet Ella Wheeler Wilcox. The specific source is the poem 'Solitude', from Wilcox's notorious volume *Poems of Passion* whose publication in 1883 drew wide condemnation for 'immoral' assertion of female desire. Wilcox defended her work – and the legitimacy of feminine passion – in a letter to a shocked woman friend: 'To one who believes dancing a sin – the act *is* wicked. If she dances, she violates a principle. But I love to dance – and believe it right' (Wilcox 1883b). For Wilcox, feminine 'virtue' was not at rest in its definition according to conventional mores, but was accessible to contestation and rewriting. *Neaptide*'s citation of Wilcox is only brief; by enlarging upon it here, I do not imply that playwright or audiences register a conscious connection. It is a linking thread, simply, and *Neaptide*'s repetitive patterns of dislocation and dividedness find their echoes in Wilcox's personal life.[20] Through Val, then, Daniels expresses in different ways the theme of women reaching out to one another across a chasm.

Val and Claire come to see that they are both 'in the same boat' (Daniels 1991: 294). It is not that the differences between them are erased, rather that the sense of societal invisibility – as it were, their shared *lack* of identity – stands as a point of connection. Each has, implicitly or explicitly, refused the nuclear family; each is disabled by that act, in society's terms. (That there is on the surface nothing 'wrong' with Val's family suggests it is the institution, rather than the individuals, that is the object of critique.) But for Daniels, what is most profoundly disabling is their isolation from other women. The necessity for women to stand by one another is a recurrent theme in her work and, as Gabriele Griffin notes, is 'a critical element in achieving change [within] Daniels' representation of women's plight under patriarchy' (2000: 199). *Neaptide* undoubtedly champions female solidarity and, especially, cross-generational support as a source of resistant strength. The inclusion of the myth reinforces that message, since the unshakeability of Demeter's resolve and the vastness of her power – whereby she can halt the earth's productivity – are highlighted here. But the myth's conclusion, conventionally and in the account Daniels employs, is that a form of compromise is effected: Persephone will pass part of the year underground and part above with her mother. Typically, the 'agricultural' reading of the myth interprets this in terms of seasonal balance. While Persephone is below ground Demeter, in her grief, permits no crops to flourish; her daughter's return to the light heralds the warmer, fertile months. The play's conclusion seemingly refuses such negotiation. Lawrence tries for everything but receives nothing. The remarkable vanishing act that Joyce contrives inverts the abduction motif central to the myth; grasping for Poppy, he clutches empty air. But although in this stratagem the women prove victorious, the spirit of *Neaptide* is not uncomplicatedly triumphalist. Where one mother keeps her daughter, another gives hers up. By pursuing Joyce's plan, both she and Claire make a sacrifice:

> CLAIRE: [...] It's not what I want.
>
> JOYCE: I don't want it either but it seemed to me that only by letting go of the two of you could any sort of solution be found.
>
> (Daniels 1991: 320)

The women must still resign themselves to separation; but, although Joyce loses a second daughter to America, she brings them closer together, in mutual understanding and acceptance, than when both were so busily present in each other's lives. Thus Daniels's re-visioning of the myth refuses its conclusion for Persephone, since Poppy is held safe within a supportive female circle, yet acknowledges the necessity of partial maternal loss.

For Katharine Worth, *Neaptide*'s conclusion demonstrates the playwright's refusal to accept half measures. Worth reads the myth as narrative of (sexual) violence:

> Demeter's grief over her daughter's rape and her successful strategy for reclaiming the girl gives Daniels the main line of action in her play. What she does not take over from the myth is its acceptance of rape as a necessary part of a cyclic seasonal process: Persephone comes back to her mother in the spring but must pass the winter underground. (Worth 1989: 14)

This reading of the myth ties in closely with the version told to Poppy.[21] The spiriting away of the young girl in *Neaptide* breaks the cycle, not of the seasons but of compromise and emotional violence. Daniels's women challenge the 'natural' authority of patriarchal law. In most accounts of the myth, Zeus is Persephone's male parent and it is he who promises her to Hades; through the father's gift of his daughter, the sky (Zeus), earth (Demeter) and underworld (Hades) will be symbolically tied together and harmony between the spheres established thereby. In this way, as Barbara Smith puts it, the 'female "body physical" [acts as] metaphor for the (male) "body politic"'; patriarchy's control of women's destinies stands for its effective mastery of the community or state (Larrington ed. 1992: 91). Daniels's re-visioning explicitly rejects this appropriation, denying the authority of the Father and resisting the heterosexual norm. As Claire reads, in Demeter's voice: '"Yea, if that be the natural fate of daughters, let all mankind perish. Let there be no crops, no grain, no corn, if this maiden is not returned to me." And she stopped the world' (Daniels 1991: 239). As we have seen, *Neaptide* does reach resolution through a form of compromise but crucially the dynamics of this settlement are negotiated according to women's terms.

As a lesbian retelling, *Neaptide* marks out a new pattern that by implication challenges the 'universality' of the archetype. At the start of the play, Claire appears isolated by virtue of her sexual orientation. But soon, through the 'scandal' of lesbian relations at the school, several other women, of different ages, 'tumble out of [the closet] like so many brooms and mops' (Shulman 1986). Through these characters, in scenes of public and private life that blur distinctions between each, Daniels examines the reasons that prevent lesbians 'coming out'. The teachers can expect at best suspicion and damaging accusations and at worst termination of their educational career; little wonder that initially we see attempts to deny the reality of homosexuality amongst their pupils also. Nevertheless, *Neaptide* insists upon the political necessity of coming out: to oneself, to other lesbians and to the 'outside' world. To pass as heterosexual within society – as initially do Claire, the headmistress and the games teacher – is, the play suggests, implicitly to condone the homophobic values embedded in its institutions. Coming out cannot satisfactorily remain at the level of private, selective confidence; only by *'public, indiscriminate, indiscreet* self-disclosure' can the full extent of heterosexist prejudice be confronted (Hodges and Hutter 1974). However, the revelation of lesbian identities in *Neaptide* does not in itself bring victory; the act may reap the reward of increased solidarity, but the values of 'the system' remain firmly intact. Claire cannot win her case, even though – as Daniels takes pains to show – all right is on her side; there is no use in fighting when 'you're up to your neck in quicksand' (Daniels 1991: 320). As a result, *Neaptide*'s ending has been challenged not only by mainstream critics – for the perceived implausibility of the older women's support for the younger – but from feminist standpoints also, for providing a 'fairy-tale' conclusion that problematically 'displaces the struggle into a utopian realm' (Griffiths 1993: 62). Yet one might argue that the flight to the 'new world' by Daniels's characters signals less defeatism, on the playwright's part, than a refusal to battle for solutions within the establishment framework. As Griffin argues, 'women indeed *cannot* survive in such situations. To suggest that they could would be a way of supporting the status quo' (2000: 206). The extremism of *Neaptide*'s solution is offered as counter-defence against the inflexibility of patriarchal law. If it is ultimately utopic, it is so only in the sense that we are urged to imagine a world organised otherwise. That Daniels's women retaliate to the exclusion of the men is not their ideal but, in the circumstances, their only course; as her title reminds us, a 'neap tide' – when the gravitational forces of sun (male) and moon (female) oppose one another – is the *weakest* tide. As the playwright insists, her work is 'not about hating men', but about putting the focus on women and saying: 'This is how it feels from here' (Stephenson and Langridge 1997: 4).

Daniels has acknowledged that *Neaptide* is very much an 'issue play' (Goodman 1993: 129). Her treatment of that issue has proved profoundly contentious and from almost contrary viewpoints. Michael Billington found the play problematically one-sided, melodramatic in its depiction of societal prejudice: most worryingly, he suggested, by 'rubbishing [...] the opposition' Daniels seriously over-simplified the problem and in so doing damaged her own case (Billington 1986). Certainly, Claire's husband is drawn as brutish and unsympathetic, his campaign for sole custody unmistakably tinged by the desire for revenge on his ex-wife; equally, the homophobic attitudes prevalent amongst Claire's work colleagues border upon caricature. It is of course entirely defensible – inevitable even – that the play should show bias; as Daniels says, the intention is to express how it feels *from here*. But as a political work *Neaptide* is weakened by its failure to dramatise the complexities of the problem and to that extent Billington's charge has validity. The play is careful to load sympathies in Claire's favour; that the verdict of the court does not reflect this might cry out at the injustice of the system, but the nature of the conflict as shown does little to explore subtler positions that might exist on either side. And if *Neaptide*'s representation of the 'opposition' is open to criticism, so too is its depiction of lesbian experience. Margarete Rubik observes that the play's more or less exclusive focus on institutional struggles bypasses any engagement with lesbianism as potential identity problem for the women themselves. Thus none of these characters

> is made to agonize over her sexual orientation in private, or suffers ostracism from her friends and family. None of them has internalised repressive social attitudes or has come to look at herself as a deviant or misfit. Although society obviously regards lesbian motherhood as unthinkable, or at least inappropriate, Claire is never made to feel uncomfortable in her role. (Rubik 1996: 18)

The point is not that female homosexuality *should* be represented as a source of anxiety; rather it is that the relative simplicity of the play's treatment of this theme – together with the fact that no lesbian relationship is directly shown onstage – arguably invokes lesbianism more as symbol of female solidarity than as concrete sexual and social practice. Such a view is reflected in Godiwala's conclusion that in Daniels's plays '*lesbian* [becomes] a trope of reassurance which says there *are* alternative ways to live', and more broadly 'a sign of women's awareness of the invisible oppressive text of patriarchy' (Godiwala 2003: 121). The risk attached to this strategy lies in the tension between an enabling metaphor for women in general and the lived experience of some women in particular. *Neaptide*'s affirmation of female bonding overcoming difference seems to imply that women will ultimately prove 'natural' allies.[22]

Neaptide's interweaving of the Demeter myth is, as I have discussed, an important means by which the playwright reaches beyond both the immediate situation of the contemporary action and the multiple constraints that attach to this. However, the allegorical level sits awkwardly at times within the play's otherwise predominantly naturalistic framework. The handling of myth here is quite unlike Rame's playful tale-telling in *The Same Old Story*,

or the more confrontational approach of *Medea*. The decision
that the action be rooted in an immediately recognisable 'present'
necessarily restricts the author's scope for abstraction. Thus certain
moments such as the storytelling scene may seem heavy-handed,
whilst for the majority of the play the myth continues only in our
heads if it has registered at all. There is some likelihood, therefore,
that in production the Demeter narrative oscillates between virtual
invisibility and a potentially distracting dominance. The majority
of original reviewers made no mention of it, implying that this
element had not shaped their reception of the play at a conscious
level. But where it was addressed, the response was frequently
dismissive: it was as if the inclusion of myth – and particularly *this*
myth, which intimates a powerfully oppositional dynamic – simply
confirmed their impressions of an overly black-and-white dramatic
world. Thus Shulman ridicules the protagonist's 'fill[ing] Poppy's
mind with Greek myths about the perfection of women and the
cruelty of men', but does not remark on the extent to which
the play signals disjunction with that model (Shulman 1986).
Similarly, Coveney asserts that Daniels uses myth 'to reinforce
her view that a perfect world was destroyed with the advent of
men', commenting caustically on a mood of 'Sapphic celebration'
that undermined the author's political intention (Coveney 1986).
However, when reading (rather than viewing) the play, the Demeter
narrative makes possible the opening up of character and theme
in provocative ways. As we have seen, there is a risk that in
performance both Joyce and Claire are received as unidimensional
and mutually opposed; the 'turnaround' of the former to support
the latter may well be judged dramaturgically and politically
deficient as a result. But a reflective consideration of *Neaptide*'s
layering encourages a more expansive analysis: when Joyce and
Claire – and indeed, the majority of the play's female figures – are
examined critically against the archetype of a 'Great Mother', both
sides of that comparison are usefully complicated.

The reception of *Neaptide* when first produced was inevitably
mediated heavily both by context of production and by the
perceptions of critics who, in many cases, had not forgiven Daniels
for *Masterpieces*. At the time, on balance, the play found little
favour: for some its arguments were too extreme, for others not
contentious enough. Rumens's review of the production is as
positive as any, yet even she judged *Neaptide* to be 'almost a period

piece, time-locked, like so much feminist thought, in the insights and prejudices of the 1970s'. To back this remark, Rumens cites the play's opening with Val as persecuted 'witch': for her such moments seem indicative of a kind of feminist extremism taken as the hallmark of earlier, less sophisticated thinking (Rumens 1986). It is ironic that a play seeking to affirm feminism as site of intergenerational connection, specifically one that invokes the power of mothers, should be found wanting for over-dependence on 'old-fashioned' models. Daniels has often been quoted for her remark that 'feminism', like 'panty-girdle', quickly became an embarrassing word: 'Once seen as liberating, it is now considered to be restrictive, passé, and undesirable to wear' (Daniels 1991: xii). But Daniels retains the word, despite this: she uses it, she has said, 'in defiance' (Goodman and De Gay eds 1996: 151). In doing so, she refuses to cut herself off from feminists before her; implicitly, this suggests resistance against attempts – characteristic of, but not exclusive to, the media – to set younger women's voices in opposition to those of preceding generations, to exaggerate the tensions between these and thereby undermine any sense of affiliation and indebtedness.[23] The relationship of mother and daughter, symbolic or literal, is of course not smoothly continuous, but marked by ruptures. It is precisely these ruptures that *Neaptide* seeks to address, not to paper over these but to imagine how and when they might be healed. The play dared to affirm the belief that common ground might be found between women despite their differences: it did so at a time when such a position was already becoming unfashionable. If *Neaptide*'s feminism is 'backward-looking', as Rumens implies, this becomes a weakness only if it does not also look forward; the present and future of feminist thought must after all necessarily be formed, and informed, by the past. Daniels's play insists not that our mothers are always right in what they say, but that we owe it to them, and to ourselves, to listen.

Notes

1 Pressure to repeal Section 28 was immense, and it was finally voted out in 2003. None the less, its effects continued to be felt; for example, it was only in January 2005 that Kent County Council finally backed down from its highly controversial policy of 'retaining

the spirit' of the law even when this was no longer a legislative requirement.

2 *Neaptide* was presented at the Arcola Theatre in London in July 2003. In March the same year a new compilation of Fo/Rame monologues under the title *The Same Old Story* was staged in Philadelphia by the Enraged Cow theatre collective. The couple's *Medea* also served as the basis for a 2006 film, directed by Vincenzo Mistretta and shot in New York, Ontario and Sicily.

3 Fo has commented that he hardly dared approach Rame since she 'was so pretty that all the men went wild over her': Farrell 2001: 33. The archive of reviews collated on the official Fo–Rame website illustrates collectively how regularly Rame's looks have been remarked on at all stages of her career: for an anonymous *Time Out* reviewer writing on Rame's Edinburgh appearance of 1986 she was 'a blonde bombshell in her mid-fifties' (22 August 1986); an Edinburgh review for the *Scotsman* sums up Rame's appeal as 'a mixture of physical allure, a husky, expressive voice, an instant rapport with the audience, a panache and an élan allied to a well practised professionalism' (28 August 1986). The full archive can be found at www.archivio.francarame.it. Accessed 13 September 2009.

4 In her English translation of *The Same Old Story* Gillian Hanna made a number of alterations to the original text to heighten this scene's relevance to a UK context, commenting that whilst English law and medical practices were more liberal than in Italy they were 'still far from embodying "a woman's right to choose"' (Rame and Fo 1991: 4).

5 The ethical status of abortion continues to be hotly contested in Italy, most recently as part of wider debate about the rights of the human embryo.

6 A criminal enquiry in 1973, conducted by the magistrate Mario Sossi, found no direct evidence of Rame's involvement, however. See D'Arcangeli 2000: 171.

7 The 1978 law included a number of caveats: for instance, that it applied only to women over eighteen, and that doctors could choose to register as 'conscientious objectors' and refuse to perform abortions (as around 70 per cent did). Equally, underfunding and inadequate resourcing in hospitals led to long delays, which meant that in reality many women found themselves past the permitted ninety days.

8 'No mothers, no longer daughters, we are destroying families.' Italian radical feminist slogan of the 1970s. Bassnett 1986: 95.

9 These images can be found at www.archivio.francarame.it.

10 Anonymous reviewer in *Time Out*. Edinburgh, 22 August 1986.

11 Although Rame's monologue plays have a single actress they sometimes imply an additional performer. In *Medea* the performer as Chorus announces that 'Jason's coming ...' and then Rame, as Medea, begins to speak to him. I have seen the play staged both with a silent male performer present and without.

12 *Time Out* in Edinburgh, 22 August 1986. The following years saw the couple's separation and reconciliation, both very publicly conducted.

13 Tony Mitchell notes that by the mid-1980s the collection of monologues had been staged in a variety of venues in Britain, Ireland, America, Canada and Australia (Mitchell ed. 1989: 62).

14 Elaine Aston has argued that Daniels is not emphatically a mainstream writer, however, since her plays have generally been presented in the smaller 'studio' spaces within mainstream venues (Aston 1995: 393–4).

15 Somewhat illogically, the initial stereotyping of AIDS as a gay disease caused lesbians as well as male homosexuals to be considered high-risk 'carriers'; for example, in 1986 the Blood Transfusion Service refused to accept a woman's donated blood once she had revealed she was a lesbian (Richardson 2000: 139–40).

16 Stonewall, OutRage! and the British ACT UP were all founded in 1989.

17 Lynne Segal notes that while heterosexual mothers would be awarded custody in 70 to 80 per cent of cases, lesbian mothers lost 90 per cent of cases (Segal 1990: 52).

18 Val's role is given some attention by Dimple Godiwala. See Godiwala 2003: 129–30.

19 Val's words are in fact a misquotation. In the poem, the line reads: 'There is room in the halls of pleasure / For a long and lordly train, / But one by one we must all file on / Through the narrow aisles of pain' (Wilcox 1883a: ll<197>21–4).

20 Devastated by her husband's death, in 1916, Wilcox determined to make contact with him – and finally did so, she believed, through spiritualism and the ouija-board (Saltzman 1960). Thus Val and the historical women that she references are all figures caught at points of extremity: a void lies before them, but they see no future in going back.

21 In Chesler's version, Hades is 'come to rape Persephone'; in the story Claire reads Poppy, he is 'come to take' her (Chesler 1997: 33; Daniels 1991: 238).

22 This was not, however, the general perception received by lesbians themselves in their affiliation with the 1980s women's movement. See Davis ed. 1987: 10.

23 Within an Anglo-American context, I am thinking here of 'postfeminist personalities' such as Naomi Wolf, Natasha Walter and Katie Roiphe, all of whom have been represented in the media principally as reacting *against* second-wave feminism.

3

Out of character

If there's a closed-off road, the curious speculate about why it's closed off, and where it might lead if followed. (Atwood 2005: 182)

The systematic disempowerment of *Neaptide*'s women provokes their refusal of the structures that sought to contain them: within the fictional world, at least, they escape it, disappearing from their persecutors' grasp as if the ground had swallowed them up. Rame's protagonists ridicule the laws that attempt to constrain them, denying their authority or, like Medea, striking out forcibly against them. The plays considered in Chapter 3 examine further such practices of resistance: that which is devalued or repressed returns with a violence that threatens to collapse 'civilised' order. Here, however, the plays address acts of collective revolt. Medea's crime might lead her to her vilification as a monster, but when a mass turns murderous there is implied threat of further contagion. Gender segregation and its damaging effects on the individual and on society as a whole is one recurrent theme explored here. When groups are marginalised they become vulnerable; the resistance of such groups may have explosive, and potentially transformative, effects. But these plays reveal subordination and denial operating within, not simply against, the self; for some characters it is an internal impulse that is deemed unacceptable and from which 'rights' are thus consciously or unconsciously withheld. Euripides' *The Bacchae* provides the chief mechanism by which such themes are addressed, a thread that runs through all three plays examined.

The Bacchae centres famously on the collision of values between Dionysos, god of wine and sensuality, and Pentheus, ruler of the city of Thebes and representative of Greek orthodoxy. Under Dionysian influence, the Theban women abandon domesticity to live wild in the mountains. In his attempt to capture Dionysos,

Pentheus becomes fatally entrapped and is eventually persuaded by the god to disguise himself as a Maenad so he may observe the women's rites unsuspected. Dionysos's punishment of Thebes for failing to honour him swiftly follows. In a scene recounted by a Messenger, Pentheus's mother Agave tears him apart, convinced in her delirium she is slaying a wild beast.[1] *The Bacchae* initially seems to set up dualistic conflicts between human and god, civilised and savage, self-control and self-abandonment, yet at the same time powerfully undermines such binaries. Dionysos is part human and has the human motive of revenge on Thebes for past rejection of his mortal mother, Semele; Pentheus is an aggressive and excitable 'hero'; the Maenads tenderly suckle animals when tranquil, but, gripped by Dionysian frenzy, will rip them into pieces. It is in part this combination of oppositions that has made the play fascinating to contemporary consciousness, in and beyond the West (Wole Soyinka's *The Bacchae of Euripides* (1973), for instance, powerfully rewrites Euripides for the African stage). The *fin de siècle* saw an acclaimed verse translation by Gilbert Murray as well as critical reassessments that revived interest in the play for a modern era (Murray 1906; Pater 2002). The anti-author-itarian fervour of the 1960s prompted further resurrection, rediscovering 'Dionysian' ecstasy in contemporary drug culture and new sexual freedoms, and resisting 'Pentheus' as embodiment of oppressive militarism – a perception intensified and contex-tualised by worldwide protests at US action against Vietnam. Richard Schechner's notorious *Dionysos in 69*, more confron-tation with the play than production of it as such, was arguably the apotheosis of such stagings; it was an event that exploited the theme of abandonment of restraints to break down conceptual and actual boundary lines between performers and spectators (Schechner 1994: 40–5). *Dionysos in 69* premiered in 1968; the signification of the title, which used no apostrophe, was primarily sexual (Hall, Macintosh and Wrigley eds 2004: 11–12). *Rites*, a Bacchic reworking by the British playwright Maureen Duffy, set in a women's public lavatory, was staged a year after this and is the first text I discuss. Duffy focuses upon versions of and constraints upon femininity: she has an all-female cast, with no Pentheus figure and Dionysos represented only by a life-size doll. It is useful to view *Rites* in context of emergent second-wave feminism: it is a one-act black farce that vividly satirises antagonism between the sexes, and articulates mounting resentment on the part of women rooted in an awareness, variously more and less conscious, of their unequal social treatment. But whilst the characters rebel against the regulatory powers that so position them, they are no activists. Their agitation is unreasoned: temporarily 'possessed', they seem modern incarnations of Euripides' Bacchants. As I will show, *Rites* is a topical and socially critical play, but far from polemic; the dream or nightmare qualities of the Bacchae narrative are clearly attractive to the author, and the mischievously bizarre scenario that unfolds gives its audience no unambiguous, proto-feminist message to take away with them. The women's violence becomes a problem for the audience to confront: its outbreak is both irrational and explicable, since it stems from a legitimate cause.

The other texts considered both emerged from late 1980s Britain, although the cultural backgrounds of their authors complicate their labelling as straightforwardly 'British' plays.[2] *A Mouthful of Birds* (1986), co-authored by Caryl Churchill and David Lan, also takes Euripides' *Bacchae* as its starting-point. *A Mouthful of Birds* is theatrically more ambitious than *Rites* and, as one might expect after two decades of feminist argument and protest, presents its audience with a deeper and more layered picture of gender identity and relations. Where *Rites* is short and tightly focused, and with an aesthetic 'pitched between fantasy and naturalism', *A Mouthful of Birds* is a stylistically complex, sprawling work, incorporating several individual and ensemble dance sequences within its overarching dramatic structure (Duffy 1969: 27). Duffy's characters are marginalised by virtue of their sex; their experience differs according to their age and class but they are at least momentarily united 'as women' in anger at their ill usage at men's hands. Churchill and Lan explore identity construction in wider terms, through a gender-mixed, culturally diverse cast of characters: all find themselves wrestling with the conflicting dictates of societal expectations – whether externally enforced, or internalised – and 'unacceptable' desires whose leakage into the everyday has become too forcibly apparent to be denied. *A Mouthful of Birds*, like *Rites*, exploits the violent content of Euripides' *Bacchae* – scenes described, if not staged – but both modern plays effect a re-emphasis. Duffy redirects attention from the conflict between Pentheus and Dionysos to turn it almost wholly upon the women. By contrast, Churchill and Lan resist altogether the notion of 'the mass' by exposing and metaphorically dismembering *all* their characters. The acronym of their title might be 'A MOB', but mob violence features only briefly, in dance-like moments that punctuate the play. These fleeting images of mass action are undercut by a strategy that emphasises difference above sameness and resists authoritarian pressures towards role conformity as inherently dehumanising and life-denying. Both plays shift repeatedly between representation of a broadly recognisable present-day world and a flight from this into an imaginative realm where orthodox rules are temporarily suspended and radical alternatives seem possible. In this way, 'myth' becomes at once the mechanism for examination of contemporary questions and the means of departure from a sphere experienced as emotionally and spiritually deadening.

The third play considered here is Timberlake Wertenbaker's *The Love of the Nightingale*, produced two years after *A Mouthful of Birds* in 1988. As a re-visioning, Wertenbaker's play differs from the other two in centring on a myth that is less familiar and of which we have no extant version in Greek drama.[3] The story of Philomela, Procne and Tereus offers a contrasting route into themes of gender and violence, specifically one whereby a murder by women is carried out not in a moment of madness or loss of control, but as a premeditated response to an oppressive act. In Ovid's version in the *Metamorphoses*, as in Wertenbaker's play, the cult of Dionysos is invoked; but in both ancient text and contemporary re-vision it is implied that its associated rituals of excess provide cover for the killing and not the motivation for it.[4] Ovid's story is far removed from Euripides' play, but both conclude with a mother killing her son. Tereus's rape and subsequent forcible silencing of Philomela to some extent presents the sisters' retaliatory crime in a sympathetic light; indeed, whilst not actually condoning the women's response, literary versions of the myth have typically been ready to place Philomela within a poetic tradition of feminine suffering regardless of her part in Itys' murder.[5] This is a myth that deals directly with the use and abuse of power: denied authorised channels of protest, victims of injustice must use illegitimate outlets through which to make themselves heard. It is a narrative well suited to Wertenbaker, a playwright whose work has always been politically charged. Like her earlier *Our Country's Good*, *The Love of the Nightingale* is highly theatrical and formally playful, but fundamentally driven by unequivocal social commitment. Wertenbaker insists that 'the theatre is a public arena [and] playwrights should use that': of the three plays discussed here, hers is the most explicit in the ideological and ethical challenges it poses for an audience (Stephenson and Langridge 1997: 145).

The narratives of Philomela and the Bacchae are not the only myths Wertenbaker draws upon here. The forbidden passion of Phaedra for Hippolytus is also deeply interwoven, through the device of a (parodic) play-within-a-play that establishes in Tereus's mind a 'precedent' that justifies his own desire for his sister-in-law. To this Wertenbaker adds the figure of Niobe, loosely inspired by classical mythology, who contributes a wry commentary on the fate of the vulnerable in a turbulent world. However, the Philomela myth provides the structure and motor of the play. Tereus's actions are horrifying but equally shocking, if not more so, is the shape of the women's response. That the stories deal with such themes is in no way unusual: violence is the stuff of classical myth, its female figures always depicted as fully capable of committing brutalities; moreover, since according to the ancient philosophers women are fundamentally less self-controlled than men, they are arguably *more* susceptible to this than men (Foley 2004: 105). But unlike the narratives of a Medea, a Clytemnestra or a Deianeira, where female characters are positioned in relative isolation, these myths show people banding together: the 'disorder' that results from their rebellion becomes dangerously multiplied as a result. Central to each of these re-visions is the perspective through which we are invited to read such acts. All three plays are informed, to different degrees and in distinct ways, by a feminist consciousness: how far, then, do they judge it necessary – or indeed possible – to 'recuperate' their perpetrators? The sociologist Belinda Morrissey remarks that women who kill have always been found especially threatening, standing as 'terrible antithesis to the myth of the good mother' and life-generator (Morrissey 2003: 2). Society suppresses the trauma such crimes engender through attempts to limit and contain the larger crisis they imply. Morrissey identifies three principal ways by which this is achieved: 'vilification' and 'mythification' operate similarly by insisting on the monstrous otherness of the offender, projecting her out of society and thereby refusing to acknowledge that she is produced by that society; the third, 'victimisation', emphasises that she has been forced into killing from a position of powerlessness.[6] Whether condemnatory or apparently supportive, all these strategies are complicit in denying agency to their protagonists, the first two by rendering the killer effectively 'inhuman', and the third by withholding intentionality. Morrissey argues that even feminist legal theorists have struggled to move beyond a model of deviant women as 'mad, bad or sad'. Traditional feminist perceptions of women's systematic oppression within heteropatriarchy have tended to reinforce victimology theses; it has proved harder for feminism to come to terms with those who cannot be regarded as acting in self-defence. Thus for Morrissey, '[m]urderesses who kill young women and children [...] form the excluded, disapproved and disavowed ground on which the acceptable violent female subjects of feminist legal discourse are constructed' (ibid.: 27).

It might seem that Philomela, manifestly offended against, could be defended as one such 'acceptable' violent female subject. What complicates such a reading is the fact that it is not her abuser but his seemingly guiltless child who is sacrificed. Wertenbaker retains this twist, emphasising that the sisters' act is lucid – although she rejects the element of the myth (graphically described by Ovid) that has them bake Itys in a pie that Tereus eats in ignorance. Similarly, Churchill and Lan approach Euripides' crazed (and thus unaccountable) Bacchants with the intent to elicit agency. Loss of control is a state the characters consciously embrace and move through, not to create a space for remorse but to reach a place where they can take responsibility for their actions and admit a capacity for destructive as well as creative choices. The implication of both plays is not of course that women's violence should be defended in the name of 'equal rights' but rather that the historical link between femininity and passivity must be broken if women are to be recognised – and recognise themselves – as social agents capable of effecting profound change.[7] Duffy's Rites undertakes no such processing of the characters' temporary anarchy: that the women declare no regret for the murder does not intimate agency, since crucially they show no comprehension either. As a form of resistance against an oppressive status quo their act has, not surprisingly, been found 'highly ambivalent' in feminist terms (Foley 2004: 106).

Whilst the theme of nonconformist femininities emerges strongly from these texts, the counter-theme of disavowed masculinities is equally raised or implied. Incorporation of the Bacchae narrative in itself invites the wider questioning of gender roles. Dionysos is, as suggested, the embodiment of transgression, a profoundly ambiguous figure at once both male and female, Greek and barbarian, mortal and immortal.[8] He is god of alcohol and excess, and his worship demands surrender of the will to ecstatic possession. Through Dionysian influence 'normal' behavioural expectations are overturned: the women leave the city to become huntresses and warriors; Cadmus and Tiresias, respected elders, are rendered undignified by Bacchic paraphernalia unbefitting to their age and status; Dionysos's most vociferous opponent, the aggressively masculine Pentheus, becomes radically feminised as his initially determined resistance to the god is broken down. By the time the king's body (clad in woman's dress) is ripped apart by the Bacchants, this action is readable as physical reiteration of a dismemberment of self already set in motion. This sense of the fluidity of role, an instability both exhilarating and hazardous, is underlined by the self-conscious theatricality inherent in Euripides' drama and manifest in its complex play of illusion and disguise. In all three plays, but perhaps most vividly in *A Mouthful of Birds*, theatre becomes at once the mechanism and the metaphor for trying on the new, entering alien spaces, performing the other.

The overturning of order that the myths imply hints at the political possibilities in dramatic re-vision. However, these plays embrace mythic territory beyond deployment of individual narratives or archetypes for their ideological potential. Here myths are not overtly or not only vehicle for social criticism, or merely suggestive of a sphere in which the fantastic becomes possible and expected. Crucially, the myths invite a different mode of thought: 'irrational' violence and the gratification of illegitimate longings promise access to ways of knowing outside the framework of Enlightenment structures. The interweaving of *The Bacchae* underscores this since the play directly stages the collapse of intellect and argument in the face of a power beyond rational explanation. The organisation of predominantly western views of reality around logocentric principles has historically privileged rational before emotional, mind over body, *logos* above *mythos*: an extension of this position would claim that attainment of knowledge, by Enlightenment principles, requires the expulsion or concealment of the latter term. The re(dis)covery of such excluded ground seeks not to replace one set of categories with another but rather to assess the radical potential of outlawed knowledges and expose the 'lived contradictions which dominant forms of reason mask' (Kemp and Squires eds 1997: 143).

In the last part of this introduction I consider how far these three plays' refusals to honour divisions that segregate and subjugate extend from content to production context. *Rites*, *A Mouthful of Birds* and *The Love of the Nightingale* were all first produced within the British mainstream, at London's Jeanetta Cochrane Theatre, Birmingham Repertory Theatre and Stratford's Other Place respectively. Given that the staging of plays by women at major venues was only marginally more common in the 1980s than in 1960s, each production in itself constituted a potential challenge to a theatrical *status quo*.[9] Duffy wrote *Rites* for inclusion within a brief season of women's work supported by the National Theatre, a special programme designed to foreground women's talent and help redress an acknowledged dearth of opportunities then available to them as actresses, playwrights and directors (Duffy 1969: 26). Such an initiative might seem wholly admirable, an encouraging move by an illustrious institution – one claiming, but manifestly failing, to represent 'the nation' – to expand their horizons of operation. At the same time, this proves problematic if the expansion in practice fulfils the function of a self-contained, carnivalesque escape from established repertory, a merely temporary departure from theatre's 'business as usual'. It is relevant that the season of which *Rites* formed a part was titled *Ladies' Night*, a label implying precisely that sense of special favour conferred by authoritative powers rather than commitment towards a permanent inclusion; one must hope that the irony of the name was intentional.

Carnival as metaphor of 'outsiderness' is an apt theme in this case. Anthony Gash draws attention to the importance in carnival of reversal, but notes two ways in which this might serve a conservative rather than a liberating function: 'The first is logical: reversals are only intelligible in terms of a normative system of rules, oppositions and subordinations. The ritual enactment of "opposites" therefore provides a mirror or map of the "true" order of things. The second is psychological: to allow inferiors to abuse or command their superiors is an attempt to exorcise aggressive impulses which might otherwise jeopardise the smooth running of a hierarchical society' (Gash 1993: 88). In the light of Gash's remarks, *Ladies' Night* could be read as a prearranged, celebratory and strictly time-limited departure from the norm.[10] The event was inherently a feminist act, not in the plays' direct promotion of an ideological stance but by seizing space for women's creativity. After the festivities, what if anything had changed? Through the fugitive bacchanalia of *Rites*, Duffy seems to pose the same question: subversive behaviours are explored within a female 'special space', and with devastating consequences, but ultimately the women return to routine, their insurrectionary impulses ostensibly exorcised. Thus, in content and context, *Rites* questions how far 'fringe' activity can impinge on the centres of power. Marking out privileged space – whether a Ladies' Night, or a Ladies' room – is one way to facilitate such activity, yet, if this is contained as a 'ritual enactment of opposites', its impact must be seriously diminished.[11] More positively, the theatrical life of *Rites* has extended well beyond its initial season. Thanks to its initial publication by Methuen in 1969, and republication in 1983, it continues to be performed (and in contexts as far-flung as New Zealand and South Africa) on top of numerous stagings in the UK, Europe and America.[12]

Unlike *Rites*, *A Mouthful of Birds* was not presented within any privileging frame; however, several reviewers considered it should have been. More than one critic challenged the legitimacy of its main stage placing at Birmingham Repertory Theatre, for example by labelling the piece a 'punishing studio exercise [that] should have stayed that way'.[13] In a similar vein, Robin Thornber of *The Guardian* considered it 'one of those perversely impenetrable and self-indulgent exercises in baffling obscurity which are so deeply meaningful to the company that they forget the need to engage and communicate with their audience' (Thornber 1986). Such comments represent *A Mouthful of Birds* as an event out of place, just about acceptable in the studio or rehearsal room but certainly unworthy of, or at least unsuited to, the main auditorium. No doubt 'the intellectuals at the Royal Court' would appreciate it when it transferred there in a few months' time, remarked the *Daily Telegraph*'s reviewer, but the Birmingham venue tended 'to expose [avant-garde] pretentiousness' and a significant proportion of the audience left at the interval (Shorter 1986). Staging it there, imply these critics, constitutes an unwarrantable disorder, in contrast with the licensed topsyturvydom by which *Rites* was framed. From these largely negative reviews emerged a degree of consensus. The stylistic eclecticism of *A Mouthful of Birds* proved a serious barrier to engagement: the unexpected jostling of naturalistic scenes with sequences of mime and dance created an 'incoherent' whole, 'fragmented' and 'bewilderingly bitty'. Thornber admits that, watching it, he longed for an 'old-fashioned scripted piece, given shape, direction and purpose by a single creative intelligence like Euripides', in other words, for the causal structure, ultimate resolution and unifying authoritative perspective of Greek tragedy. What he received instead was something closer to the carnivalesque: in the words of another more positive review, 'the profane rituals of [a] contemporary bacchanal' that allowed a cacophony of authorial voices to coexist rather than cohere (Rissik 1986).

The Love of the Nightingale was more favourably received than *A Mouthful of Birds*. Praise dominated responses to the opening at Stratford's Other Place: for many it was a significant literary as well as dramatic achievement, a work spun from 'a narrative of Homeric thrift, with cadences which owe some of their authority to Eliot' (Schmidt 1988). By the time the play transferred to the Barbican, however, the critics had discovered more to criticise. There was now less readiness to receive it into the dramatic canon, *The Financial Times* disparagingly labelling it 'Christopher Fry with added sex' (Hoyle 1989). Writing for *The Guardian*, Nicholas de Jongh judged the author guilty of hubris: 'Some grave theatrical business is being transacted. Timberlake Wertenbaker is trying on the mantle of the classic Greek tragedian. It does not fit' (De Jongh 1989). By dressing in the robes of the masters, here as it happens male, the playwright, here as it happens female, has made a spectacle of herself; she falls short of the level of those whose work she sought to emulate. De Jongh's criticisms seem curiously misdirected: the parodic metatheatricality of *The Love of the Nightingale* suggests that the borrowed robes are not meant to 'fit' but are adopted self-consciously as costume. Indeed, his complaint might productively be appropriated as apt metaphor for a re-visionary project that probes and challenges conventions of the classical theatre.

Like *A Mouthful of Birds*, *The Love of the Nightingale* attracted some criticism for presuming to (re)write 'classical' drama. It was not the case, however, that women theatre-makers more generally were judged unable to rise to its level at this time. Discussing the critical reception of Wertenbaker's plays, Susan Carlson draws attention to reviews of Deborah Warner's production of *Electra*, presented by the RSC at the Pit shortly after *The Love of the Nightingale* had opened in Stratford. *Electra* was termed 'thrilling', 'searing' and 'electrifying', its design – featuring a river of blood that split the stage – highly admired, and the piece as a whole acclaimed for its presentation of 'naked emotional violence' and 'moral ambiguity' (Carlson 1993: 271–2). This representation of Greek drama met with greater general favour than Wertenbaker's more ironical treatment. In sharp contrast with the explosive staging of *Electra*, Wertenbaker's theatrical interweaving of myths was experienced by some as peculiarly detached and unemotional, a 'cool, even calculating work' (Spencer 1989). As Wertenbaker stated at the time, her own play is 'about passion', but this is not its tone; it examines violence but does not revel in it (Gore 1989). The ending resists closure, yet the play as a whole nevertheless asserts an unflinching ethical stance, less appealing to many than the more fashionable 'moral ambiguity' of *Electra*. Like *Rites* and *A Mouthful of Birds*, *The Love of the Nightingale* stages a reversal: here, less of performance repertory and context than of dramatic convention and audience expectation. It is unsurprising, perhaps, that these interventions should meet friction as alternative values and combative claims are pitched into the theatrical mainstream.

Nothing sacred: Maureen Duffy's *Rites*

In a world in which the human faculties and needs are arrested or perverted, autonomous thinking leads into a 'perverted world': contradiction and counter-image of the established world of repression. And this contradiction is not simply stipulated, is not simply the product of confused thinking or phantasy, but is the logical development of the given, the existing world. (Marcuse 1965: 112)

Get a man, she says. I'll get him right where I want him. He thinks because I'm flat on my back he's got me but I've got him; caught, clenched as if I had my teeth in him. (Duffy 1969: 23)

The Bacchae was inspiration rather than direct model for *Rites*. Duffy takes its most horrifying action, the Maenads' frenzied murder of the king, and audaciously relocates this to a women's public lavatory. Familiarity with Euripides' drama or its mythic roots is not a prerequisite for appreciating Duffy's, although as she states an audience would find 'pleasure in knowing, in adding another layer' (1969: 27). Connections with the ancient narrative are implied rather than stated; *The Bacchae* dissolves into *Rites*' modern action, its characters refigured for the new context, or removed. A further digression from the classical text is in *Rites*' focus, not on Pentheus and Dionysos but on the 'madness' of the female characters, yet Duffy's dramatic framework draws inspiration from their conflict none the less. In *The Bacchae*, Dionysos seduces his opponent by manipulating the latter's suppressed curiosity towards that which he outwardly condemns. His final snare is to hint that the king might like 'to *see* those women, sitting together, there in the mountains'. Pentheus' curiosity is caught: 'Yes, indeed; I would give a large sum of gold to see them' (Euripides 1954: 206). Supposedly scandalised and repelled by their ecstasies, he nevertheless desires to know them more intimately. By relocating *Rites* as she does, Duffy reinvents this theme of voyeurism, tantalising her audience with anticipated revelation of women's dirty secrets. The contrast with *The Bacchae*, set 'before the royal palace', could hardly be greater. Euripides' *mise-en-scène* reinforces classical tragedy's conventional focus on the fortunes of high-level characters, their significance then expanded to implicate the community as a whole. Duffy's irreverent re-vision challenges expectations by drawing more lowly figures to the heart of the dramatic action – lavatory attendants, office assistants, a bag lady – but framed to give perpetual reminder of their socially degraded status. By exposing a prescriptively 'female' world to a gender-mixed audience, *Rites* teasingly plays on men's supposed curiosity about the 'women's room', breaks the rules, blurs the boundary lines of private and public.

Rites has twelve roles, all female. Men are not simply not included in its dramatic circle, but actively prohibited entry. They are allowed – required – to prepare the site but not to share in the women's mysteries. As prologue to the play proper, the lavatories are elaborately erected on stage by a procession of workmen, wall by wall, complete with perfume spray and notice about VD clinics; their labour completed, the men exchange bows and leave. Several critics have interpreted the sequence as physical embodiment of 'patriarchal construction' at the symbolic level (Hersh 1992: 419; Wandor 1987: 98; Winkler 1993: 221–2). The pomp and ceremony of the presentation ironically highlights the littleness of the privilege granted. The women's room offers no utopian life apart but serves rather as clubhouse, or safe house, limits defined and occupation temporary. What is revealed once when the men depart is a world both farcical and realistic, disorientating and familiar: a slice of 1960s Britain through a distorting lens. Women arrive at the toilets, but do not go: with no acknowledgement or explanation they simply gather, disconcertingly, like human embodiments of Hitchcock's birds. Initially they are driven not by vicious intent but by the imperative to perform femininity's 'rites'. First of these is self-adornment:

> ADA: Now look what you've done. I've stuck me pencil in me eye. I've told you before. Don't excite me when it comes to the eyes. Very delicate work the eyes. You can't do nothing without them and you've made the left one run.
>
> (Duffy 1969: 13)

For supervisor Ada, make-up is more than a prettifying tool. It is war paint for a sexual and economic battleground in which a clever woman will exploit those weapons she has, 'tart[ing] it up a bit to sell it high' (*ibid.*: 14). The others, too, join in these rituals of beauty: like a music hall double act, widows Dot and Nellie remove hats, comb already tidy hair, swap hats, retrieve the originals; the giggling office girls dab on cheap perfume and gaze at their reflections, fantasising romance, 'wind-tossed hair like the adverts', and escape from the sterility of workplace routine (*ibid.*: 17). For all the women these rituals are habitual, and superstitious, with much invested in their correct enactment. But Ada, the play's voice of cynicism, is manifestly no true believer. Hers is a literal making up, a self-construction: duplicitous endorsement of an idealised feminine becomes for her a strategy of resistance. The others have learned to play the (heterosexual) dating game, but where they are largely content to 'be girl', to employ Jane Ussher's terms – subscribing to its rules without questioning their legitimacy – Ada 'does girl', harnessing femininity for her own ends in knowing masquerade (Ussher 1997: 445–55). Beauty is her currency; as she explains to meek assistant, Meg: 'You have to live.

Know your market, it says. You want to read more. It's all on the back pages of the paper, just before the sport, if you know where to look. They think we don't read that far' (Duffy 1969: 14). Ada is Duffy's Agave, reincarnated here as overseer of the lavatories: queen of her territory, mistress of feminine arts – and, like her classical counterpart, undisputed ringleader in what follows.

A second rite is the exchange of stories. Through conspiratorial gossip, reminiscence and small confessions, the constant theme is the power of men. Nellie tells tales of her late husband's whims and her endless accommodation of them, ranging from picking out fishbones to accepting his ruling that she would not go out to work. The young women mock so submissive a generation, yet themselves show little revolutionary spirit as they swap stories of office tedium and petty rebellions against their bosses: day after dreary day of 'take it down Miss Smith, lick it, stamp on it', but 'when he goes out of the room we have a laugh and a chat' (*ibid.*: 18). Sex is discussed with a freedom that scandalises Dot and Nellie, yet this seeming enjoyment of the bawdy is belied by their reaction on emergence from the cubicles primly shocked by 'disgusting' graffiti on the walls: 'No decent woman'd write things like that. You must have had a bloke in here.' Turned suddenly puritanical, the girls recite a litany of 'filth' that concludes in staccato unison: 'Only men, only men, only men do that' (*ibid.*: 15). They have their own set of sexual stereotypes to impose, it appears, a story of the social in which aggression and perversity are assigned exclusively to the male. The dangerous rigidity of these binaries hints at their instability. Where in *The Bacchae* Pentheus defines himself against the 'effeminate' god, *Rites'* women refuse to admit the possibility of anything 'masculine' in their make-up; ancient Greek orthodoxy is replaced by 1960s liberalism, but gender boundaries remain in place and policed by women as well as men.

The women's complaints, jokes, frustrations and cynicisms suggest an underlying stasis; in themselves, they amount to no more than ritualised release of tensions. However, the gradual direction of the plot presents these as backdrop for a potentially radical act of rebellion: outbreak of ferocious, collective violence directed against a (supposedly) male intruder. Three earlier moments in the play prepare us – at least partially – for this climactic scene. First, a boy is brought into the lavatories by his mother, his presence there tolerated but none the less distrusted. The child, here a life-size doll of cherubic and androgynous appearance, is all the presence Duffy grants to 'Dionysos'. In a scene that is both comic and genuinely unnerving, the women stand the 'boy' on a chair and undress it. The sight of its genitals stimulates awe and resentment in equal measure:

> FIRST WOMAN: Mummy's big boy. (*She strokes its body.*)
>
> MEG: I had a baby brother once.
>
> ADA: Looks so harmless all quiet there. A pity they ever have to grow up. Snaps and snails and puppy dogs' tails.
>
> DOT: Cause all the trouble in the world they do.
>
> (Duffy 1969: 21)

Casually, Ada suggests castration: 'It'd be so easy, and then nobody'd know the difference.' *Rites*' recasting of Dionysos as the women's toy – which, like all-powerful small girls, they may mutilate if they choose -refuses the god his influential force. This change from Euripides demands that we review the characters' actions. It is tempting, from a feminist standpoint, to read the Bacchants' desertion of conventional duty as resistance to authoritative control, yet such an interpretation is problematic when we know them to be plagued with madness and hence not acting through conscious will. As the Messenger who describes Agave's attack explains: 'It was no strength of hers that did it; the god was in her fingers and made it easy' (Euripides 1954: 217). Allison Hersh argues persuasively on this point that, since Euripides' characters are possessed as part of Dionysos' scheme for vengeance, 'any act of revolt or resistance undertaken by the Bacchae is automatically qualified and dismissible' (Hersh 1992: 411–12). By contrast, the violence that escalates in *Rites* does not result from the wrath of a god but from the repressions of daily experience. The women do not act on Ada's impulsive proposal, denying any wish to hurt the boy. They insist there is 'no harm in looking': the outcome of both plays demonstrates the reverse.

The sudden discovery that the hitherto silent occupant of cubicle two has slashed her wrists heightens already mounting resentment. Aided by the other women, who staunch the blood with sanitary towels, the failed suicide is too weak to say more than one word – 'Desmond!' – which for her rescuers is evidence enough that '[a]nother bleeding man' has caused female suffering. The revelation provokes a collective tirade against all men, building to an jubilant chorus: 'We don't need them. Don't need them' (Duffy 1969: 23) This impression of solidarity is short-lived, however, since when an old, homeless woman emerges nervously from cubicle one – where she has been for the duration of the action – she immediately becomes a target. Hissing they encircle her, launching into a nightmarish version of 'Knees up Mother Brown', a song popularly associated with victory celebrations of postwar England but that here heralds increase rather than termination of conflict. The women's aggression reaches a frenzy that leaves her cowering in fear. She is saved only by the appearance of a new victim, 'suited and coated, short-haired and masculine', who emerges from cubicle seven:

> ADA: Look a bloody man. In here. Spying on us. *(They stop and all turn panting towards the FIGURE which tries to back away.)* He's trying to run for it. Don't let him out. *(Some of the women run behind him and edge him in.)* You think you can get away with murder, that we've no place we can call our own. Coming down here to see what we get up to when we're alone.
>
> *(Ibid.: 24)*

In fury they attack the figure *en masse*, the old woman joining in. When they finally step back we see from the broken and bloody body that the 'intruder' is dead. It is not until Norma examines the corpse and exclaims 'Christ! It was a woman' that the women realise their mistake.

Thus in a state of hysteria – one not divinely induced – these modern Maenads have slaughtered no man, but one of their own. As 'radical protest', the act has proved utterly self-defeating. Wandor offers one plausible reading of what might initially seem a puzzling twist: the ambiguous figure is a lesbian, the women's 'violent hatred of men spill[ing] over into a hatred and a violence against lesbians' (Wandor 1987: 99). The play does not support this conclusively but it is clear at least that this sisterhood cannot tolerate those they perceive as 'other'. The earlier attack on 'Old Mother Brown' reinforces this, albeit that her sex is not in question. The old woman represents a threat because she *is* one of themselves. Old age, wrinkling and cracking the feminine façade appal them not least for the fall in 'market value' that accompanies it. As Ada spits angrily: 'That's how we all end up'

(Duffy 1969: 24). Duffy's women are the true product of a society that represses and categorises. Their temporary community is already exposed as internally riven, hierarchical and selective even before the play's vicious climax. Symbolically, the bloody slaughter cries out against societal constraints; ironically, the revelation of the victim's identity demonstrates still more starkly the system's dangerous limitations.

It is illuminating to compare this murder with its counterpart in *The Bacchae*. Simply by staging it, Duffy breaks implicitly with the ancient taboo against direct presentation of violent action. The Greeks feared that to show was to invite imitation and thereby admit brutality into common culture: hence the mediation of such events through witnesses. *Rites* exposes the transgression in all its horror, in dreamlike release of savagery already present in the 'civilised' – but the nature and implications of the act are changed. Agave kills what she believes is a wild beast, later to discover it was a man and her son: one of her own. Duffy's women attack what they believe is a man, but turns out to be a woman: one of their own. Thus, despite the avowed motivation behind *Rites*' slaughter, what connects the plays is less the motif of spying man than that of fatal misrecognition. The women's discontent is genuine and well grounded, but the play's outcome highlights the distortion of perception that accompanies this. Effectively maddened by the restrictive, contradictory character of imposed femininity, they are unable to identify their enemy.

Another significant departure from Euripides' play is the absence of judgement passed on *Rites*' women for their crime. That they have killed in error is interpreted by Lynda Hart as punishment 'for their separatist desires', yet this analysis seems inadequate since discovery of the mistake produces no effect beyond an initial shock (Hart ed. 1992: 10). No punishment is registered; ironically it is the women rather than men who, in Ada's words, are allowed to 'get away with murder'. The corpse is efficiently dispatched via the incinerator, a monster that seemingly *requires* such nourishment: 'It's hungry. Listen to it roar. We'll feed it.' The evidence gone, routine is effortlessly re-established. The visitors leave; Meg and Ada bring out mop and make-up. *Rites* concludes more or less as it began:

> MEG: When you get your promotion you won't leave me here, will you? You'll let me come with you now, won't you? (ADA *goes*

on with her make-up. MEG *sits down at the table.*) What's he like, your Friday feller?

(Duffy 1969: 24–5)

The contrast with Euripides' final scenes is pointed. In agonies of grief over Pentheus's body, Agave finds herself 'justly punished; for in pride I blasphemed the god Dionysos, and did not understand the things I ought to have understood' (Euripides 1954: 224). The worst revenge Dionysos can exact on the Thebans is not to destroy their leader but to manipulate them into doing this themselves. Ada and her followers draw no lessons from what has happened; they have still not understood. They are products of a system that has dulled their perceptions and led them to attack substitute targets whilst their true oppressor – a complexity of structures material and ideological – remains firmly intact. The play opens a window on to a 'perverted world', in Marcuse's terms: *Rites* reveals deviance not as the province of 'Bastard men!', nor of maddened and resentful women, but as underside to and logical development of a 'normality' that arrests potential and disregards need.

That Duffy's characters simply continue, as Elizabeth Winkler observes 'never entirely conscious of their own positions, and never articulating any vision of a different social organisation', leads the critic Ruth Hazel to interpret *Rites* as gloomy pronouncement on the futility of women's rebellion and, by extension, of the feminist movement itself (Winkler 1993: 219). The absence of male figures reinforces this, Hazel argues, its implication that Duffy's company of women effectively self-destructs (Hazel 2000). For those who find *Rites* invigorating and not depressing, this reading will be unsatisfactory; it would also be curiously at odds with Duffy's own consistently vigorous political engagement.[14] Moreover, whilst feminism might attract angry women, angry women do not equal the feminist movement. The play's action is metaphoric; this is after all myth, not history. Duffy has likened it to a vivid dream, adding that 'it need be no more real than that' (Duffy 1969: 27). The moments of surreally synchronised movements, the women's chants, the abrupt and 'irrational' shifts of mood: all these undercut the surface realism of setting and dialogue and reveal the scene as distortion rather than reflection of the ordinary. *Rites* pushes an idea to its extreme, shocking like a joke that goes way beyond the borders of the acceptable. In so doing, the play invites us to retest all our boundary lines for their validity. This seems appropriate for a play first produced in the late 1960s, a period marked by contestation and rewriting of rules actual and implied. Amidst more general counter-cultural fervour, the so-called sexual revolution – not least, the development of the contraceptive pill and decriminalisation of abortion – signalled a break with ideologies that had sought to contain women's desire within heterosexual marriage. In 2001 Duffy published a critical history of English culture, and within this comments that the sexual dilemmas of the 1950s – 'How far can you go?' – were decisively answered in the following decade: 'As far as you like' (Duffy 2001: 244). As if too hastily accepting that invitation, *Rites*' characters, following impulse, go as far as *they* like. Within Duffy's surreal and mischievous fantasy the result is murder, but this does not make the play an argument for reduction of liberties. Rather, *Rites* presses home the need to tackle further and perhaps still more fundamental impediments to sexual democracy: a challenge that the feminist movement would meet, if not necessarily resolve, in the 1970s and 1980s.

'I don't know what got into me': Caryl Churchill and David Lan's *A Mouthful of Birds*

> Some stories float; others are held under
> until someone sees a small series of bubbles and knows
> there's a body to be dredged.
>
> (Natasha Sajé, 'Tongues', 1994: 26)

Caryl Churchill is one of the UK's best-known playwrights and has produced more than twenty plays for theatre, radio and television since she began to write professionally in the late 1950s. She has long been regarded as a 'feminist voice' in the British theatre, although the shape this has taken has fluctuated over time, as one would expect from a career spanning more than five decades. Her work combines enduring social commitment with constant artistic experimentation, the latter stimulated especially through collaborations with choreographers and composers, and by writing for companies whose methods require her to be unusually flexible and responsive. A number of her plays have rewritten myths, in the sense discussed here: her examination of the 'witch' in *Vinegar Tom* (1978) juxtaposed historical persecution of women with contemporary prejudices; *The Skriker* (1994) explored a nightmarish fairy underworld that suggested the damage wrought within a human sphere fatally corrupted by materialistic self-interest. I limit discussion here to *A Mouthful of Birds* (1986), which like *Rites* takes inspiration from *The Bacchae* but from a later historical vantage point.

A Mouthful of Birds was co-written by Churchill with the playwright and anthropologist David Lan, their shared authorship reflected in the co-direction of the original Joint Stock production by Les Waters and the choreographer Ian Spink. The approach to the project was interdisciplinary and collaborative therefore, inviting less a combination than a deliberate collision of intellectual and aesthetic perspectives. The diversity of 'authorial' voices – which must include the actors, particularly given the improvisatory creative method Joint Stock then employed – helps account for the play's episodic structure and dislocating effect: qualities that, as already mentioned, left some reviewers bewildered and frustrated. *A Mouthful of Birds* is a multi-voiced text in more ways than one: it 'contains' a plurality of authors, and sets *The Bacchae* – or rather, fragments of it – as parallel text against seven contemporary narratives that do not explicitly interconnect. *A Mouthful of Birds'* evocative title connotes the savagery of the Maenads but perhaps also suggests a struggle to control potentially competing impulses within a single expressive structure. However, this perceived incoherence in the work does not derive solely from juxtaposition of contesting creators and texts. Crucially, it comes from the very instabilities inherent in the myth it revisits and emphasised by Euripides' drama. *The Bacchae*'s characters, human and divine, shift from one state to the radically 'other', or inhabit both simultaneously; individuals and institutions alike seemingly split open at Dionysos's touch. The Dionysiac experience implies ecstatic release – through alcohol, music, dance, emotion – from constraints and responsibilities: it demands the relinquishing of control. Whilst the catastrophic outcome arguably demonstrates the dangers to society that arise from indulgence of such impulses, the play has equally been read as critical of any tyrannical 'order' that allows no space for these (Euripides 1954: 24–32). Like *The Bacchae*, *A Mouthful of Birds* tackles abandonment of restrictions, exploring the risks, pleasures and possibilities that attach to this. The collapsing of conventional divisions is, moreover, embedded in its fractured and disconnected form. As I will argue, the result of the re-visioning process is a text that is 'schizophrenic', both ideologically and aesthetically.

A *Mouthful of Birds* requires seven performers, each of whom is protagonist in a self-contained narrative and takes on additional roles in others. Each character becomes temporarily possessed by the spirit of *The Bacchae*: two transform into Dionysos; others are taken over by Pentheus and Agave, or by the Bacchant women. *The Bacchae* exists as an explosive force, for the characters a life-changing or perhaps life-destroying energy. Through the seven stories, Churchill and Lan explore the forms 'possession' might take in a contemporary society, how apparently ordinary lives can be radically disrupted. The design of the original production extended this theme of invasion of the wild/unknown into the civilised/familiar: a number of box-like rooms were arranged to resemble an opened dolls' house, suggestive of a tenement block, yet with a tree growing fantastically out of the staircase (Churchill and Lan 1986: 59). Dionysos dancing – a man, dressed in a white petticoat – is the first image of the play. There follow seven narrative fragments: Lena preparing dinner, but unable to touch the dead rabbit; Marcia at a switchboard, shifting rapidly between West Indian accent and 'neutral' telephone voice; unemployed Derek working out intensively at the gym; Yvonne, acupuncturist, giving up her break to treat a client with the bad manners to fall asleep; businessman Paul playing chess, impressing his mother-in-law with strategies and deals; Dan, a vicar, coping with a barrage of questions spiritual, political and pragmatic; finally, Doreen attempting to explain to an angry partner why she ran away – again – and slept in the open. From these first moments, points of overextension and frailty are evident, although nothing that could prepare us for the anarchy or sheer surreality of what unfolds. Fragmented verbal and danced sequences express desires, fears and appetites beneath the narrative surface; overtaken by the disordering Dionysian spirit, each of the characters is brought to a position of extremity, to what Churchill refers to as an 'undefended day' in which normal constraints are abandoned (*ibid.*: 5). This state of unleashed energy coincides, in the mythic parallel text, with the violent murder of Pentheus. Once Dionysos's influence is withdrawn, the seven pick themselves up and go on with their lives, but these are not the same lives they had before. Metaphorically, the characters stay on the mountain; where Euripides' Agave wants only 'to go away and die', these contemporary Bacchants hold on to their experience and take responsibility for its consequences, using the knowledge gained in the final choices they make (Euripides 1954: 223). Thus formerly squeamish Lena, who when possessed kills her baby, works now as carer for the elderly, sickness and death a part of routine. In the first of seven monologues that conclude the play, she explains:

> LENA: Every day is a struggle because I haven't forgotten anything. I remember I enjoyed doing it. It's nice to make someone alive and it's nice to make someone dead. Either way. That power is what I like best in the world. The struggle is every day not to use it.
>
> (Churchill and Lan 1986: 70)

Of the characters, only Doreen can offer no reflection on her experience, because she is still wrestling with it: 'It seems that my mouth is full of birds which I crunch between my teeth. Their feathers, their blood and broken bones are choking me' (ibid.: 71).

Churchill records that she and Lan began the project with two distinct interests, which converged in The Bacchae: in women's violence, and the idea of possession. The impetus to explore the first was inspired less by evidence that this phenomenon was on the increase than by the desire to challenge a perceived over-readiness, in the contemporary climate, to dissociate women from such behaviour (ibid.: 5). The Greenham Common 'peace protests' against nuclear weapons that began in 1981, extensively covered by the media, were at first gender-mixed but later became strictly women only. Such strategies, valid and even admirable in themselves, nevertheless risked reinforcing culturally inscribed oppositions whereby women became identified as inherently peace-loving, and men as aggressive. Prescriptive and radically divisive accounts of this kind necessarily ignore evidence of violence in women, except where it occurs in self-defence, and dismiss socio-historic factors that have placed men in contexts where violence is legitimised and expected. Still more dangerously, reframing cultural patterns as natural laws creates a tyranny that, in its turn, demands suppression of impulses that might undermine its stability. The Bacchae, dealing both with barbaric women and feminised men, gave the authors a provocative starting-point. In

Euripides' drama, this behaviour 'out of character' is compelled by Dionysian ecstasy. To know ecstasy is, literally, to be 'dis-placed' (from the Greek, *ex* = out of; *histani* = to place). In *A Mouthful of Birds*, ecstatic possession is reframed within the new context of consumer culture, whose constant business it is to stimulate desire and provide means for gratification: hence the playwrights' decision to expand their definition to include 'any form of behaviour that is not entirely under one's own control' (*ibid.*: 6). Violent urges, addictions and transgressive passions, as well as spirit possession, are thus encountered here. Lan especially was intrigued by the political possibilities of this. His claim that possession could, in some contexts, be a covert practice of revolt is supported by the anthropologist Ioan Lewis's observation that in some parts of the world women's possession cults – which may also include 'downtrodden categories of men' – although ostensibly concerned with curing disease, actually serve as 'thinly disguised protest movements directed against the dominant sex' (Lewis 1971: 31–2). It is for the audience to consider how far, if at all, these stagings of loss of self – necessarily and problematically implying absence of agency – could be found subversive, either in themselves or in their effects. The play neither glorifies nor condemns the characters for their behaviour whilst under 'Dionysian' influence: scenes eccentric, ludicrous and horrifying are offered apparently without judgement.

Like Pentheus dismembered, each of *A Mouthful of Birds*' characters metaphorically comes apart as the play progresses. Thus, at the beginning, Trinidadian Marcia is already under pressure in her job through society's refusal to tolerate her otherness. Her suppression of voice, at first a self-conscious manoeuvre, becomes more extreme when later we see her practising as a medium and unable to shake off possession by the spirit of Sybil, a white upper-class woman. Before her 'own' voice disappears altogether, she is able to tell a friend:

> MARCIA: I am bein' worked on [...] My doctor said I'm just not
> feeling right in myself. She understands me. I got to go back
> home and find myself. I lost myself. I don't know where.
>
> (Churchill and Lan 1986: 36)

For Marcia, the movement 'out of place' that ecstasy provokes is a literal dislocation. The climax to 'Baron Sunday', which leaves

her as speechless body, the voice that was hers now coming from
Sybil's mouth, seems to symbolise her aggressive absorption into
the dominant order. Churchill suggests that all the protagonists
are peculiarly 'open to possession': displacement from home makes
Marcia potentially and then literally so (*ibid.*: 5). Yet Marcia as
medium – eventually, mere instrument for identities that (ab)use
her – becomes also potent metaphor for a 'schizophrenia' characteristic to the culture within which all these figures exist and
act. I borrow this term from the Marxist critic Fredric Jameson,
who argued in his seminal essay 'Postmodernism and Consumer
Society' (1983) that the discontinuity, isolation and fragmentation
that distinguished schizoid experience were qualities mirrored in,
or simulated by, postmodern culture. Jameson's use of these terms
is descriptive and not diagnostic, though he begins with a psychoanalytic model. His comparison derives from Jacques Lacan's
account of schizophrenia as essentially a language disorder, a
condition emerging from 'the failure of the infant to accede fully
into the realm of speech and language' (Jameson 1983: 118). In the
schizophrenic, signification processes are broken down: concepts
of personal identity and temporality are dissolved. As this occurs,
says Jameson,

> the experience of the present becomes powerfully, overwhelmingly
> vivid and 'material': the world comes before the schizophrenic with
> heightened intensity, bearing a mysterious and oppressive charge of
> affect, glowing with hallucinatory energy. But what might seem for
> us a desirable experience – an increase in our perceptions, a libidinal
> or hallucinogenic intensification of our normally humdrum and
> familiar surroundings – is here felt as loss, as 'unreality'. (*Ibid.*: 120)

Jameson's account of schizophrenic detachment from the 'real',
which he parallels with a wider alienation in contemporary living
– an effect produced by the emergence of multinational capitalism
and theorised in post-structuralism's radical critique of individualism – is powerfully suggestive of possession as interpreted by *A
Mouthful of Birds*. Certainly Jameson's terms evoke the characters'
ecstatic trances, perhaps in particular that of Doreen/Agave who,
in 'Hot Summer', is simultaneously 'completely full of this awful
sickness' and so psychically 'charged' that she can will objects,
and later a male intruder, to fly across the room (Churchill and
Lan 1986: 58–66). But, more than this, Jameson's representation

conveys the daily world they inhabit *before* the Dionysian spirit overpowers them. The playwrights' re-vision thus positions its myth not simply as energy that bursts from the past to disrupt the order of the present but as metaphoric expression of a culture already fractured, hallucinatory and consuming.

Schizophrenia, in Jameson's sense, pervades the play. Increasingly unable to cope with what is asked of them, the characters defensively throw back 'Excuses' (Act 1 sc. 8) that seem randomly compiled from some collective, mediatised memory bank: 'I can't go to the disco, the army's closed off the street'; 'I know it's my turn to collect them but the kitchen's flooded'; 'I can't meet the deadline. The chairman's been struck by lightning' (Churchill and Lan 1986: 23). This scene immediately precedes 'Psychic Attack', the development of Lena's narrative. Here 'schizophrenic' experience is overtly communicated through fragmentation of the verbal text. A virtually silent Lena endeavours to listen to the rantings of her belligerent husband, and to resist the promptings of a malefic spirit who rails against him. A conversation between the couple – effectively an exchange of clichés – is persistently disturbed by provocations to violence:

LENA: Don't forget to get a lightbulb.	SPIRIT: The order is to kill the baby. The order is to kill the baby. Because the baby is directly / connected to him. The baby is directly connected to you. The baby is directly connected to me. / When you kill the baby you'll be free of him. You'll be free of yourself. You'll be free of me. That's why you're going to kill the baby.
ROY: Mind you I'd like a break.	
LENA: Sure you don't want an egg?	
ROY: No.	

(Ibid: 26)

The spirit seems to embody Lena's unthinkable desire: to lash out violently against this family, the husband who 'swallows the air' leaving her breathless and disempowered. Finally, she submits: after wrestling verbally and physically with the spirit, she drowns the baby in the bath. She tells the appalled Roy: 'It wasn't me that did it' (*ibid*.: 28). The words suggest she cannot own the act; the continuing presence of the spirit after the drowning symbolically confirms this. But her bewildered defence provokes the audience, similarly, to distance the crime from the person. The spirit is more than expression of Lena's private unconscious. We can read her, like Marcia, as channel through which societal energies flow: her pronounced sense of non-existence and desperate attempt to combat this articulate the repercussive impulse for self-assertion amidst pressure of suffocating expectations and demands.

For Lena and Marcia, possession results in recognition of strength, but brings no exhilaration in the moment; neither is granted even the fleeting glory that Agave believes her own deed has won. Yvonne, becoming alcoholic, fares little better; dancing drunkenly, she quickly breaks away to retch (*ibid.*: 57). However, this bleak interpretation of 'ecstasy' is not repeated throughout. Of all the seven, Paul seems initially the most at home in his culture. Champion of high capitalism, he embraces the dissolution of barriers that would limit exchange; the animals he exports, which exist for him merely as profit-making commodities, can the more easily be mechanistically shifted 'from Birmingham first to Berlin then to Boulogne' (*ibid.*: 22). Possession for him comes when – ridiculously yet movingly – he falls in love with a pig, which here literally dances itself into his consciousness.[15] In this tender and bizarre romance we might see mischievous reinvention of the Bacchants' transgressive yet strangely idyllic intimacies with the 'young gazelle, or wild wolf-cubs' to whom they give 'their own white milk' (Euripides 1954: 203). But equally, given Paul's construction as Businessman, his irrational, unstoppable love for the pig paradoxically becomes metaphorical extension and consequence of the deterritorialising processes of the capitalist machine. The effacement of divisions that the latter requires – 'That way we make more profit' – is exposed as its Achilles' heel, since, after the obsession or possession leaves him, Paul drops entirely out of the life he knew before. Not selling, not consuming, he simply sits in the street and waits: 'I can't stand small pleasures. If there's nothing there's room for something to come' (Churchill and Lan 1986: 71). The schizophrenia that here so decisively collapses borders hints at more strongly subversive possibilities than Jameson's account predicted.[16] It suggests rather the radical position of Gilles Deleuze and Félix Guattari, who have claimed that to embrace capitalism's 'schizophrenic' drive, rather than resist or seek to 'cure' this, would be to dismantle its mechanisms. For these theorists, the alienation produced by schizoid experience situates the subject outside oppressive ideological constructs, escaping their codes and an affront to their logic. Similarly capitalism,

> through its process of production, produces an awesome schizo-phrenic accumulation of energy or charge, against which it brings all its vast powers of repression to bear, but which nonetheless continues to act as capitalism's limit. For capitalism constantly counteracts, constantly inhibits this inherent tendency while at the same time allowing it free rein; it continually seeks to avoid reaching its limit while simultaneously tending toward that limit. (Deleuze and Guattari 1984: 34)

Paul's experience pushes him beyond the limit. That his transformation is irreversible, rather than a freedom allowed and then inhibited, is emphasised by his final condition; Paul's choice in the last scene to do 'nothing' symbolically refuses the reterritorialisation that, for Deleuze and Guattari, is the means by which capitalism perpetuates itself (*ibid.*: 257–60).

The proposal that 'decomposition' of identities and territories might prove empowering is played out further through the narratives of Dan and Derek. In 'Dancing', we rediscover Dan inexplicably metamorphosed from progressive vicar into convicted multiple murderer who kills by performing 'precisely the dance' that each of his victims longs for: watching it, they die of pleasure (Churchill and Lan 1986: 37). For certain characters it is possible to find, in their opening scene, the seed of what they later become; for Dan, the relationship is essentially alogical. The key is in his doubling with Dionysos: Dan's resistance to religious dogma – 'I don't believe God is necessarily male in the conventional …' – is the barely visible thread that ties his former self to its re-embodiment as godlike figure, creative and destructive, both male and female (*ibid.*: 22). In this new incarnation Dan, like Dionysos, frees his followers from the structures that confine them; like the god, he grants their release only at the cost of absolute submission of will. Androgynous, Dan proves literally unplaceable by the prison authorities:

FEMALE POLICE OFFICER: You admitted him.
MALE POLICE OFFICER: Her.
FEMALE POLICE OFFICER: Her.

MALE POLICE OFFICER: It was him when we admitted her. I can guarantee that.

FEMALE POLICE OFFICER: Guarantee? [...] You tell me it's Tuesday, I'm going to write down Easter Sunday, that I guarantee.

(Ibid: 37)

Dionysos is similarly uncontainable: 'I alone with effortless ease delivered myself', he states. Pentheus's soldiers never held him, in their delusion shackling a bull in his place (Euripides 1954: 200). Dan's weapon is his own hypnotic and destructive energy, which cannot be taken from him and which flows through the 'corridors, the workshops, the latrines' of the jail to leave dead bodies in its wake. In the end, to protect those still living, the female police officer simply lets him go. Dan, possessed, is perhaps the most *strangely* terrifying of the play's seven protagonists: the Dionysian spirit – where ecstatic celebration combines with savage, even nihilistic energy – is most concentrated in him. But in *A Mouthful of Birds* even the god does not escape dismemberment: we find intoxication in Yvonne; through Paul comes blurring of civilised and savage; in Marcia, shape-shifting and ventriloquism; in Lena, infanticide; through Doreen, a dangerously volatile female community; and in Derek, an unpicking of gendered identity.

Derek's transformation during the play from aggressively masculine to refashioned feminine is symbolically underpinned in his doubling with Pentheus. At first, both try to combat crisis with force. Avowedly, Derek distances himself from his father's equation of productivity with masculinity – 'He thought he wasn't a man without a job' – but obsessive bodybuilding suggests over-compensation for the sense of failure. Unemployment, a common condition in the 1980s and underside to the capitalist boom, leaves Derek anchorless and undefined. Writing in this period, the sociologist Victor Seidler has argued that, for men, work 'is more than a source of dignity and pride. It is the very source of masculine identity, so that without work [...] it is as if men cease to exist at all' (Seidler 1989: 151–2). Derek's possession in Act 2 offers him radical redefinition of self, through the spirit of the nineteenth-century French hermaphrodite Herculine/Abel Barbin.[17] The playwrights discovered Barbin through Foucault, from whose edition of Barbin's memoirs they quote directly. In a speech that is almost dreamlike stream of consciousness, Herculine recalls a past marked by unnameable desires and irresolvable confusions. Speaking, she offers Derek objects – a book, rose, scissors and comb, a crucifix, shawl and petticoat – and, accepting them, he 'becomes' her. Herculine's words, repeated, are now his; her memories are rediscovered as his own submerged knowledge. But the gifts are withdrawn and, as each object is given up, this fragile 'feminine' identity dissolves. His despairing cry 'couldn't you have stayed?' is a call not only to Herculine's beloved Sara but to a self he has been forced to deny. Turning back, Herculine tenderly kisses him on the neck, creating an image that, as Diamond points out, startlingly suggests the 'impossible' two-headed hermaphroditic body (Churchill and Lan 1986: 53–4; Diamond 1992: 276).

Derek's possession and dispossession communicate the pain of socio-sexual alienation. In his preface to Barbin's memoirs, Foucault asks whether 'we *truly* need a *true* sex', whether sexuality might instead be conceived as acceptance of the materiality of the body and the intensity of pleasures it affords (Barbin 1980: vii). Derek's final monologue, celebrating his new transsexual physicality, seems to affirm this: 'My skin used to wrap me up, now it lets the world in. Was I this all the time? I've almost forgotten the man who used to possess this body. I can't remember what he used to be frightened of.' The 'killing' of Pentheus/Derek in *A Mouthful of Birds* is thus not the destructive and vengeful act that it is in *The Bacchae*. Dismemberment – here, a surgical ripping apart – has led to the creation of a re-membered self, one in which he can, at last, be 'comfortable' (Churchill and Lan 1986: 71). In her memoirs Barbin fantasises that, one day, doctors will 'make a little stir around [her] corpse; they will shatter all the extinct mechanisms of its impulses, will draw new information from it' (Barbin 1980: 103). Churchill and Lan 'stir' Pentheus's broken body; rather than compose it for burial, their re-vision reorders the limbs into an alternative and less repressive 'whole'. This pattern is echoed in our final glimpses of the other protagonists, with only Doreen left in pieces. There is an arbitrariness in this, a kind of random cruelty. In the surreal schema of the play, her transgressions are no worse than the others; it is as if she is forced to carry the trauma of what has occurred but denied the ability to process this. Like Agave she is condemned to live in exile; unlike her mythic counterpart she cannot leave for a foreign land: 'I carry on my work as a secretary'

(Churchill and Lan 1986: 71). In the beginning, Doreen sought only 'peace and quiet', not Bacchic revelry. Moreover she fulfilled her desire, by herself, before Dionysos overtakes her; as she tells Ed: 'I was happy' (*ibid*.: 22). Possession has not proved liberating in her case. Nauseous and choking, pulled in contrary directions, she seems more schizophrenia's victim than embodiment of radical resistance.

The play's final speech conveys Doreen's entrapment. But its closing moment – mirroring the beginning – shows Dionysos dancing. The dancing body has been as powerful a mechanism of expression, in *A Mouthful of Birds*, as the speaking body – perhaps more so, since it is through dance that the disruptive spirit of possession is made manifest and primarily this that 'voices' the myth's violence. Lena faces her merciless demon in dance; Paul's old life falls away as he dances with the pig; Dan's divine dancing annihilates those who witness it. We know that Dionysos sets his followers 'dancing, [...] delirious, possessed' (Euripides 1954: 186). Celebration of body here comes through surrender of will, an implied division reiterated through western cultural tradition in the association of the body with the primitive and pre-linguistic. The body, Helen Thomas suggests, typically becomes classified as

> the dangerous 'other' to culture: as a thing that speaks of nature, it has to be surrounded by [...] rituals and controlled through manners and covered in appropriate dress and adornments, in order to prevent it seeping out or breaking through into and contaminating its privileged 'other', culture, reason, civilisation. (Thomas 1995: 7)

Culture and nature are set in opposition in *The Bacchae*; the outcome suggests less that the latter overtakes the former than that this division was overstrained and unsustainable. Initially, *A Mouthful of Birds* holds these potentially contesting spheres apart through deployment of contrasting performance languages: the excesses of its myth-world are conveyed by dance, with the deadening reality from which the contemporary characters long to escape played out in fragmented naturalism. But increasingly there is seepage, to use Thomas's term, and the ambivalence of that relationship becomes more acute. Formal separations begin to break down: notably, by the time of 'The Death of Pentheus' – a dance of murder performed by the whole company – all the actors apart from Derek, clothed by Dionysos in his own feminine dress, wear the costumes of their main characters. Paul/Dionysos and Dan/Dionysos watch as the women tear their victim to pieces. Agave and the Bacchants become quiet when they realise what they have done:

> AGAVE: I broke open his ribs. I tore off his head.
> *She gathers his limbs together.* LENA, YVONNE *and* MARCIA *get up and start to go.*
> AGAVE: Where are you going?
> LENA: Home.
> MARCIA: I'm late for work.
> YVONNE: I have to look after someone.
>
> (Churchill and Lan 1986: 70)

Mythic and modern are fused in this moment, but still schizo-phrenically so: alone amongst the women, 'Agave' is unwilling or unable to withdraw.

The climactic ensemble sequence incorporates and reframes fragments of action from earlier in the play; in dance, 'civilised' and 'savage' come together and are indistinguishable. Individuals fleetingly become a mob: but as we have seen these identities were always already internally inconsistent, a compression of desires and not a coherent whole. In *A Mouthful of Birds* the disorderly Dionysian spirit is reimagined through figures who, to borrow once more from Deleuze and Guattari, are themselves not 'clearly defined personalities, but rather vibrations, flows, schizzes and "knots"'. Although singled out as open to possession, they are also ordinary figures forced into recognition that 'everyone is a little group and must live as such' (Deleuze and Guattari 1984: 362). For some, this realisation provokes a kind of liberation: not in the overthrow of some external authoritative power but in subtler counteraction of essentialist ideologies through newly found identifications with generative, democratic values and a deepened ethical awareness. The extreme violence at the heart of the myth is used here to explode regulatory constructs and imagine a space where new discoveries are possible. But whilst *A Mouthful of Birds'* makers are attracted to the Dionysian – for choreographer and director as for writers this is manifestly source of tremendous creative momentum, as well as metaphor for subversion – their re-vision is not straightforwardly celebratory: the fragility of the subject makes this a place of risk, of vulnerability as well as a potentially revitalising fluidity.

Making silence speak: Timberlake Wertenbaker's *The Love of the Nightingale*

> When you accept the parrhesiastic [truth-telling] game in which your own life is exposed, you are taking up a specific relationship to yourself: you risk death to tell the truth instead of reposing in the security of a life where the truth goes unspoken. (Foucault 2001: 74)

> I wouldn't want to live in a world that's always shifting. Questions are like earthquakes. If you're lucky, it's just a rumble. (Wertenbaker 1989: 22)

In a 2001 lecture at Oxford University, Timberlake Wertenbaker asked the assembled academic audience why the contemporary era, far more than those that preceded it, should have so insatiable an appetite for the tragedies of ancient Greece.[18] Quantities of productions, adaptations and retranslations stand as evidence of this resurgence of interest. Of the plays Wertenbaker herself has written to date, three are rooted in classical drama – *The Love of the Nightingale* (1988) was succeeded by *Deianeira* (1999) and *Hecuba* (2001), both for radio – and another stage play, *Credible Witness* (2001), has strong connections with Euripides' *The Trojan Women* (see Freeman 2008). *Hecuba* was based on Wertenbaker's own translation from Euripides; she has also translated Sophocles' Theban dramas (1992) as well as Euripides' *Hippolytus* (2009). Whilst Britain is her adoptive country, Wertenbaker has lived and worked extensively in Greece; the persistence of her personal interest in its theatre and mythologies is unsurprising. However, she suggests a broader societal answer to the question posed. The destructive conflicts of the last century – the Second World War, Vietnam, Afghanistan, Iraq, amongst so many others – lead us to the frightening conclusion that, for all the advances our civilisation has made, 'we do not seem to progress morally as human beings: we know more, but we seem to understand less and less about ourselves. And so the human being is truly an object of fear and pity' (Wertenbaker 2004: 366). In such moments of crisis, she argues, we turn above all to the Greek playwrights: and, in the narratives of the ancient tragedies, we find our contemporary anxieties already mapped out. The modern loss of faith in a subject who is rational and knowable finds its reflection here, in characters who do not have a conventionally 'Aristotelian' plot line – of pride, fall, realisation and acceptance – but who in Wertenbaker's eyes remain ultimately unresolved, irrational, blinded to themselves: a Medea, an Electra or an Oedipus. These dramas require us to face the unknowable, yet that recognition need not be pessimistic, because

> if you look at, write, see in performance the unknowable human being, you will not close off with the conclusions that have brought so much destruction on our world: you will not insist – even to the death – that this is the right way to love, this is the political system that works, and you are the one who knows best. (*Ibid.*: 366–7)

In other words, the plays of the Greeks expose egocentricity; they demand we confront the limits of our knowledge and power. This is a theme central to *The Love of the Nightingale*, whose central image – of the cutting of a tongue – forcibly expresses that moment when no more answers are possible.

The myth at the heart of Wertenbaker's play is recounted in Book 6 of Ovid's *Metamorphoses*. Here Procne, Philomela's elder sister, marries the Thracian king Tereus and leaves her native Athens. Lonely, she asks Tereus to fetch Philomela to be her companion. He complies, but is overcome with passion for her; raping Philomela on the journey to Thrace, he then cuts out her tongue so she cannot expose his crime. Nevertheless Philomela, like many other women in Greek myth, contrives to 'speak' through the one means of expression she is allowed: spinning and weaving. Philomela's tapestry, delivered to Procne, tells her what has happened and sisters are reunited. Together they kill Tereus's son and serve the cooked flesh to his father to eat. When Tereus learns the truth he moves to kill the women, but as he does so all three are transformed into birds (Ovid 1955: 145–53). Ovid's version is the basis of Wertenbaker's drama, but there are two notable changes: first, theatre, not weaving, is the means by which Procne discovers her sister's treatment; second, Itys is killed but not eaten. Despite these departures, the twin themes of violence and speech, and the suppression of speech, emerge strongly from both texts and are combined in a moment pivotal to each: the cutting of the tongue. Both authors emphasise this offence more strongly than the earlier violation of rape. Ovid alludes to the latter through metaphor, offering poetic analogies for Philomela's suffering: she was 'like some timid lamb', or 'like a dove, its feathers matted with its own blood'. By contrast, he conveys the severing of her tongue in graphic detail: 'he grasped her tongue with a pair of forceps, and cut it out with his cruel sword. The remaining stump still quivered in her throat, while the tongue itself lay pulsing and murmuring incoherently to the dark earth' (1955: 148–9). Wertenbaker's dramaturgical decisions are in some ways comparable: the earlier crime is displaced offstage, but the latter enacted in front of us, leaving Philomela – in *The Love of the Nightingale* called Philomele – '*crouched in a pool of blood*' (Wertenbaker 1989: 36). This question of what is revealed or spoken and what concealed or silenced is critically revisited throughout the play.

A further source drawn upon by Wertenbaker is what remains to us of Sophocles' lost play *Tereus*.[19] Two fragments from this are quoted in the Foreword to her published playtext, both of which appear to be attributable to Procne. The first speaks eloquently of women's vulnerability within a social system that 'markets them out' to men of whom they know nothing, and with whom – 'after the yoking of a night' – they have no choice but to be content. The second, briefer passage evokes an experience of alienation: 'Much / I envy thee thy life: and most of all, / That thou hast never had experience / of a strange land' (Wertenbaker 1989: xi). Both extracts reveal the ways that ancient Greek culture marginalised women: that in themselves they 'are nothing', their wishes disregarded or simply unheard. The very title of Sophocles' play implies this inequality. Jennifer Wagner observes that a drama called *Tereus* suggests one in which the '"tragic" intemperance' of the king takes centre stage, but a modern audience, reading these disconnected fragments in their programme, might be provoked to wonder 'what a tragedy called *Procne* might sound like? or one called *Philomele*?' (Wagner 1995: 231). The decision to preface *The Love of the Nightingale* with this broken and partial text signals Wertenbaker's concern with the mediation and transmission of narrative, inviting us to question which stories survive and which disappear as well as how circulation of narrative might correspond to circulation of power.

Unlike *Rites* and *A Mouthful of Birds*, *The Love of the Nightingale* does not transpose its myth(s) into contemporary times but is set in an imagined ancient past. It requires a sizeable cast, of eight men and eight women, which allows the author to people the stage with a density that recalls the scope of the Greek tragic theatre. Wertenbaker's dramatic structure echoes the pattern of Ovid's narrative: the action opens in Athens, and concludes in Thrace. The majority of stage time is devoted to the voyage upon which Philomele is raped and mutilated by Tereus, events 'recorded' by a Male Chorus; this narrative is intercut with scenes of Procne, waiting in Thrace, attended by a Female Chorus with whom she believes she has no common language. The importance of each Chorus is highlighted in the play to the extent that they become 'protagonists' in their own right. Both groups initially sideline themselves from the central action: the Male Chorus by claiming an impartial role: 'We are only here to observe, journalists of an antique world'; the Female Chorus, less assertive and sensitive to their lack of power as women, by trying 'most of the time [...] to keep out of the way' (Wertenbaker 1989: 14; 20). However, *The Love of the Nightingale* ultimately disallows those positions, for the characters and by extension for the spectators: no one can hold themselves aloof from injustice, whatever the risks attached to speaking out.

Perhaps surprisingly given the savagery of its subject matter, *The Love of the Nightingale* is a cool and often witty play. It is a tale of cruelty – pitilessness marks the sisters' revenge, as well as Tereus's offences – told critically: we are not to lose ourselves in the horror of the story, but to listen to it and consider what could be learned from it. To say this conveys the impression of didacticism but, despite the play's frequently confrontational style, this is only partially its effect: we are urged to reflect seriously on its questions, but are not given answers. This, Wertenbaker has suggested, is effectively how plays *must* work if they seek to exert political effect; the theatre will not provoke its spectators to revolution, but can lead them 'to question something, [...] by intriguing them, or giving them an image that remains with them. And that little change can lead to bigger changes' (Wagner 1995: 252). In *The Love of the Nightingale*, as in others of her plays, Wertenbaker highlights the theatre's functional role through a sustained metadramatic discourse that asserts itself in diverse ways: through a play-within-a-play; in moments of direct address from a Chorus whose detached perspective suggests a parallel with the spectator's own; and by anachronistic real-life references that jar with the dominant theatrical frame. Metadrama is familiarly a source of comedy, and the author exploits it as such. Thus Philomele, hurrying in to watch the performance of Euripides' *Hippolytus* – 'We're late! I've missed Aphrodite' – is reassured by her father: 'She only told us it was going to end badly, but we already know that. It's a tragedy' (Wertenbaker 1989: 9). At the same time, such devices can be usefully disorientating, producing in us, the real audience, the sensation of seeing double. Thus in *The Love of the Nightingale* the behaviour of Wertenbaker's onstage audience promotes speculation on how we in our turn receive theatre. King Pandion insists that plays help him think, but in practice demonstrates the reverse; isolated pronouncements of the characters are seized superstitiously, making it easier for him *not* to think. Tereus, unfamiliar with playgoing, takes all literally. Echoing the arrogance of Hippolytus, he condemns Phaedra outright: 'Why should we pity her? These plays condone vice' (*ibid.*: 10). Yet later he will seize on her example to justify his case, telling Philomele: 'The play. I am Phaedra. (*Pause.*) I love you. That way' (*ibid.*: 29). His parallel is false, however, since the passion of Phaedra is never consummated. Indeed, where Euripides' Phaedra resists attempts to make her speak it aloud – hoping thereby 'to bring honour out of shame' – Tereus enforces quiet on the object of his desire (Euripides 1974a: 93).[20] Philomele's reaction to the play is the most complex. She pities Phaedra, recognising in her the depth of feeling that Hippolytus lacks; as spectator, she questions, comments and challenges, but in the end she weeps: 'It's the play, I am so sorry for them all' (Wertenbaker 1989: 13). Touched and troubled by the drama, Philomele understands that its meaning extends beyond individual praise or blame.

That *The Love of the Nightingale*, too, is 'about' more than the story it centres upon is strongly hinted by the Male Chorus, who also double as Tereus's soldiers. On the voyage back to Thrace, while Philomele's 'fate' moves ever closer, they contemplate the nature of myths:

MALE CHORUS: What is a myth? The oblique image of an
    unwanted truth, reverberating through time.

MALE CHORUS: And yet, the first, the Greek meaning of myth
    is simply what is delivered by word of mouth, a myth is speech,
    public speech.

MALE CHORUS: And myth also means the matter itself, the
content of the speech.

(*Ibid*.: 19)

We may not wish to adopt these definitions universally or uncrit-
ically yet they are helpful in pulling apart a word within which many
meanings are concentrated. Watching Wertenbaker's re-vision, we
might well respond first to the content: to the narrative, as it were,
at face value. In so doing we could be led to receive the whole as
'about men and women, yes, you think, a myth for our times, we
understand' (*ibid*.: 19). However, the Chorus have said that the
image myth offers is *oblique*. This view is reiterated in the following
scene, where the Female Chorus's use of metaphor to communicate
danger – 'The sky was so dark this morning' – is (perhaps wilfully)
misread by Procne: 'It'll rain. It always rains.' Gently, she is reminded
that images 'require sympathy', '[a]nother way of listening'; the
caution is for the contemporary audience too (*ibid*.: 20–1).

The second, more pragmatic definition the Chorus offers is perhaps
the more fundamental to Wertenbaker's purpose. At its root, a myth
is an act of speech. To speak a myth or create new myths is to assert
one's part in shaping discourse if not in mastering it. In *The Love
of the Nightingale*, both sisters embrace the beauty of words and
their right to utter them. For Procne, Athens was a place where
'[e]verything that was had a word and every word was something.
None of these meanings half in the shade, unclear'; a stranger in
'barbarian' Thrace, it is she who is the foreigner, deprived of speech
(*ibid*.: 7). Language for her sister is at first a sophisticated game.
Philomele plays moral philosopher for the Captain: 'I will begin by
asking you a lot of questions. You answer yes or no. But you must
pay attention' (*ibid*. 15). But more often her speech is impulsive,
disorderly, her unrestrained tongue earning perpetual reproof;
indeed, before she has uttered her first line in the play we gather she
has breached decorum: 'Don't say that, Philomele' (*ibid*.: 2). The
admonition presages the later confrontation with Tereus, following
the rape. Infuriated by her mockery, he struggles to silence her:

TEREUS: I said that was enough.

PHILOMELE: I will say more. They will all know what you are.

TEREUS: I warn you.

PHILOMELE: Men and women of Thrace, come and listen to the
truth about this man –

TEREUS: I will keep you quiet.

PHILOMELE: Never, as long as I have the words to expose you.
The truth, men and women of Thrace, the truth –

(TEREUS *cuts out* PHILOMELE'*s tongue*.)

(Ibid.: 36)

Philomele takes on the role of truth-teller: in classical terms, that of the *parrhesiastes* whose duty it is to speak out with frankness despite danger. Discussing this concept of *parrhesia* – ordinarily translated as 'free speech' – Foucault explains that the risk attached always comes from the fact that the truth is capable of hurting the interlocutor. Truth-telling becomes a 'game' of life or death: 'It is because the *parrhesiastes* must take a risk in speaking the truth that the king or tyrant generally cannot use *parrhesia*; for *he* risks nothing' (Foucault 2001: 11–24). When Tereus cuts his victim's tongue he performs a literal act of oppression; metaphorically, he strikes at the heart of the constitution. The act is an assault upon a culture centred upon the word. As John Heath notes, for the ancient Greeks 'to be able to speak freely in public [...] was the primary definition of citizenship in their democracy' (Heath 2005: 177). Enforced silence in the public arena was thus the equivalent of non-citizenship; mutilation of Philomele's tongue seemingly grants tyranny free reign. Yet despite this suggestion of entitlement withdrawn, we should remember that the democracy of the classical *polis* did not extend to women; like slaves, barbarians and children, they could not speak in public and were thus excluded from the discourse of governance. Tongueless, Philomele is 'more beautiful' to Tereus than before. We might read this as further evidence of his barbarity; nevertheless, his preference accurately reflects the orthodox perception in the classical world that 'silence graces women' and is their proper condition.[21] It seems that Philomele's faith in what she can do with words, instilled from childhood, was misplaced; as woman, and non-citizen, her access to *parrhesia* was already violently cut off.

The image of a severed tongue can be extended – with the 'sympathy' urged by the Female Chorus – to encompass the ways that women's language is denied authority within and beyond the frame of the play. Onboard, Niobe's talking is dismissed as inconsequential chatter by Philomele and Tereus alike. Yet the

old woman's garrulousness is more purposeful than her charge
understands:

> TEREUS: Do you want to be married, Philomele?
>
> NIOBE: Oh, yes, my lord. Every young girl wants to be married.
>   Don't you, Philomele?
>
> PHILOMELE: Niobe, go to bed, please.
>
> NIOBE: No, I can't. I mustn't. I will stay here. I must.
>
> (Wertenbaker 1989: 17)

Recognising what threatens Philomele, Niobe tries to distract and
frustrate. But her words can only do so much: 'I could have warned
her, but what's the point? Nowhere to go. It was already as good
as done.' The rape of the girl seems as inevitable to her as the
aggressive colonisation – by democratic Athens – of her own 'small
island' (*ibid*.: 30). Tereus devalues the words of all women, giving
the lie to his earlier, flattering claim that marriage to Procne would
import 'civilised discourse' to Thrace. His wife and her attendants
talk about '[w]hat women talk about' and Procne, divorced from
her Fatherland, initially shares that view: the speech of the Female
Chorus is incomprehensible to her, meaningless 'muttering', literal
non-sense (*ibid*.: 16; 20–1). But the Thracian women, unlike the
Athenian sisters, intuit the limitations of their speech, recognising
their exclusion from the language of power:

> HERO: Sometimes I feel I know things but I cannot prove that I
>   know them or that what I know is true and when I doubt my
>   knowledge it disintegrates into a senseless jumble of possibilities,
>   a puzzle that will not be reassembled, the spider web in which I
>   lie, immobile and truth paralysed.
>
> HELEN: Let me put it another way: I have trouble expressing
>   myself. The world I see and the words I have do not match.
>
> (*Ibid*.: 20)

Such words as they have are like a foreign tongue; as women,
they cannot make it theirs. Yet the Female Chorus, like Niobe,
recognise that their language, however inadequate, is none the less
necessary. Women must seek alternative ways to communicate: by
imagery and metaphor; in silences; with a tapestry; or through the
performance of 'irrational' Bacchic rites.

The explosive Dionysian myth is more tightly restrained in
The Love of the Nightingale than in either *Rites* or *A Mouthful*

of Birds. Where the violent energy of the disempowered quietly seethes underneath Duffy's play, and altogether pervades that of Churchill and Lan, the predominantly 'rational' frame that Wertenbaker establishes for a long time keeps this stilled. When it finally emerges, it does so with a vengeance. In *The Love of the Nightingale*, the women's rituals are associated with the barbarian practices of Thrace and are initially rejected by Procne in consequence. But severed from her sister, whom she believes to be dead, she is forced to turn at last towards her companions; joining their festival, she discovers another 'way of listening' previously inaccessible to her. On this one 'strange night' of the year, the normal restrictions on women's behaviour are lifted: as Bacchae, they can stream through city and woods, temporarily uncontainable. Wertenbaker reimagines this ritual frenzy as the means by which the tongueless Philomele can 'speak', as well as that which disguises the murder of Itys. Appropriately here, sister communicates with sister through theatre instead of weaving: Philomele's brutally parodic, defamiliarising dumb show redraws Wertenbaker's wider drama in cruder colours. Through huge dolls that evoke carnivalesque effigies, Philomele and Niobe re-enact Tereus's assault for a jeering crowd. Niobe's involvement in this seems accidental; in her struggle to restrain the 'mad girl' the older woman unwittingly plays out the rapist's part. Laughter gives way to an uneasy silence when Philomele re-creates the cutting of the tongue. The onstage spectators drift away to leave Procne – and ourselves, the theatre audience – to deal with this ugly and unwanted truth.[22] Philomele's grotesque, wordless drama is far harsher than the sophisticated entertainment of Athens, and when Procne recoils from it her sister makes a spectacle that is starker yet: she opens her mouth. It is an image that reveals to Procne, as nothing else could, 'what the world looks like' (*ibid.*: 41).

Denied *parrhesia*, Philomele has no choice but to learn a new kind of speech. If this is the language that women must use, then it is with this bitter speech that they will tell Tereus what they now know. For him, the spectacle will be the body of his own child. As audience, we do not see the murder initially; our perspective is that of the soldiers who try to spy upon the women's 'mystery'. This is the same voyeurism that *Rites* exploits in its provocative staging, a curiosity tinged with resentment – at the reversal of power that forces the men, unfamiliarly, to the margins – and, unmistakably, with fear. Yet the soldiers lack even the deluded courage that marks Pentheus's intrusion; instead they manipulate Itys, lifted on their shoulders, to look for them. Seeing a 'slave girl' with his sword, the boy runs in to challenge them. For the men, what follows is 'Nothing. Nothing. Nothing' (*ibid.*: 45). By contrast, the Female Chorus are now able to confront that from which the men turn away, and require the audience to face this too. Before replaying the murder onstage, they speak to us in a flood of questions that pour 'out' of the theatrical frame. The moment sharply reconnects mythic and modern, transgressing the conventions the play itself has established:

> IRIS: We can ask: why did Medea kill her children?
>
> JUNE: Why do countries make war?
>
> HELEN: Why are races exterminated?
>
> HERO: Why do white people cut off the words of blacks?
>
> IRIS: Why do people disappear? The ultimate silence.
>
> ECHO: Not even death recorded.
>
> HELEN: Why are little girls raped and murdered in the car parks of dark cities?
>
> (*Ibid.*: 45)

In a culture where aggression is ingrained, violence becomes invisible and 'silent', out of discussion. We have been told that for some questions there are no answers; there is still, the play insists, the moral responsibility to ask.

When Itys bursts into the women's space this second time we are shown what the soldiers claimed they 'did not see': his murder, a ritualised sacrifice carried out in silence. The scene is far removed from the Bacchants' frenzied dismemberment of Pentheus. Wertenbaker attracted some criticism for her decision to rewrite the myth as she does at this point, sparing the sisters from cooking the boy and Tereus from eating him. Charles Spencer suspected positive discrimination: 'Good feminist that she is, Miss Wertenbaker cannot permit such womanly barbarism' (Spencer 1989). We might equally read this change as the attempt to redress what Sarah Annes Brown terms the typical 'scapegoating of society's female victims', whereby the story's grotesque conclusion threatens to eclipse Tereus's tyrannical acts (Brown 2005: 101–2). However, I would argue, given the scenes that have preceded this, that the preservation of Itys' corpse significantly allows the women to present a further *spectacle*. The sight of Philomele, battered and bloodied, is not sufficient for Tereus to comprehend the enormity of his offence. He cannot explain or defend himself; he lacks the words. To shock him into language, Procne reveals the body of his son: 'If you bend over the stream and search for your reflection, Tereus, this is what it looks like' (Wertenbaker 1989: 47). This has become the shape of women's speech. It is not 'rational': but as image, as metaphor, it is lucid. Wertenbaker has emphasised:

> I [...] feel very strongly that if you can't speak, if you don't have the language, the only way you can express yourself is violently, and I think we have evidence of it all around. If you can speak, you can at least make your claims, hope to be listened to, make more claims, listen to the other side. Without that, yes, I think there will be nothing but violence. (Stephenson and Langridge 1997: 143)

Seen in this light, the slaughtered body of Itys is effectively the only reply they can make.

Following Ovid, Wertenbaker refuses Tereus further bloody revenge. The protagonists metamorphose into birds: Philomele becomes a nightingale, Procne a swallow and Tereus a hoopoe.[23] The final scene is a coda to the play. Philomele-as-nightingale instructs Itys, here granted afterlife, in the art of questioning. If he wants the reward of her song, he must earn it by permitting no 'truths' to pass unchallenged. That Philomele was punished for her own questions makes it more rather than less urgent that Itys – symbolic of an imagined future – should refuse to accept authoritative pronouncements at face value. The two use the philosophers' method of question and answer. But again this language fails, to be replaced by a different kind of speech:

ITYS: What does wrong mean?

PHILOMELE: It is what isn't right.

ITYS: What is right?

(*The Nightingale sings.*)

Didn't you want me to ask questions?

(*Fade.*)

(Wertenbaker 1989: 49)

Itys must find his own answer in her wordless song. It is appropriate that this play, which opens in confident articulacy then destabilises and undermines this, should conclude with the language of birds. In classical literature, the 'ceaseless chatter' of the birds is a recurrent metaphor for the speech of women; for the 'gibberish' of foreigners; and for the language of the unquiet dead (Heath 2005: 186; 200; 60). None is silent, but all speak a barbarous tongue that persists beneath the 'rational' speech of the recognised citizen. This is the voice of the marginalised, the disempowered and the disappeared: resisting mastery, striving to make itself heard.

Notes

1 Euripides' version of the myth emphasises aspects of the story (such as Pentheus's disguise) which have the effect of adding to Pentheus's humiliation, but which do not feature in every account. Drawing off Theocritus and Ovid, Robert Graves's version says simply that Pentheus chased after the Bacchants but the women, 'inflamed by wine and religious ecstasy, [...] rent him limb from limb' (Graves 1961a: 105).

2 Caryl Churchill was born in England, but grew up in Montreal. David Lan was born in Cape Town to a family with Lithuanian roots and did not move to Britain until he was in his twenties. Timberlake Wertenbaker is French-American by birth, was raised in the Basque country and has lived extensively in Greece; of this 'plurality', she remarks: 'I feel I am an American but not completely [...] I grew up in Europe so I am not an expatriate. Really, that's just narrow nationalism and I don't know why people can't accept that you can have several cultures. The whole thing about being a writer is that you can have a floating identity anyway' (Carlson 1993: 268–9).

3 The myth of Philomela, Procne and Tereus has received a number of famous literary treatments in addition to Ovid's account in the *Metamorphoses*. See for example Geoffrey Chaucer's *The Legend of Good Women* (c. 1385); John Gower's *Confessio Amantis* (c. 1390); Matthew Arnold's 'Philomela' (1853); Algernon Charles Swinburne's 'Itylus' (1904); T. S. Eliot's 'The Waste Land' (1922).

4 In Ovid, it is Procne who carries out the murder of Itys. The Dionysian revels make her act possible: she 'pretended that she was being driven by Bacchus' frenzy' and although 'dressed [...] in the costume of one of Bacchus's worshippers', she is not one of them (Ovid 1955: 150–1).

5 Later readings (and retellings) have challenged the representation of Philomela as victim. See for instance Tennant 1975; Cutter 2000.

6 The notorious case of Myra Hindley and the 'Moors Murders' of

the early 1960s demonstrates Morrissey's thesis. Although Hindley's partner Ian Brady was equally implicated in the crimes (the serial abuse and killings of several children), in the public consciousness Hindley was perceived as doubly monstrous because she was a woman. She was 'vilified' as unnatural and inhuman. She was also 'victimised', through arguments that she was effectively one in a line of Brady's victims, led on and abused by him and hence not truly responsible for her actions. The now-iconic snapshot of Hindley taken in 1966, with her peroxide hair swept up and a fixed expression in her eyes, regularly attracted the description 'Medusa-like', as if only 'mythification' could adequately convey the magnitude of evil she seemed to symbolise.

7   Alana Barton has argued that the association of femininity with passivity is so pervasive and deeply ingrained that women have been dismissed as social agents even when, historically, they have engaged in action that constituted a serious political threat (such as the suffrage activism of the nineteenth-century women's movement) (Barton 2005: 27).

8   The anthropologist Barbara Smith states that in classical iconography Dionysos 'was usually depicted as effeminate, bisexual or homosexual [...], a beautiful young man, bearded but not patriarchal' (Larrington ed. 1992: 67).

9   The small percentage of women's plays staged at major venues during the 1980s can be paralleled with the extent of recognition accorded to women within the British theatre industry as a whole at this time. Mary Remnant quotes a 1987 survey conducted by the Women's Playhouse Trust which showed that 'for every level of appointment that might be expected to have a significant impact on theatre policy, where women hold such posts, they are disadvantaged financially, and therefore artistically, compared with men in the same posts. In most posts, women are more likely than men with the same job title to be working with small theatre companies with low levels of funding, with small-scale touring theatre companies without a permanent building base, or in theatres with small auditoria [...]' (Remnant ed. 1988: 7).

10 The *Ladies' Night* plays were staged not in fact at the Old Vic Theatre (then the National's base) but at the Jeanetta Cochrane Theatre, which the National was then using 'as a kind of studio theatre'; evidently marginal, the work did not have the chance to penetrate the National's 'main space' (Duffy 1969: 26).

11 The question of the potential and limits of carnival as mechanism of social subversion has been widely, and heatedly, debated. *Rabelais and His World*, by the Russian philosopher and literary theorist

Mikhail Bakhtin, is a classic work on the subject; Stallybrass and White (1986) provides a useful commentary on and analysis of Bakhtin's arguments, roughly contemporaneous with the later plays considered here.

12 *Rites* was presented by the University of Kwazulu, Natal, South Africa (1980), and by the Riccarton Players, Christchurch, New Zealand (1982); later in the century, stagings were mounted by the Los Angeles City College Academy (1992) and the Tübingen Anglo-Irish Theatre Group, south Germany (1998).

13 Review of *A Mouthful of Birds* at Birmingham Rep. *The Observer*, 7 September 1986. Unreferenced cutting supplied by the Theatre Museum, London.

14 Looking back on her adult life in interview, Duffy remarked: 'I've always been a politically active person. When I was teaching I was the secretary of the local teachers union, I marched with CND and I stood around for animal rights, with anti-fur banners outside Harrods, and all that' (Bode 1999: 96).

15 Amidst the cynical reactions of many critics to the play, the sequences between Paul and the pig were grudgingly singled out for praise. For Shorter (1986), the scenes were 'strikingly theatrical and almost touching'; Hoyle (1986) similarly notes that the *pas de deux* between Phillippe Giradeau's businessman and Stephen Goff's pig 'linger[ed] in the memory'.

16 Jameson feared that in consumer society art might lose all subversive potential: postmodernism's erosion of divisions, particularly between 'high' and 'popular' forms, implied its absorption into capitalist mass culture and hence an undermining of its capacity to oppose this. The conclusion to his essay avowedly 'leaves open' the possibility that postmodernism might yet be able to resist capitalist logic, but the overriding tone is one of scepticism (Jameson 1983: 125).

17 Herculine Barbin was raised as a girl at a convent school, but was eventually recognised by doctors to be a man. This was established as her 'true' identity and her civil status changed as a result. Dislocated, mentally and socially, but physically unaltered, Barbin committed suicide.

18 Lecture given at the Archive of Performances of Greek and Roman Drama, University of Oxford. 28 February 2001.

19 For details and discussion of the fragments that remain (some 57 lines extant) see Sutton 1984: 127–32.

20 For a detailed and thought-provoking consideration of the interaction of the Phaedra and Philomela myths in Wertenbaker's play, see Winston 1995.

21 The line, from Sophocles' *Ajax*, is delivered by Tecmessa but actually

quotes Ajax: 'Woman, silence graces women' (Sophocles 1912: 135). Classical association of women with silence is discussed in detail in Heath 2005: 185–92.

22 Wagner observes that the disappearance of the onstage crowd 'is only in body, as it were, for the burden to "react" to this spectacle becomes our own. [...] Philomele's parody of her own rape has the ultimate effect [...] of once again forcing the theater audience to confront its own kinship to the on-stage audience, who are able to laugh at violence, and to effectively shut their eyes to the real implications or consequences of their gazing upon those events' (Wagner 1995: 244–5).

23 The earliest Greek versions of the myth had Procne as the nightingale and Philomela the swallow (despite the fact that the word *philomel* meant nightingale in ancient Greek). The Roman poets reversed this, as Robert Bell suggests 'perhaps because the irony of having a tongueless woman transformed into a sweet singer was too much to resist' (1991: 364). Ovid avoids the problem, choosing not to specify (1955: 152).

4

Stages of subjectivity

So long as we do not put aside 'character' and everything it implies in terms of illusion and complicity with classical reasoning and the appropriating economy that such reasoning supports, we will remain locked up in the treadmill of reproduction. (Cixous 1974: 387)

In 'The Character of "Character"', Cixous attacks fundamental assumptions of subject representation. The very concept of 'character' is a straitjacket, she insists: promising subtlety, it is in the end always a reductive puzzle whereby the subject exists in order 'to be *figured out,* understood, read' (1974: 385). As readers, our engagement with 'character' becomes an ideological transaction in which the text ultimately confirms and endorses that which we have been conditioned to see. Fetishised as whole, conscious and knowable, 'character' cannot by definition embrace that which does not yet exist; it prohibits in advance what Cixous describes as 'the open, unpredictable, piercing part of the subject, this *infinite* potential to rise up' (*ibid.*: 384). The production of 'character', she concludes, is a process of mastery, resting on principles of selection and exclusion through which we are all reduced, distorted and dehumanised. Her examples are largely literary, but the illustrative metaphor she chooses is explicitly dramatic: when we say '"character" or "*personnage*" we are in the theatre, but a theatre that offers no exit, that takes in everything, that substitutes itself for a nonrepresentational reality' (*ibid.*: 386). The way out of this ideological trap, for Cixous, is through the invention of texts that resist narrow interpretation: reaching out in multiple directions, retaining contradictions, and thus liberating the subject from 'character' and its restrictive codification. The plays I examined in Chapter 3 initiated such a movement 'out of character', both thematically and formally.

The recurring motif of Bacchic possession offered a means by which writers could imagine the consequences, empowering or appalling, of stripping away control mechanisms; at the same time, these radical departures from the habitual found expression in formal interruptions to 'representation' through verse, dance, role-doubling, puppetry and direct address. But if the plays of Duffy, Churchill and Lan, and Wertenbaker present characters that are later 'undermined', the texts I consider now move still more decisively towards abstraction. As re-visions, these plays affirm the expansive, unfathomable dimension of myth narratives in which passions are embodied by figures that have not yet hardened to become 'characters', in Cixous's sense of the word; perhaps paradoxically, these plays seek freedom within the patterning of the archetype. They are like the stagings of dreams; in moving away from the concrete and immediate, their authors attempt to expose the 'open, unpredictable, piercing' parts of subjectivity and discourse that the patriarchal symbolic order represses.

If such plays propose that myths can help us understand and potentially 'remake' the self, the same principle is as firmly embedded in psychoanalysis. Freud and Jung both regarded the activity of mythmaking as a necessary manifestation of the human psyche and myths themselves as symbolic articulations of 'primitive' instincts. Both also emphasised the close correlation of mythic structures and symbols with the patterns and imagery of dreams. Released from the prohibitions that shape waking life, Freud claimed, our dreaming minds – provoked 'invariably and indisputably [by] *a wish from the unconscious*' – reach instinctively towards territories that appear dangerous or actually forbidden (Freud 1958: 561). Freud judged the creation of such stories (in myths or dreams) a necessary outlet for urges that if acted on would make assimilation within the social order impossible. Jung's view, by contrast, was that dreams were expressions of something effectively 'missing' from the dreamer's consciousness. For Jung, engaging with myths and learning to listen to dreams were both part of the individuation process whereby preconscious impulses could be gradually returned to conscious awareness. The eventual goal was the achievement of new psychic wholeness: a self in balance, divested of 'the false wrappings of the persona' but neither in thrall to 'the suggestive power of primordial images' (Jung 1953: 172). Both men believed that myths were culturally persistent because they found resonance in psychic patterns common to all humanity. To propose interpretive frameworks that are universally applicable is inevitably to draw charges of essentialism and neither Freud nor Jung proved immune to such criticism. Contemporary psycho-analytic practices are more likely to recognise a pluralistic conception of difference, permitting a more sensitive theorisation of connections between individual subjectivity and structures of thought and feeling that may be culturally specific.

Some decades after Freud and Jung, Jacques Lacan championed, and in important respects transformed, Freudian thinking. Lacan proposed that the structures of the unconscious mapped the structures of conscious awareness in a direct interrelationship governed primarily by the experience of language. Thus where Freud found in the Oedipus myth the basis for his theory of the Oedipus complex, reflecting submerged sexual impulses, for Lacan the child's desire for the mother – in his view, a 'desire for her desire' – and growing recognition of the authority of the father marked stages in the civilising process of language acquisition (Lacan 2001: 219). Lacan acknowledged that, chiefly through Freud's endeavours, psychoanalysis as a discipline had re-established the connection between the modern mind and ancient myths; he was similarly well versed in classical mythology and regularly drew on its narratives to elucidate points of theory. More than once he employed the myth of Actaeon, for example, as metaphor for the psychoanalyst in pursuit of truth. Ovid describes how Actaeon, a hunter, leaves his companions to wander with his hounds, only to stumble upon a grotto where the goddess Diana is bathing with her nymphs; offended to be seen naked by a mortal, Diana punishes Actaeon by turning him into a stag so that he will be hunted and torn apart by his own hounds (Ovid 1955: 84–7). In 'The Freudian Thing', Lacan represented Freud as 'an Actaeon perpetually slipped by dogs that have been tracked down from the beginning, and which he strives to draw back into pursuit, without being able to slacken the chase in which only his passion for the goddess leads him on' (Lacan 2001: 137). Actaeon's hunt was comparable to the analyst's search, but for Lacan the quarry, 'truth', resided not in the person of the goddess but in the hunt itself. He underlines the point in *The Four Fundamental Concepts of Psychoanalysis*, using the same myth: 'The truth [...] is that which runs after truth – and that is where I am running, where I am taking you, like Actaeon's hounds, after me. When I find the goddess's hiding place, I will no doubt be changed into a stag, and you can devour me, but we still have a little way to go yet' (Lacan 1981: 188). The myth is one of metamorphosis: the hunter-analyst is transformed as a result of the desire that drives him on. It is clear that, for Lacan, the analyst is not nor could be divided from the processes under scrutiny. This recognition of the fluidity of affect and an accompanying undermining of common assumptions about the authority of 'rational' discourse have helped make Lacan's metamorphic (re)readings of Freud to a degree more serviceable for subsequent feminist analysis than Freud's work in its original forms; that said, the Lacanian model has also been challenged as 'elitist, male-dominated, and itself phallocentric' by some feminist thinkers, Cixous among them (Grosz 1990: 147).

The discussions of this chapter draw on the thinking of Freud, Jung and Lacan since the plays considered here are closely bound into such debates. In the first two re-visions examined, the territory of myth 'stands in' for the unconscious. I begin with *Demeter Beneath the Sand*, co-created by Serena Sartori and Renata Coluccini of the Milan-based Teatro del Sole and first staged in Padua in 1986. Few readers will have come across the piece, yet as Bassnett observes, in notes that accompany her English translation, it might nevertheless be considered 'in many ways absolutely typical of the best of Italian women's theatre work in the 1980s' (Sartori and Coluccini 1995: 112). In this work Sartori and Coluccini play women trapped in a dreamlike, ahistoric landscape where rocking chairs and tea sets lie half-buried in sand. Their monotonous interactions are periodically disrupted as each woman is 'invaded' by archetypes of myth (in a manner that in some respects recalls the possession sequences of *A Mouthful of Birds*). Jungian psychoanalysis was one of many influences on the production. By physically staging 'the self', the artists take the Jungian model in a direction Jung himself implicitly endorsed. In the way he chose to describe 'the living process of the psyche', Jung insisted he 'deliberately and consciously' privileged 'a dramatic, mythological way of thinking and speaking', since he believed – controversially – that this was 'not only more expressive but also more exact than an abstract scientific terminology' (Jung 1959: 13). *Demeter Beneath the Sand* attempts to negotiate a similar balance of expressive metaphor with concrete application; the piece enacts tensions between acknowledged and hidden parts of the self, an effortful struggle mirrored in a making process marked by personal and artistic risk-taking.

The second work considered is Cixous's opera *The Name of Oedipus: Song of the Forbidden Body*, first performed at the 1978 Avignon Theatre Festival. Cixous contributed the libretto, with the score supplied by André Boucourechliev. Cixous's re-vision is informed by Freud and Lacan and challenges both. Her drama imagines the retrospectively transgressive sexual relations of Oedipus and Jocasta as source of a radically 'unfixed' subjectivity, of an ideal harmonised self, freed from the violence done by law and language. Jocasta is the centre and motor of her play, with the potential for transformation located within the maternal feminine. The theme of the maternal as creative force is repeatedly evoked in Cixous's work, linked specifically to the idea of a feminine practice of writing. The connection was most vividly articulated in her call in the mid-1970s for an *écriture féminine* written in women's 'white ink': 'In women there is always more or less of the mother who makes everything all right, who nourishes, and who stands up against separation; a force that will not be cut off but will knock the wind out of the codes [...] Because the "economy" of her drives is prodigious, she cannot fail, in seizing the occasion to speak, to transform directly and indirectly all systems of exchange based on masculine thrift' (Cixous 1976: 882). Such writing, Cixous claimed, could shatter the restrictive structures of language and restore to the culture voices long suppressed. The proposal of *écriture féminine* and feminist critical responses to this is considered briefly in Chapter 1 and further debated in this section. Both *The Name of Oedipus* and *Demeter Beneath the Sand* adopt strategies that could be associated with the ideals of *écriture féminine*, as originally conceived; my own concern is less to establish how far either play endorses or actively stages *écriture féminine* than to identify ways in which incorporation of myth texts support or undermine that process.

After writing *The Name of Oedipus*, Cixous became increasingly involved with theatre, most notably through her association with Ariane Mnouchkine; she now regards her early drama as 'pre-theatrical' (Prenowitz ed. 2004: 1–2). Acknowledging this, I also discuss a later play, *The Perjured City, or The Awakening of the Furies*, first staged in 1994 by the Théâtre du Soleil. Admittedly, inclusion of *The Perjured City* stretches the boundaries of the chapter somewhat, since it is not primarily concerned with the relations of myth and female subjectivity. It is also an explicitly political play, didactic even, which again distinguishes it from those examined first: on the surface the story of an unspecified plague a city has brought on itself, the play unmistakably references France's blood scandal of the mid-1980s, an affair which saw the country's Centre for Blood Transfusion distribute products it knew to be infected with the HIV virus to over four thousand patients. *The Perjured City* is far removed from *The Name of Oedipus*, in thematic concerns, in formal structures and in performance style and scale; the difference between them reflects a more general development in Cixous's drama, described by Julia Dobson as the movement 'from self to other, from solitude to multitude, from personal narrative to world history' (Dobson 2002: 12). Yet there are also evident continuities in Cixous's work and these are highlighted when the plays are assessed side by side. The theme of the maternal feminine is equally important to *The Perjured City*, its central protagonist 'the Mother', a woman seeking justice for the death of her children. Here too the struggle the play dramatises is rooted in language, since the Mother's unashamedly emotional tale of criminal irresponsibility is shown as vulnerable to erasure in the moment that History chooses to 'write the story for eternity' in 'an account stripped of the passions / Which horribly distort still too recent events' (Cixous 2004: 96). Finally, both plays reveal the ultimately imprisoning logic of 'authoritative' narratives and seek to articulate a utopian space beyond this. And, in each, that space is gendered feminine, whether more or less explicitly: in *The Name of Oedipus*, the ideal is a radically reconceived subjectivity that reincorporates the devalued feminine; in *The Perjured City* it is the vision of female characters that shapes the afterlife staged in the epilogue, yet in this play 'the feminine' seemingly describes a polemical model that is not literally gender-exclusive but which in practice includes a multitude of outcast 'others'.

Inclusion of these three plays in this chapter opens several related lines of enquiry. My discussions of *Demeter Beneath the Sand* and *The Name of Oedipus* explore how a myth, or myths, may be harnessed in a project of critically reconfiguring (especially women's) subjectivity. Since these are plays that inhabit a place outside 'real time', each risks attracting criticism for choosing, as it were, to bypass social and other contextual forces that would present the self as subject *in process*, shaped by and acting upon history. This is a danger attached to re-visioning myth in general for, as previous chapters have shown, gestures towards mythic abstraction concurrently necessitate a departure from the immediate and specific, even if the departure is temporary. Deployment of myths that aim to explore female subjectivity – or 'consciousness', 'psyche' or 'internal life' – are fraught with such difficulties and, regardless of a project's depth or complexity, could seem perilously close to popular psychology's exhortations that women should release their 'goddess within', whether it be an Aphrodite, an Artemis or a Hera, as if such figures were independent, untrammelled energies rather than fictions of western philosophic tradition. Such proposals could serve to reinforce a set of psychological and social choices already entirely familiar to women, rather than to invite the imagining of liberating alternatives. With this in mind, I consider the kinds of interrogations that these first two plays pursue and the forms they assume, to see how each negotiates the risks of, on the one hand, seeming to stage an unrealisable utopia, and, on the other, effectively endorsing culturally prescribed gender roles. My examination of *Demeter Beneath the Sand* will comment in detail on production context, revealing how a piece that appears initially to retreat from the social and political was in fact firmly tied, during creation and in reception, to the changing realities of contemporary women's lives. Cixous's *The Name of Oedipus* pursues a self-consciously dislocated exploration of the feminine, but *The Perjured City*, considered last, by implication suggests another way that such journeys might be reconnected to a modern world that is unmistakably *today*: a 'today' that in Cixous's words is 'never [...] rigidly tied to current events, but a present' (Prenowitz ed. 2004: 12). Both the socio-political dimension of this last play and its overt engagement with the actual and metaphorical disappearance of the marginalised make its ethical concerns explicit. As I shall argue, *The Perjured City* strives to reunite self with other, solitude with multitude, personal narrative with world history, by combining self-consciously anachronistic re-vision of myth with a representation of the contemporary or 'real' that is itself to a degree mythicised.

The voices within: Serena Sartori, Renata Coluccini and *Demeter Beneath the Sand*

> Not for a moment dare we succumb to the illusion that an archetype can be finally explained and disposed of. Even the best attempts at explanation are only more or less successful translations into another metaphorical language. [...] The most we can do is to dream the myth onwards and give it a modern dress. (Jung 1968: 271)

When they created *Demeter Beneath the Sand* (*Demetra sotto la sabbia*), in the mid-1980s, Serena Sartori was director of the Teatro del Sole and Renata Coluccini an artist within the company. Carlo Formigoni originally founded this Milan-based collective in 1971. The Del Sole has always been first and foremost an actors' theatre, with great emphasis placed on the improvisatory skills of the performers and their ability to create a theatrical language that is richly physical as well as verbal. In production, the actors' bodywork is framed by scenography usually more evocative than directly representative. *Demeter Beneath the Sand* is informed by this creative ethos but equally bears the marks of Sartori's and Coluccini's own preoccupations as artists and as women. They created the piece primarily through improvisation, but at points drew on other texts that attracted them, such as Heinrich von Kleist's 1808 tragic drama *Penthesilea* and Marguerite Yourcenar's 1936 prose poem *Feux*. Sartori and Coluccini performed and subsequently toured the play, 'owning' it to the point where it feels difficult if not impossible to envisage it staged by other actors. This is a very different kind of theatre from, for example, the polished *scenarii* of Franca Rame and Dario Fo: and while Sartori did spend some years in the early 1970s with Nuova Scena (founded by Fo and Rame), *Demeter Beneath the Sand*, although shaped by the same improvisatory tradition, has none of the apparent transferability that makes Rame's monologues so widely adapted. One reason for this might be the layered, expressionistic *mise-en-scène* Sartori and Coluccini adopt, an effective opposite of the virtually bare stage – a platform, literally and in the political sense – on which Rame's solo plays are typically presented. A second explanation is the strong personal dimension of the piece: archetypal figures are employed that had special significance for those performers, meaning that the boundary line between actor and role is blurred.

Third, it is clear from interviews with each that the entire project was coloured by the nature of their relationship. They were friends and fellow artists, but Sartori was also the director of the Teatro del Sole (from 1985 to 1995) and Coluccini's teacher; there is a gap of eighteen years between them. Undoubtedly all these elements fed into the mother–daughter dynamic central to the piece and the myth of its title.

Demeter Beneath the Sand was one of three works developed within a larger project of the Teatro del Sole that aimed to explore myths through performance (the others were *L'era dell'Abalia* and *Persefone rapita*). The plays were created simultaneously, by different groups of artists from the company, and originally staged literally side by side in separate rooms within an old Venetian villa in Arlesega, Padua; the villa was also the home of the Centro Internazionale della Maschera, a renowned centre for the study of mask in performance that was managed at the time by Sartori's brother, Donato Sartori. The audience for the show arrived at the villa through a park, passing between lighted bonfires, and then moved from room to room to watch the performances. The event ended late at night: Sartori has said that it felt as if the audience had been taken on a journey into the underworld (Sartori 2006). Two years later in 1988 the entire project was transformed into a single large show, renamed *Racconti d'inferno*, which toured all over Europe. The piece was revived again in 1990, under Sartori's direction, for the Teatro Stabile of Reutlingen.

One of the most striking features of *Demeter Beneath the Sand*, detailed in the English version of the text, is the stage environment that was created. Its dominant colours are white, black and red: the white of hanging washing that shapes the playing space, and white garments that seem at once to suggest women's lingerie, nurses' uniforms and swaddling clothes; black for the variously styled costumes assumed by the archetypes; the red of nail varnish, lipstick and startlingly red blood that at one point is poured from a white teapot into white cups. Set and costumes are carefully stratified: what the audience initially see is stripped away to reveal a buried image, or is covered up as if to obliterate the first. The props, too, become animate in unexpected ways, as in the example of the teapot, above, or in the use of a black and white radio that periodically transmits female voices and hoarse laughter that seem to emanate from another world. Strewn everywhere in the space is sand, half-obscuring the objects that are there: the top of a white rocking chair is just visible. The complex layering of the stage picture suggests an analogy for the myth of Demeter and Persephone in which someone or something becomes lost, buried underground while still alive, enacting an 'endlessly repeated drama of coming-to-be and passing-away' (Jung and Kerényi 2002: 146). Symbolically the sand suggests the earth, here arid ground that implies the absence of vitality and growth. Psychologically, the different levels connote hidden layers of the self: aspects repressed, forgotten or disallowed. But one might also read this as a space for children's play; the repetitive games and rituals of the contemporary women in white could seem to reinforce this. Moreover, on a simple physical level, the sand directly impedes the actors' movements, weighs them down; the trivial means of time-passing of the women in white – such as ritual tea-making or testing each other with a 'personality quiz' – appear the more ridiculous by contrast with the heavy, elemental environment in which they are placed. It is an extremely rich interpretative space, deeply suggestive for an audience even before the action 'proper' begins; one might say that the setting has a presence as strong as that of the human players.

This stage environment is also framed and marked in every way as a feminine space. The visual elements suggest the sphere of women, through social convention, as with the tea set, a vase, washed linen and make-up, or biological association, through a bloodstained sheet or naked doll baby. All the play's characters are female: the two women in white, who represent a contemporary world, identified in the script as R. and S. (signalling Renata and Serena), and the archetypal figures of myth, dressed in black, who 'possess' the women in white. Male figures come to us only mediated by the women, whether in the form of the blandly generic 'superb specimen' of a seduction fantasy described by R. and S., or as an Achilles or a Hippolytus, as it were lightly sketched in by the actors because necessary to situate the passions of Penthesilea and Phaedra. *Demeter Beneath the Sand* makes femininity and femaleness its focus; it concerns itself with the cultural forces that have limited women's potential but does so without turning its gaze on men, or even 'the patriarchy', in any direct way. Given this emphasis, it is perhaps unsurprising that women in the audience and female critics reviewing the production typically received it with greater warmth and enthusiasm than did their male counterparts. The two artists suggest that men watching the finished work seemed to recognise that their experience was in some important way outside that being shown. Sartori recalls that the noted critic Ugo Volli, reviewing the show for *La Repubblica*, commented that he felt unable to apply the same logic that he would normally use to evaluate a piece of theatre, since the rules or laws of this performance remained a kind of mystery to him (Sartori 2006). Volli's response was none the less appreciative; by contrast, Coluccini remembers another review whose title, 'The crime of being male', suggests a more hostile reaction (Coluccini 2006, my translation). I will return to this self-conscious choice by the artists to make a play so thoroughly about and for women – one offered like a gift to female spectators as well as to an implied wider 'female community' – and consider how far expressions of opposition within this privileged space may be reconciled with the desire to impact critically and positively upon the broader social domain.

At the beginning of the performance, there is little evidence of the impulse towards resistance in these characters. *Demeter Beneath the Sand* opens with dreary acceptance, by R. and S., of a world in which the two *'have been condemned to "eternal Sunday afternoons", where time hangs uselessly and feeling is almost blotted out'* (Sartori and Coluccini 1995: 114). The women in white do not so much live as exist, and in a present that feels unbearably thin: they have no past and no future because no sense of purpose. The first words of the play actually come from the radio, a blur of whispers that gives way to audible phrases:

> THE WHISPERING VOICES: Here they are ... those women with no memories in them ... now they'll have to remember our stories ... They're flitting from one memory to another, one to another, with their false pearls and frowsy feathers ... Look at them ... they're coming ... sand ... sand ... memories – dancing on the memories means dancing on the sand ...
>
> (*Ibid.*: 115)

That the radio is black and white implies it connects the play's two worlds, or at least transmits messages from an unseen place to the one before us. There is ambiguity in the line 'they're coming': the action of the performance shows archetypal forces that come forcibly to invade the empty spaces of contemporary women's experience; yet as words uttered *by* the archetypes of myth, the line seems rather to prophesy these figures' own burial, forgotten by successive generations of women who it seems have 'no memories in them'.

Yet whilst R. and S. appear purposeless on the surface, their potential for resistance, at least, is hinted at in an evident dissatisfaction with their lot: the women drum fingers, tap feet, propose activities then reject or abandon these. R. yearns to 'love and be loved by a man close to me', a desire coloured by a fear of ageing that sees her refuse to face her reflection in a mirror; S. craves an alternative landscape, one she has never seen but nevertheless intuits: 'I want to go somewhere, but I don't know where it is [...] but I know the place exists and I know it's wonderful' (*ibid.*: 118). In marked contrast to these compromised longings are the unadulterated impulses that motivate the figures in black, women of myth who return to life through the bodies of R. and S. in the course of the performance. The structural patterns of the piece are quickly established. Demeter, Phaedra, Hecuba, Clytemnestra, Medea and Penthesilea emerge from 'under the sand', their appearance signalled by donning a black jacket over a white dress, or removing white garments to reveal black ones underneath. Each archetype arrives as if when needed: hence a game or apparently idle conversation will unexpectedly trigger some deeper reaction in R. or S., a memory that serves as a channel for a mythic figure to make herself heard. In this way, the moments when R. and S. are 'invaded' actually represent a meeting of desires between contemporary and ancient, ordinary and mythic; it is as if there is compulsion from both sides to come together in order to express a passion that has long lain dormant or unacknowledged. In Jungian terms, these encounters could be considered illustrative of the attempt to bring to awareness that which was previously unconscious or preconscious, in order to transform and ultimately reintegrate this within the self.

The archetypal characters introduced into the action can be broadly differentiated as 'Great Mothers' and 'Great Lovers', although some, like Clytemnestra, cut across categories. The artists explain that in the rehearsal process each chose figures that felt urgently 'alive' at that point in their own lives. For Sartori, then in her forties and with a twelve-year-old daughter, the theme of motherhood and the maternal was uppermost; in the piece, she personifies Demeter, Hecuba, Medea and a Clytemnestra seeking vengeance for the sacrifice of Iphigenia (Sartori 2006). Coluccini was drawn to the theme of all-consuming love: what attracted her above all was the opportunity to explore such desire 'in an age where emotions are impoverished, controlled and often rendered unfamiliar' (Coluccini 2006, my translation). She plays Phaedra, Clytemnestra the lover, and a Penthesilea, inspired by Von Kleist, whose passion for Achilles sees her bite into his flesh (Von Kleist 1988). The myth of Demeter and Persephone provides a frame for the whole and loosely contains the other narratives. In this myth it is Demeter's daughter who disappears below ground, yet the play's title positions Demeter herself under the sand and, by extension, all women. Coluccini explains:

> Women in many cultures have had daughters who had to be eliminated, suffocated, buried under the sand. To bury a daughter is to bury a woman, and a mother. To die beneath sand, so light and so heavy at the same time, is a small metaphor for all in women's lives that is lost, suffocated, hidden, silenced. (Coluccini 2006, my translation.)

We can find reflection of this view in Jung's commentary upon the myth, in which he proposes that 'every mother contains her daughter in herself and every daughter her mother, and [...] every woman extends backwards into her mother and forwards into her daughter'; for Jung this recognition should lead a woman to regard her life not narrowly but 'spread out over generations' (Jung and Kerényi 2002: 191–2). Jung did not direct this observation to overtly political ends, but the ethical implications of this imaginative extension of self are evident. Foregrounding the myth of Demeter and Persephone carries many resonances in the piece, therefore. It is a means of articulating Sartori's experience of childbirth and mothering; it gestures towards the seniority of Sartori as mentor to Coluccini, whilst acknowledging the latter's development into a mature artist; and, for both, the myth symbolically expresses forces – cultural, psychological, political – that historically have limited women's potential; it stresses equally women's struggle to resist. The myth further represents, through metaphor, the experience of dividedness. A mother and daughter are separated: by implication, so too have women become disconnected from one another and individually and collectively weakened in consequence. In *Demeter Beneath the Sand*, Sartori and Coluccini take this narrative of rupture and re-examine it through a creative process and production structure that by contrast emphasised female friendship, responsiveness and community.

Demeter the Earth Mother is also a figure that features prominently in many cultures as part of a philosophy of origins. I have commented on the 'mother goddess' theory, proposed by some anthropologists, that postulates worship of a female deity in prehistory (see Chapter 1). From that perspective, the myth of abduction of Demeter's daughter speaks of violent overthrow of the symbolic order of the 'Great Mother' by an emerging patriarchal order that is warlike and hostile towards nature. Sartori references this theory in her commentary on the thinking behind the project:

> Demeter the Mother Goddess, the great creator and destroyer that all we women are potentially, has been trivialised in memory as a little myth, close to a fairy tale. Who today knows of the Eleusinian Mysteries, the great initiation rites that celebrated the Mystery of Mother and Daughter, of Life and Death, that were like a religion and that lasted 2000 years? (Sartori 2006, my translation)

However, Sartori is less concerned to make a historical case than to reinvigorate action and development in the present. She goes on:

> In modern western society one speaks of women's emancipation, equal rights, etcetera, but one does not speak of the originary power of Woman. Demeter separated from her daughter [...] becomes the destructress. But Demeter 'whole' is the Origin, the Principle. For that reason, when the two protagonists are drawn to the sand, it is to retrieve from underground the forgotten fragments of Demeter, for self-transformation in a powerful theatrical way. (*Ibid.*)

In this piece, invocation of Demeter the Mother Goddess is principally the means to expose psychic impoverishment within contemporary women's experience and re-engage with the possibility of psychological wholeness. Whether as subsequent dramaturgical decision or merely natural extension of these underlying conceptual impulses, the production ultimately staged had, in its character and 'feel', something of the spirit of the Mysteries to which Sartori refers: a meeting between theatre and ritual, in which the feminine is (re)invested with a power verging on the magical.

Significant to both artists, framing the performance as a whole, Demeter is the first archetype that penetrates the thin skin of the play's contemporary world. I comment on an early sequence in detail to illustrate how the central motif of the piece operates in practice: the possession of a recognisably modern character – although one curiously two-dimensional or depthless – by an ancient figure of myth. First, a banal guessing game sees R. challenge S. to discover, 'telepathically', what number she is thinking of. Through the 'clue' that this is between four and six, S. finally gets it right:

S: Why five?

R: Five because there were five of us in our family before father
   went blind. (*As she says this, she folds the sheet that was
   covering the chairs. They look at each other, playfully.*) There
   was my father, me, my sister, yes ... her ... and my two brothers
   who died. Shhhh!
   (*They both look round as though they can hear voices and
   sounds in the air that are trying to stop them talking. R.
   continues. S. is gradually taken over by this memory, and as
   the other woman speaks she starts to undress, removing the
   childish white garment to reveal a long, tragic black gown.
   Her face, gestures, expression all change too. S. is becoming
   the Mother, her body relives the rape and loss of her daughter,
   Persephone. Mother and daughter, dual aspects of a single
   essential being, theirs is the first great female separation.*)

(Sartori and Coluccini 1995: 116–17)

Most notable in R.'s account is the absent mother. The words 'yes ... her ...' could refer to a mother who cannot somehow be named or signal discomfort or disturbance around the figure of a different woman: a sister. In either case the feminine is weakened in the description. Next, the effective removal of two brothers 'who died' leaves only father and daughter, as it were Hades and Persephone (although the reference to blindness might gesture towards Oedipus and Antigone also). The sequence is represented as R.'s memory, yet it is S. who is primarily affected. It is perhaps R.'s failure at first to acknowledge existence of a mother that sparks the older woman's awareness of loss. When R. does recall her mother, it is through an account of coming upon 'a lovely yellow dress, my mother was wearing it yesterday, it had been left on a chair ...'. The image of abandoned clothing is an evocative one: it highlights the wearer's absence; it connotes the garments of the deceased. At the same time it is invested with potency, since, R. adds, 'all the light and silence in the room were gathered into that dress' (*ibid*.: 117). In a fleeting exchange across 'worlds', the two women appear both as daughter and mother, communicating over a chasm, and as a guide or witness assisting a figure entranced. R. hints at her own abduction in words that have a contemporary ring: 'When mother came home she found the house deserted, the doors were torn off their hinges, the windows hanging open, the clothes torn to shreds...' S.'s response suggests rather archetypal grief:

> My daughter, the other half of myself! The daughter I longed for, the daughter I loved, created by me. The daughter I was myself before I became mother! Stolen from me! My golden haired spring, the ripe corn of my harvest. I want her back! (*Ibid*.)

R. speaks '*as though she wants to push S. even deeper*' into this transformation. R. appears to desire the return of the mother, here reborn in the body of S.; then, when the moment fades she herself assumes the maternal role, dressing S. in white again, 'slowly, affectionately' (*ibid*.: 118). The daughter becomes the mother, or perhaps we are seeing the child grown mature, caring for a parent who has become dependent in her turn.

The description of the yellow dress and its meanings additionally mirrors the strategies of the play itself. It is precisely through devices such as touching or putting on clothes simultaneously alien and familiar that the performers mark the transition from one state of being to another. Central to the creative process were Sartori's and Coluccini's own memories, as well as personally significant items of clothing or other objects used as stimuli for improvisation. Sartori describes a rehearsal process where one actor working alone would 'end the improvisation as from a kind of dream'; the other would then offer feedback on that which had communicated most powerfully. This was a tried and tested method of the Teatro del Sole, in this instance establishing what Sartori calls 'a true atmosphere of creative trance in which the actor becomes other than herself and creates without "knowing" what it is that she is creating' (Sartori 2006, my translation). It is clear from the comments of both artists that drawing on myth, specifically, coloured this process in profound ways. Coluccini similarly characterises their way of working as a departure into the unknown:

Confronting myth is like setting out on a journey where you don't know exactly where you are being carried, both in terms of the show and in terms of your life. I'm talking about meeting, clashing with archetypes that speak to the depths of your soul. I'm talking about uncovering the origins of your being, your thoughts, your feelings. (Coluccini 2006, my translation.)

Sartori makes this point about submission to the material even more forcefully: at each stage of creation and selection of material, she states, 'the Myth was our guide [...] with its great mysterious force'. At the same time, however, the process remained both personal and empowering: 'I was also guided, as I have said, by my own maternity, which had been a kind of rebirth for me as well. The Myth gave me the chance to understand what I had experienced and the joy of sharing this as an artist' (Sartori 2006, my translation). It is clear from both women's accounts that engagement with myth and archetype was both mystical and yet grounded in their own lived experience. Equally, the improvisatory process may 'carry' them to unfamiliar territory, but this does not imply passivity on their side; the emphasis is rather on establishing an open and receptive state that will allow the women to reach and uncover emotional 'places' less travelled but already present within each. At the point of presentation, too, the artists must continue to balance the relinquishing of control with the focus necessary to keep the performance coherent. One might say that this is simply the job of acting: to be simultaneously inside and outside, to 'go with' the energy or spontaneity of the moment whilst retaining a directorial eye on the effect produced. However, to perform *Demeter Beneath the Sand*, suggest Sartori and Coluccini, was more like engaging in a rite: for both, 'to begin the show means to enter into a kind of emotional trance, as an experience always new. Really, a ritualistic piece' (*ibid.*, my translation).

For Coluccini, the guiding archetype was the Lover. The most striking embodiment of this figure is through the 'rebirth' in R. of Penthesilea, in the last of the play's possession sequences. In an earlier, comic scene, R. and S. measure each other's sexuality with a quiz that has just three possible outcomes: 'Let's do the "are you normal women, are you frigid or do you have a strong sex drive" one.' S. poses a predicament: R. is alone on a desert island when a 'magnificent' man appears, who has 'just been hunting or fishing, something or other', saying '"Woman, I've only got five minutes, just five minutes. Say you'll be mine." But there's a problem – you've only got one big bed and there's sand in it. What do you do?' (Sartori and Coluccini 1995: 119–20). Sand, dominant environmental element of the performance and vivid metaphor for the passage of time and suffocation of the self, is in this example reduced to a literal 'irritation'. Later in the piece, as part of 'pretend cooking', sand stands in for food: flour, sugar, powdered milk. With seeming cruelty S. takes their game too far, commanding R. to 'Eat …' Yet here, as before, the role of one is to push the other where she most needs to go, whether the latter is conscious of this or not:

> *Eating evokes memories. R. goes into another dark trance. She takes an X-ray plate from the sand, her voice rattling in her throat. S. undresses her down to her slip, then holds the X-ray plate against her. It is like a suit of armour that exposes her heart and her bones, a symbol of absolute nakedness. This is Penthesilea […].*
>
> R: I … I … Achilles. I … I, Penthesilea, I who from henceforth will no longer have a name, I went forward to meet the young man who loved me and whom I loved, I hurried in the passion of my youthful feelings, with the horror of battle and the burning desire to possess him […] And he, drenched in his own blood, touched my sweet face and said: 'Penthesilea, my bride, why have you done this to me? This is not the day of feasting you promised me.' But I had torn off his breastplate, competing with the hounds. His blood ran from my mouth and hands, and I kissed him to death. I kissed him to death. (*She collapses.*)
>
> (*Ibid.*: 125–6)

The motif of unpalatable food, stimulus for R.'s metamorphosis into Penthesilea, has the same interpretative richness as the cast-off dress. R. all but chokes on the food S. is offering her, a daughter pushing aside what her mother has prepared. Her reluctance to swallow might signal an eating disorder; it might imply the lack, or fear, of sexual appetite. Potentially those two interpretations are connected: it is familiarly argued that resistance to 'normal' eating, which would foster the body's development, represents subconscious refusal of sexual maturity.

In classical mythology Penthesilea is an Amazon queen, a woman warrior. In her association with Achilles, the figure of Penthesilea arguably conflates two archetypes therefore, Lover and Warrior, that might ordinarily be thought to conflict. Achilles is the most handsome of all Greek heroes, central character of Homer's *Iliad* and, famously, almost invulnerable in battle. The passionate encounter of these two – between extreme femaleness on one hand and extreme maleness on the other – is in classical as well as modern versions one in which both parties are damaged or destroyed. Traditional mythography has Achilles as Penthesilea's killer, with violence and passion inextricably entwined. Several accounts state that Achilles fell in love with the Amazon after slaying her and committed necrophilia on her corpse (Graves 1961a: 675). We might read in Achilles' treatment of Penthesilea the forceful imposition of patriarchal order: Penthesilea is a dangerous female figure, unafraid of men or battle; it is only upon her death – in other words, when she is rendered unthreatening – that he falls in love with her. *Demeter Beneath the Sand* chooses instead to draw chiefly on Von Kleist's *Penthesilea*, a text that effectively reverses the two protagonists' positions: Von Kleist's play dramatises the sexual frenzy of Penthesilea that leads her to devour the still-living body of Achilles.[1] In *Demeter Beneath the Sand* this act is not staged (nor is it in Von Kleist's text) but confessed by R., as if '*dragged out of her*' (Sartori and Coluccini 1995: 126). Her words describe a moment of almost unthinkable violence; the effort of confession brings her to collapse at its conclusion. At the same time, the visual addition of the X-ray plate lends the sequence an air of detachment and irony. An X-ray enables scrutiny of the 'inner self' in the most literal terms. Given the Jungian influences on the production, one might interpret this touch as self-parody; alternatively, the juxtaposition of text and image could signal the artists' recognition that exploratory engagement with ancient myth none the less comes from and retains connection to the contemporary moment.

The opening words of R.'s confession – 'I ... I ... Achilles. I ... I, Penthesilea' – convey that the figure before us has become an amalgamation of both; or that the literal swallowing of Achilles identifies him as a 'masculine' force within the woman. We might read the moment as dramatic embodiment of Jung's principle of the *animus*, the supposed masculine inner personality of the female. For Jung the *animus* is normally repressed in waking life, although it may appear in dreams; it nevertheless influences interactions with and attitudes towards the other sex. From this perspective, R.'s fantasies of love yet hesitation around consummation could be thought to stem from her repression of the physicality of desire and horror of where self-abandonment might lead. The archetype staged here precisely voices these tensions. In her passion and the way she acts upon it, this Penthesilea directly breaks down the boundaries that had divided her from the object of her love: through the kiss that bites, she takes Achilles inside her, actually as well as figuratively. The X-ray scans her body for what exists beneath the skin. The episode of choking on sand, which initially provokes the possession sequence, similarly implies the need to regurgitate and so expose something swallowed that will not quite go down.

The unfolding action of *Demeter Beneath the Sand* does not suggest that either Penthesilea or Demeter archetype is, in itself, positive or empowering: they are not disowned, but neither is straightforwardly celebrated. Furthermore, the status of both figures within the piece is implicitly qualified by the presence of others that Sartori and Coluccini have also included. The Mother archetype is represented not by Demeter alone but additionally through the multiple and at times conflictual voices of Medea, Hecuba and Clytemnestra. Sartori's Medea, for example, is driven by despair to kill her child – here a doll – and then, filled with horrified realisation of what she has done, to bury it under the sand. This wordless sequence does not provide a context; nothing is included that would explain or justify the murder. (Indeed, spectators might not necessarily register that this *is* Medea.) Where Demeter rages against the theft of her daughter, Medea actuates the separation of mother from child. Such figures personify extremes: inclusion of so many insists that we recognise them as fragments of a whole and so imagine beyond a mother labelled 'wronged' or 'guilty'. By the same means the archetype of the Lover acquires diverse shades of meaning, here through reincarnation of Phaedra, and another Clytemnestra, before its already complex representation in the person of Penthesilea. Indeed, one of the strengths of this production as re-vision lies in the engagement with many myths as opposed to a single narrative. *Demeter beneath the Sand* deliberately uncouples the protagonists from the stories that traditionally contain them; each is kept distinct, yet all are connected through the bodies of R. and S. In this way – and in contrast with the majority of plays discussed in this book – the piece sidesteps some of the problems inherent in attempting to rewrite a myth narrative in its entirety. The killing that Medea performs, for example, is deliberately taken 'out of context' in the desire to engage with and understand the simple horror of that sacrifice: the sequence also acknowledges the reality of (especially female) infanticide, a concern of the artists remarked upon previously.

For R. and S. the discovery of energies previously buried but now forcing acknowledgement can be interpreted, I have argued, as release of hidden impulses within the self. Importantly, this journey begins with a *specific* self – here, the selves of Sartori and Coluccini – rather than some universalised, presumed 'self' of Woman. That said, it must be desirable from a feminist point of view that an exploration grounded in the personal extends beyond this to uncover potential connectedness or shared significance. We can identify the same expansive gesture within individuation: Jung emphasised that just as the individual is 'not just a single, separate being, but by his very existence presupposes a collective relationship, it follows that the process of individuation must lead to more intense and broader collective relationships and not to isolation' (Jung 1971: 448). The search for wider resonance is equally an imperative for artistic development. With improvisatory creative work, it is clear that the studio-based experimentation of the artists must, at some stage, be translated into a performance accessible to 'outsiders'. Sartori's comments on the rehearsals indicate as much: 'For many weeks the piece was close to psychodrama, with joy, play, catharsis, tears and laughter, passion ... then we began to make selections from our material and to structure the piece, choosing that which had come out of our closeness that could be turned into something coherent and understandable' (Sartori 2006, my translation). While Sartori's account consistently stresses the role of myth as guide in both creative and shaping stages of the work, Coluccini puts equal emphasis on the project as outcome of a particular social moment. Asked about the choice to work with archetypes and the style of the piece that resulted, Coluccini responded that 'everything came from a sensibility born and developed in times in which woman was rediscovering herself, searching within herself and was, above all, speaking' (Coluccini 2006, my translation). Deeply internalised feelings and conflicts, particular to Sartori and Coluccini yet meaningful to other women (if not *all* women), are at the same time shaped by the forces of culture and history. Acknowledgement of these 'suffocated selves', to use Coluccini's words, is considered as essential for women's psychological and social advancement as the determination that economic and other inequities be challenged in the public sphere.

Demeter Beneath the Sand expresses in theatrical form the results of an extended study of the 'feminine psyche' mediated through the imagination, lived experience and exposed impulses of two women artists. For Jung, acknowledgement of the 'shadow self' is in fact the defining characteristic of the truly creative; he claims that 'the very advantage that such individuals enjoy consists precisely in the permeability of the partition separating the conscious and the unconscious'. However, Jung argues that the progress of civilisation essentially represents triumph of the conscious mind over the unconscious, something he acknowledges as a 'very heavy sacrifice'; he explains that, by extension, for all kinds of work that require 'continuity and reliability' such exceptionally creative people 'are as a rule of little value' (Jung 1969: 70). The practice of Sartori and Coluccini, and perhaps the wider project of feminism, refuses that diagnosis: it insists rather that suppression or denial of the 'shadow' – whatever form it might assume – renders the results of such progress flawed and so inherently unstable.

Politicised engagement on the artists' part does not mean that their play concludes on a note of empowerment: it does not. Gradually *'coming round'* after her possession by Penthesilea, R. starts *'trying to tidy up'* remarking baldly: 'Right, that's it. It's all over.' She exits leaving S. in a panic: *'(despairingly)* No, look, it can't be over. It isn't over for me. (*She rummages in the sand, picking up objects.*) It can't be over, I'm still searching for it ... It can't be, I have to find it ... I need to find it ...' (Sartori and Coluccini 1995: 126). From the evidence of the script one might well find the ending pessimistic. S. cannot find what she is looking for and at the end is driven from the stage by the sound of laughter from the radio; before leaving, she sets the space *'back in order, ready for it all to start again'* (*ibid.*). The women in white do not appear to have changed, learned or moved forward therefore. However, according to the artists, the play in production produced quite the contrary effect. Coluccini states that above all the message of the piece was one of 'travelling, searching, shouting, laughing, crying, being defeated, but struggling. Never be silent! There is no solution but there are different ways of tackling the journey, the world, others' (Coluccini 2006, my translation). Sartori concurs, insisting that 'to understand it it's necessary to *see* it: in performance the conclusion was very positive, it was an incitement to dig and so uncover buried strength' (Sartori 2006, my translation). Equally, one would not be aware from the text published that in production the performance was followed by discussion sessions with the audience, inscribing the opportunity to seek out resonance of this material, or resistance to it, in the experience of spectators. Sartori adds that in these post-show conversations 'the women in the audience were fired with enthusiasm and spoke about themselves, their hidden desires, the "goddess" within themselves and the wish to reawaken her' (*ibid.*). The responses of male spectators were typically more equivocal. According to Coluccini, some men reacted with a certain '*disagio*', a word carrying the multiple meanings of 'discomfort', 'embarrassment' and 'unease'. It would be fair to assume that, to a degree, all these translations would have been applicable.

Demeter Beneath the Sand is a work that seeks to expose a hidden landscape: literally, through physical action that has characters and objects pulled from the ground; metaphorically, by interrogating a realm of forgotten or repressed energies. It is a landscape represented as archetypal yet differently contoured for each individual. Myths prove to be ways of describing the terrain; confronting the archetypes of myth – not for simple imitation but to see where connections may be found – is a task undertaken by the artists, dramatised through the figures of 'R.' and 'S.', with the invitation to follow suit extended by implication to women watching. The play demands we attend to that which lies buried within the psyche and insists that the shadow self and the very activity of searching are bound to, and essential, for productive growth. This is a work above all addressed to women and which takes feminine self-transformation as its central theme; it makes a virtue of looking inward, yet while doing so, I have argued, produces a work that is neither depoliticised nor problematically essentialist. Recollecting this project conducted more than twenty years ago, Sartori dwelt in interview primarily on the mystical aspects of their creative journey while Coluccini tended to emphasise what was for her an ever-present political dimension.

There is no conflict between their accounts; the two together give rather the impression of a rewarding and challenging dialogue in which the internal-spiritual and external-social form complementary parts of a total process of engagement.

Hélène Cixous and the scene of the unconscious: *The Name of Oedipus: Song of the Forbidden Body (Le nom d'Oedipe: chant du corps interdit)*

> We are living in an age where the conceptual foundation of an ancient culture is in the process of being undermined by millions of a species of mole [...] never known before. When they wake up from among the dead, from among words, from among laws. (Cixous 1986: 65)

The second half of this chapter examines two of Cixous's myth re-visions. *The Name of Oedipus* comes near the beginning of Cixous's engagement with drama; *The Perjured City* exemplifies her output as a mature playwright. Reflecting on the earlier piece, she acknowledges that whilst she was concerned with 'reanimating and resuscitating the legend of Jocasta and Oedipus [...] I think the element of surprise was textual, aesthetic, and not dramatic'. Here, as with the earlier *Portrait of Dora* (1976), she 'had not [yet] opened the door to the *event*' (Prenowitz ed. 2004: 2). The door was opened decisively when Mnouchkine suggested Cixous should write a play for the Soleil, a company renowned for imaginative, collaboratively created performances on an epic scale. The invitation resulted in *The Terrible but Unfinished Story of Norodom Sihanouk, King of Cambodia* (1985) and this marked the beginning of a now firmly established artistic partnership. Cixous observes the Soleil's rehearsals and will modify the script to take account of the discoveries of actors. She has explained in interview that this is, in part, an ethical choice: it proves a way 'of bearing the marks of the others very, very quickly' (Blyth and Sellers 2004: 106). Typically, she does not write the final scene until a few days before the opening so that all involved 'experience uncertainty' and thus exist fully 'in the present' (in Prenowitz ed. 2004: 33–4). The recognition of theatrical performance as live exchange has proved inspirational to her as a philosopher as well as a playwright, and she has increasingly privileged theatre, in interviews and elsewhere, as the site *par excellence* of alterity; in 'Enter the Theatre' (2000), she calls theatre 'by definition the stage where the living meet and confront the dead, the forgotten and the forgetters, the buried and the ghosts, the present, the passing, the present past and the passed past' (Prenowitz ed. 2004: 28–9). Thus, if the experimentation of her early plays was primarily confined to textual elements, Cixous subsequently embraced theatre's larger possibilities: as embodied, imagistic, scenographic, relational and ethical.

As one would expect, Cixous's theoretical writing has also changed and developed over the decades. None the less, Blyth and Sellers remark that her name is still more often than not associated with 'The Laugh of the Medusa' and 'Sorties', essays that sounded a clarion call for women to 'come' to writing and through this to rediscover their own 'forbidden' bodies. Cixous urged: 'Write your self. Your body must be heard. Only then will the immense resources of the unconscious spring forth' (Cixous 1976: 880). It is not surprising those essays had such impact: they are extraordinary and unforgettable pieces of utopic writing, wide-ranging, poetic, satirical and impassioned. Nevertheless, the result of critical preoccupation with these texts has been the perpetuation of Cixous the thinker in 'sketchy caricature', meaning in turn that production and reception of her output as a whole has regrettably been limited (Blyth and Sellers 2004: 2–3). In what follows I pay some attention to these essays and to 'Aller à la mer', since it is clear that ideas articulated here are to an extent reflected in *The Name of Oedipus*, written in the same period; this does not mean that the play can be regarded straightforwardly as the practical realisation of theoretical proposals. In addition, I draw on later writings by and interviews with Cixous, to illustrate some of the shifts that have occurred for her by the time of *The Perjured City* and in years following.

The Name of Oedipus is a complex and in some ways inaccessible work, especially so if approached only through the libretto (which will generally be the case, since the opera is rarely revived). With few stage directions, one gains little impression of physical action or even of entrances and exits. Scene divisions are marked but it is not always apparent what changes they indicate. The cast list shows that the main roles of Jocasta, Oedipus and Tiresias were doubled between singer and actor, although the written text does not clearly distinguish between the sung and spoken parts; this use of doubling deliberately undermines the figures' 'wholeness', revealing them not as characters in the conventional sense but as something closer to the animation of ideas. Where Sophocles' play is plot-driven, building towards a climactic moment of revelation, *The Name of Oedipus* is non-linear, heavily marked by repetition, with knowledge of the entire myth narrative inscribed from the beginning. All these qualities contribute to an impression, for the reader, almost of falling into the play, or of circling around within it. But from even this rather dreamlike engagement with the text, two themes nevertheless emerge strongly: passionate desire and equally passionate resistance. Appreciation of the nature of the struggle the text strives to articulate depends on some understanding of the theoretical issues with which its author has been preoccupied. For this reason I will outline some central ideas that inform the play before returning to consider the text itself in more detail.

At the time of writing *The Name of Oedipus*, theatre was for Cixous already a site of special significance. In 1977 she had published 'Aller à la mer', a manifesto that accused western theatre of sadism in its perpetual reinforcement of the patriarchal family structure that insisted woman assumed the position of victim: sometimes, '[l]ike Electra or Antigone, she is eliminated'; or, 'like Ophelia [...] condemned to be buried alive'; if she has the strength to resist the father's authority, 'like Cordelia [...], she will die'. Weary of this endless repetition, Cixous states that she stopped going to the theatre altogether: 'it was like going to my own funeral, and it does not produce a living woman or (and this is no accident) her body or even her unconscious' (Cixous 1995b: 133). Cixous called instead for a new theatre in which all that had been absent would be made present: there would be real, living women; women's bodies, thoughts and speech; women's selfhood. The theatre she anticipated would be attuned to all the senses, rather than privileging the visual, able 'to hear the silences and what lies beyond them'; there would be 'no need for plot or action', only for the single gesture of 'a text, a body decoding and naming itself in one long, slow push'. Given not just this lyrical evocation of a new, woman-centred stage but the strongly polemical note the essay strikes overall – '[i]f I go to the theatre now, it must be a political gesture' – we can legitimately assume that Cixous's plays of the period attempt to answer this call (*ibid.*: 134). *The Name of Oedipus* foregrounds Jocasta's role, and circles, plotless, in what one might well call a 'long, slow push' to make a female 'self' recognised. None the less, it is worth re-emphasising that 'Aller à la mer' describes a theatre yet to be, rather than one already in existence: *The Name of Oedipus* may more fairly be regarded as an experimental step towards this than ideal fulfilment in practice.

Cixous's contribution to the development of feminist thought, although significant, has remained controversial. In the mid-1980s, Toril Moi's *Sexual/Textual Politics* summarised concerns, particularly of Anglo-American feminists, that Cixous's investigations into 'the feminine' were damagingly essentialist. The emphasis on 'writing the body', together with frequent recourse to metaphors of bodily fluids, such as blood and milk, seemed to imply that *écriture féminine* was biological imperative rather than conscious tactic. Moi concluded that, whilst Cixous's writings were invigorating, they were flawed by naivety: '[s]tirring and seductive though such a vision is, it can say nothing of the actual inequities, deprivations and violations that women, as social beings rather than as mythological archetypes, must constantly suffer' (Moi 1985: 123). It is clear, however, that Cixous did not consider *écriture féminine* disconnected from the daily experience of 'social beings'. The opening sentences of 'The Laugh of the Medusa' establish this by aligning the poetic with the socio-historical: 'I shall speak about women's writing: about what it will do. Woman must write her self: must write about women and bring women to writing, from which they have been driven away as violently as from their bodies – for the same reasons, by the same law, with the same fatal goal. Woman must put herself into text – as into the world and into history – by her own movement' (Cixous 1976: 875). Since writing is identified as a practice of liberation, the proposal is inherently political: it does not follow either that the release of the repressed will be easy or that imagination can immediately be translated into action.

Écriture féminine was proposed as a radical opposition to patriarchal language, which for Cixous was a 'universal battlefield', marked by the unceasing struggle for supremacy (Cixous 1986: 64). The proposed 'feminine' discourse would seek to undo binary thought and thus open up multiplicities of meaning. Ever controversial, Cixous named this new language 'bisexual'. She insisted this was not, however, 'the classic conception of bisexuality, which, squashed under the emblem of castration fear and along with the fantasy of a "total" being (though composed of two halves), would do away with [...] difference'; Cixous's use of the term was intended to affirm the presence within one's self of both sexes, a kind of 'self-permission' which allowed for a 'multiplication of the effects of the inscription of desire' throughout the body (Cixous 1976: 883–4). It is not surprising that assertion of the transformative potential of bisexuality should lead Cixous to the Oedipus myth, which has at its centre a sexual union implying a plurality of relational possibilities. Cixous has had much to say about Freud and is far from dismissive: 'let's do as modern people do, let's use the contemporary means of transport. We owe Freud the exploration of the unconscious' (Blyth and Sellers 2004: 25). At the same time, she emphasised that to subscribe to his belief that the feminine condition is defined by lack would be to participate 'in condemning woman to death' (Cixous 1986: 81–2).

The Name of Oedipus engages not only with Freud but with Lacan, the latter an acknowledged influence to whom she is regularly indebted. Lacan drew parallels between the infant's entry into language and into society, like Freud emphasising the importance of the triadic relationship of father, mother and child. Lacan's 'Symbolic order' denotes the realm of the social. To enter this, the child must forgo narcissistic over-identification both with the mother and with the child's own self-image in the mirror. Lacan termed the authority of the Symbolic *le Nom du Père*, the phrase playing upon the homophony of *nom* (name) and *non* (no); Cixous's title exploits and adapts the same linguistic device. For Lacan, resistance to entering the Symbolic order or failure to obey its laws could lead the subject into the third order of the Real, a sphere that 'stretches from the trauma to the phantasy' (Lacan 1981: 60). Oedipus's act of self-blinding, which for Freud represented castration, for Lacan also signified the fragmentation and collapse of the communicating subject. Thus while Lacan's perception of the Oedipus complex in some respects rewrote Freud's, both defined the feminine position in terms of an inherent deficiency. Acceptance of these terms as Juliet Mitchell explains means there can be no meaningful answer to the question 'What [...] does the woman [the little girl] want?' The question itself is found false: 'she simply *wants*' (Mitchell and Rose eds 1982: 24). Lacan's emphasis is less anatomical than Freud's, but his identification of the female with the Imaginary still positioned women as, in a sense, outside society. Jacqueline Rose adds that Lacan was undoubtedly 'implicated in the phallocentrism he described, just as his own utterance constantly rejoins the mastery which he sought to undermine' (Mitchell and Rose eds 1982: 56). Both Freud and Lacan used the Oedipal narrative to demonstrate that rebellion against the father and over-identification with the mother would lead to the collapse of the individual subject and by extension to the breakdown of society; indeed, Lacan's analysis of Sophocles' *Antigone*, through which he retraces critical steps to Oedipus and Jocasta, regards desire of the mother as the very origin of destruction (Lacan 1997: 243–90). Given that Cixous's aim is to open the subject to the possibility of erotic and linguistic pluralities in a move towards individual and ultimately social transformation, rewriting this narrative constitutes a necessary act of resistance.

Rejecting the linear development from ignorance to knowledge that structures *Oedipus Rex*, Cixous instead organises her play, over fourteen scenes, in ways that foreground issues of language and naming. This preoccupation is evident from the start through the incantatory prologue, performed by the whole cast. In this, the voices of Jocasta, Oedipus, Tiresias and the Chorus overlap; through the confusion we receive only fragments of language, fleeting images. The fear and pain of estrangement are repeatedly evoked: in the separation of mother from child, the experience of bereavement and the loss of a lover. Each voice hints at foreknowledge of the drama, but it is Jocasta especially who demonstrates this awareness. In the opera's first scene she pleads with her lover to remain with her, not to turn towards the city and not to accept his name:

JOCASTA: Forget the world

　Forget the town

　Forget the time.

　Do not be someone

　Today [...]

JOCASTA: *No, Oedipus! Do not be Oedipus,*

　Today, you are not the one

　They are calling.

(Cixous 1994: 255)

From the beginning, Cixous's Jocasta recognises what 'the name of Oedipus' signifies. To agree to be Oedipus means to accept the obligations and laws of the city; it is to set in motion the mechanisms of separation from Jocasta; it signals submission to the determinism of the mythic narrative. In Lacanian terms, to 'be Oedipus' is to enter the Symbolic order and so, of necessity, to leave the realm of identification with the mother. In Sophocles and Cixous, Oedipus is horrified to discover the truth of his 'unnatural' relations with Jocasta. In an instant, her sexuality becomes appalling, unthinkable: the perceived sanctity of motherhood has been hideously perverted. Cixous's decision to foreground Jocasta's role in her reworking thus serves to voice the forbidden desire of/for the mother, but more broadly to protest against both the repression of female sexuality and the silences imposed upon the female subject. For Cixous, Jocasta stands for Everywoman: the author's cover notes to the French edition emphasise that '[a]ll women, forbidden from the body, from language, forbidden from being a woman, are Jocasta' (Dobson 2002: 36).

Cixous's Oedipus resists Jocasta's pleas and attends instead to the city, here characterised as a rival lover who calls to him in *'a trembling voice / Of love, of shyness'*. He is flattered by the city's need, the Chorus tells her: *'That is normal. He is a man. / He is a child. Never adored enough'* (Cixous 1994: 261, 262). The majority of the play explores the consequences of Oedipus's choice. Early scenes show the characters as it were suspended, frozen as at 'the crossroad' that Oedipus recalls when he reflects upon the battle he fought with a stranger, so long ago (*ibid.*: 273). Cixous's text implies a stretching out of time, the creation of a long moment of decision in which a future, with known and fatal consequences, lies before the characters, but where liberating alternatives are still glimpsed as possible. A great burden of guilt seems to hover all around this Oedipus. At the same time, Jocasta speaks/sings love and acceptance of him, over and over. This extract will illustrate their respective stances:

> JOCASTA: Again I say to you: I love you
>> Absolutely, every day,
>>> In all the motions of your life. Ever since your first breath,
>>>> Before that and without end.
>
> OEDIPUS: You would forgive me the worst?

JOCASTA: *Between you and me there is no worst*
　　No god, no law, no time,
　　No thought
　　Only us, Naked.

(Cixous 1994: 275)

Cixous's libretto takes such an exchange and plays out endless variants upon it. Time is slowed down, or metaphorically enlarged, in the effort to break the momentum that propels Sophocles' drama. The structure of *The Name of Oedipus* is not simply non-linear or straightforwardly cyclical: rather it is fluid, dreamlike, with moments expanding and contracting, as if in search of a single instant that, as Jocasta says, would be '[p]rofound enough, / Present, ancient enough, / So our entire story may be relived in it / All at once' (*ibid.*: 257). Such lines seem to speak of the work of re-visioning myth more generally: 'the story' extends before and behind the writer at the same time.

Oedipus answers the city and submits to the oracle, here described by the Chorus as a '*voice that encloses the world. Like a wall*' (*ibid.*: 269). Upon learning 'the truth' of his identity he turns from Jocasta in horror. Where she insists that 'no revelation would prevent' her from moving 'closer still', he recoils: 'Do not say that! Do not! / If fate had decided that you were my ... ? / No. Not to be said' (*ibid.*: 283). His unfinished sentence leaves 'mother' unvoiced, an anticipation of Jocasta's erasure and by extension, suggests Cixous, that of every woman 'forbidden from the body, from language, forbidden from being a woman'. But in *The Name of Oedipus* it is first of all Oedipus who turns mute, his silence a substitution for blindness that reflects Cixous's emphasis on the centrality of language. His rejection of Jocasta and especially his refusal to speak – 'Three weeks without a word' – seems to plunge her into a dark void (*ibid.*: 294). She is stubborn, both in her love and in her resistance to their 'fate'; in this, she is quite unlike the Jocasta of Sophocles, who slips obligingly from the play to a reported suicide. Still, Cixous's Jocasta must die also. She is granted no reconciliation with Oedipus, but is given only a kind of flashback (scenes 11 and 12) that allows her to relive their first encounter and mutual passion. This sequence moves back in time, yet simultaneously expresses utopic possibility:

OEDIPUS: The moment I saw you all laws and limits were abolished.

The doors of the universe swung open.

The Earth became the sea. I was born.

You were there, you would be there, the future had arrived.

(Ibid.: 301)

In Oedipus's lines and these two scenes, their relations are blurred: he is at once husband and son, she his child, mother and wife. Theirs is the playful talk of lovers in which anything seems permitted and all roles are fluid. There is innocence in their exchange: undoubtedly, the scenes are 'idealistic', yet we might read this quality in a number of ways. Backward looking, the sequence nostalgically recalls their love and dwells upon what appeared then to be limitless potentiality and promise. Jocasta is now effectively on her deathbed, her life unravelling as Tiresias stands guard over her. At the point of her disappearance, Cixous strives to articulate, through the extremes of tragedy, the larger significance of this loss. Equally, the play's fluid temporality invites us to view these scenes as an enactment of radically alternative *future* relations.

Despite the transgressive, even explosive, potential inscribed in these sequences, one cannot easily read the play's conclusion as celebratory. The final scene opens with Oedipus's return and, in the same instant, the death of Jocasta. He has come back to her, he announces: 'My love! My strength! I am here, / My beloved, my child. / He has come back for you!' (Cixous 1994: 319). It is a moment of dramatic irony, one that recalls classical drama in the sense of a revelation come tragically too late. But remembering Cixous's 'Aller à la mer', his words can be understood differently: it is surely no accident that only when the woman is 'relegated to repression, to the grave, [...] oblivion and silence' does Oedipus's 'strength' return (Cixous 1995b: 133). Cixous's Oedipus grieves when he realises Jocasta's loss, but that grief evaporates as he begins to experience the growing sensation of her presence within and around his body: '*Without possessing you, / Nor you possessing me, / I feel you rejoin me / Elsewhere, at last.*' The play closes with these lines:

OEDIPUS: *And we are entering each other*
   My mother,
   My child.

My flesh is restful here.
I shall cease to suffer.
I have forgotten everything.
I no longer know who is dying.

(Cixous 1994: 326)

The play's conclusion is profoundly ambiguous, which explains why critics have been able to regard it in more or less diametrically opposing ways. Most optimistically, the ending could seem to suggest that male and female, parent and child, are now joined in a single 'bisexual' body that is at last able to accommodate difference (see Freeman 1998: 244–6; Miller, in Cixous 1994: 250). This interpretation could be supported by the recognition that Tiresias sings to Jocasta as she dies, since in myth Tiresias lived as both man and woman.[2] However, the fact remains that Cixous's play closes with Oedipus alive and Jocasta dead; we might be sceptical, then, how far this new 'dual being' has moved on from the oppositional structures in which the masculine term suppresses or devalues the feminine (see Pavlides 1986: 158; Canning 1999: 312). It is possible, of course, to argue a critical middle ground. Jocasta may not achieve liberation, but she does at least resist; her eventual death could be read not as the acceptance of patriarchal exclusion but as a refuge from this, a departure to an imagined time 'before the Symbolic took one's breath away' (Cixous 1986: 93).

To come to terms with the outcome of *The Name of Oedipus* and with Cixous's re-visioning practice more broadly it will be helpful to recall the philosopher Adriana Cavarero's work, briefly discussed in Chapter 1. Here I outlined the basis of Cavarero's *In Spite of Plato*, a feminist re-examination of a number of philosophical and literary texts from Greek antiquity. Cavarero's strategy not of rewriting these so much as seeking out 'loose threads' which, if tugged, might herald the unravelling of an entire discourse, seems to me akin to Cixous's own process of excavation: referring back to the quotation which heads this section, to a process of undermining – of digging into and under – 'an ancient culture', by a persistent species of (feminist) 'mole [...] never known before' (Cixous 1986: 65). Cavarero's purpose is to re-present voices in ways that allow conflicts between them to be heard: neither by her nor Cixous is it suggested that a repressed subject will achieve

'liberation' as a result. I summarised Cavarero's rereading of
Penelope, a figure perhaps selected by the author in part because
of her strong association with passivity: her position seemingly
one of locus for competing masculine desires rather than that of
active female subject. Penelope's act of repetitively unweaving then
reweaving a shroud for Laertes is interpreted by Cavarero as a
practice of motion without progress, a halting of time; her actions
metaphorically carve out an almost magical space within which
she can hold herself back, albeit provisionally, from the possessive
claims of men and the forward momentum of the myth narrative
(Cavarero 1995: 11–30). One might regard Cixous's treatment
of Jocasta in *The Name of Oedipus* as somewhat comparable.
In Sophocles, Jocasta is less a figure of action than one upon
whom the desires and fears of others are projected. Unable to
release her protagonist from the structures – narrative, discursive,
cultural – that bind her, Cixous instead creates the impression of
arrest: we are invited to look both ahead and back, as well as to
press down upon the myth to discover its weak places or pressure
points. In conclusion, although her Jocasta can be granted nothing
more optimistic than a form of refuge that gestures towards an
undefined 'elsewhere', we are left with an Oedipus who has at least
been comprehensively 'undermined'.

However, as is the case when reading any script independent
of theatrical production, the ambitions and achievements of *The
Name of Oedipus* exist at the level of potential only. There
are no records readily available to suggest how critics or the
wider public received the original event. In addition, as already
noted, Cixous herself has downplayed the work's status as drama,
inviting readers to consider it more closely correspondent to a
tone poem: what kind of performance should we imagine, then,
when we engage with the text as readers? While the script reflects
the author's call for a theatrical *écriture féminine* in its rejection
of the linear, its attentiveness to sound, to silence and to conflict
within and between voices, the play's formal experimentation is
largely confined to linguistic strategies which in some cases are
not easily translated. There is also, I suggest, a strongly cerebral
quality to Cixous's re-vision. Aside from the irony of this, given
her insistence elsewhere on the imperative that women 'write the
body', the implications are twofold and interrelated: we must
ask first how far ideas embedded in the script are readable in

performance; second, we could usefully examine the ways in which specific dramaturgical choices might shape the experience of spectators.

Charlotte Canning offers a helpful commentary on a 1991 production at Yale School of Drama for which Canning acted as dramaturg. Canning describes in detail a series of visual additions introduced by the director Marya Mazor and the designer Monica Raya that seem designed to open up a physical dimension largely unexplored in the original (Canning 1999: 313–20). There is much that is intriguing in this account, not least choices of cross-racial casting that 'unmoored the play from its relentlessly white European roots' and costume designs that confined one Jocasta within a striking cage-like dress of metal (*ibid.*: 314–15). Canning does not mention any shortcomings in the project and, if there were difficulties attached to a directorial strategy that allowed characters – physical 'realizations of feminist critiques' – to remain more or less static, '[r]arely moving' and addressing 'no one but the space in front of them as they lamented, pleaded or explained', these are not elaborated (*ibid.*: 314, 319). The essay is of course not unusual in offering theoretical justifications for performance choices – and understandable, given Canning's role as dramaturg – without dwelling upon audience reception of these; admittedly, reception is difficult to gauge in any event. But it may be useful to highlight comments from one review of a subsequent production by the same director in 1998, the work retitled *Jocasta* to signal clearly who is the protagonist as well as to reflect Cixous's emphasis on the importance of naming (Mazor 2010). After leaving Yale, Mazor went on to co-found with Jean Wagner the New York-based theatre company Voice and Vision, a group dedicated to developing work by and about women and girls. Mazor's remounting of the opera with this group, this time with a new score by the German composer Ruth Schonthal, employed not two but three Jocastas: an actress, a soprano and a Butoh dancer (the last addition suggesting a concerted resolve to draw out bodily as well as aural languages from the piece). Reviewing the show, Anthony Tommasini of the *New York Times* praised the cast's sensitivity to the material but considered that the work as a whole remained seriously hampered by the 'long, philosophical and poetically stylized' libretto that in performance proved heavy-handed and overpowering. Ultimately, he concludes, '*Jocasta* gets draggy and ponderous' (Tommasini 1998). In quoting this I do not seek to endorse Tommasini's criticisms but rather to highlight challenges inherent in the text and difficult to meet in practice. The idea of critically exploring 'motion without progress' is more immediately workable in (Cavarero's) philosophical analysis than in (Cixous's) drama; and equally, while 'The Laugh of the Medusa' argued that theatre in the future feminine had 'no need for plot or action', can the difficulties an audience might experience watching actionless, plotless theatre be ascribed simply to their insufficient education in contemporary stage languages? Mazor comments that *Jocasta* tended to divide spectators: some were straightforwardly bored but others, perhaps more willing to accept the lack of narrative advancement, were excited by it (Mazor 2010). All the same, it is evident that dramatic re-visions of myth that adopt such forms and that voice, above all, themes of repetitive struggle without apparent reward may struggle to convince audiences that their project is ultimately productive.

The scene of history: Cixous's *The Perjured City, or The Awakening of the Furies* (*La ville parjure, ou Le réveil des Erinyes*)

Cixous's collaborations with Mnouchkine to date could hardly be further from the 'pre-theatrical' experimentation of her early drama, in terms of the sheer scale of events created – often with huge casts and a playing time of several hours – and an ambitious scope of reference that attempts to present on stage the complex narratives of contemporary history. Linguistic and aural elements predominated in *The Name of Oedipus*, at least as originally conceived; by contrast, Mnouchkine's productions have always been fully theatrical – music, dance and mask work regularly feature – and Cixous's plays for the Soleil sustain this tradition. There is no shorthand to describe the company's performance style, since through almost half a century of practice it has continually privileged innovation, experimenting with familiar forms and actively seeking 'other' theatrical languages that could reshape their practice. Asian performance traditions have been especially influential: the play cycle *Les Shakespeares* (1984), for instance, was strongly coloured by the structures and techniques of Noh, Kabuki and Kathakali theatres, Mnouchkine finding there the ritual form and non-realistic stage language she hoped would enable fresh examination of the texts and simultaneously underline their distance from the present day (Déprats 1999: 93). Through this and other productions the Soleil has sought to develop art that is epic in scope and stature but nevertheless contemporary in reference; Cixous's contributions precisely reflect this dual ambition.

In 1990 the Soleil mounted a series of four Greek tragedies, with Euripides' *Iphigenia in Aulis* (1990) preceding productions of the three plays of Aeschylus's *Oresteia* (1990–92). All four were presented as a cycle, *Les Atrides*, which toured internationally to considerable acclaim. Mnouchkine's decision to preface her *Oresteia* with this rarely performed play that deals with Agamemnon's sacrifice of his daughter in the name of war explicitly invited a feminist perspective on the work as a whole. Presentation of a *four*-play cycle served effectively to highlight 'the ambition, violence, misogyny and sheer political expediency of the militaristic patriarchy'; the ordering brought out sympathy for Clytemnestra's position and criticism of the patriarchal Greek empire, attitudes that, in Mnouchkine's view, were already inherent not just in Euripides' play but in Aeschylus's trilogy also (Bryant-Bertail 1999: 180). Cixous's role in this project was chiefly that of translator for *The Eumenides*, and this activity along with the larger experience of *Les Atrides* inspired her next authored play, *The Perjured City*.

The Perjured City opened in Paris in May 1994 and was awarded the Prix de la Critique Dramatique the same year. The production played at the Avignon Festival and later toured to Belgium and Germany; the play has since been staged twice in America, in Bernadette Fort's translation, and in Australia.[3] Its scale is epic, the original production running at seven hours. There are twenty-one scenes, followed by an Epilogue, and around thirty individual roles plus a Chorus of unspecified number. *The Perjured City* appropriates and adapts elements of Greek tragedy in a work that turns its gaze upon present-day France, considering the implications of the notorious blood scandal described by Bernadette Fort as 'one of the most alarming examples of individual and collective failure to have occurred in our supposedly enlightened and humane democracies' (Fort 1997: 425). In 1991, the world was shocked to learn that the National Centre for Blood

Transfusion had in the 1980s knowingly distributed contaminated blood products to haemophiliacs, resulting in the deaths of thousands; it was eventually proved that doctors in authority had been aware of a heating procedure that would render the virus inactive, but had elected to sell off the infected supply and wait for the release of French-produced heat-treatment equipment rather than purchase from abroad. The Centre's director, Dr Michel Garretta, subsequently received a four-year prison sentence and fine; the then Prime Minister Laurent Fabius was acquitted, as was Georgina Dufoix, the Minister for Social Affairs; the Health Minister Edmond Herve was convicted but not given a punishment. There was widespread popular feeling – not least amongst victims and their families – that the acquittals were dishonourable, the trial 'fixed'.[4] The affair, shot through with political and private economic interests, was for Cixous an extraordinarily pregnant metaphor of tragedy today:

> What is the thorn, what is it that makes us shudder? How did we find ourselves in a scene that is awash with blood? [...] Then, all of a sudden, this story of contaminated blood struck us in the face as the metaphor of sickness of the kingdom when this kingdom is called democracy. Because nothing spreads faster than bad example. It was so enormous. I hesitated for a while because, like the audience, I needed to assure myself that this absolutely monstrous thing was indeed as it appeared to us: iniquitous and unique in its iniquity. (Fort 1997: 430)

The choice to write about this subject was in Cixous's phrase 'over-determined', given the Soleil's staging of *Les Atrides* and her own work on *The Eumenides*, a play for which blood-guilt is a driving theme. The challenge was finding the form to articulate an affair of such magnitude, one in which there were still victims dying. It was absolutely necessary, she concluded, to relocate the story within a mythical universe to acknowledge its scale and significance – in effect, to allow it to claim the status of tragedy – as well as to protect those presently suffering who might be there, watching, in the audience (Prenowitz ed. 2004: 18). Ironically, however, this mythological dimension has been expressly criticised by some critics who consider that the effect of the relocation is to obscure contemporary reference points and so weaken the play's power of critique (Bradby and Sparks 1997: 98; Dobson 2002: 111–12). In what follows I examine the place of mythological elements within the play and assess the opportunities and the risks of their inclusion.

In line with Cixous's conviction that the plot should be distanced from its original context, *The Perjured City* speaks of an anonymous 'plague' in which thousands, many of them children, have been allowed to die. The Mother has left the city for the cemetery located at its outskirts and now seeks justice for the deaths of her two sons: the ghosts of these boys, Daniel and Benjamin Ekekiel, haunt the play.[5] To support the Mother's cause, Cixous borrows the Eumenides themselves, from Aeschylus, from myth. These vengeful spirits flare up in *The Perjured City* as if from under the ground, or from within the unconscious. These 'old childish women' are unruly; they shout; they will not be pacified, bribed or silenced. The Furies still know 'the wording of indignation' and have the energy to sustain their protest; they are needed here, Cixous comments, precisely because such abilities are too little in evidence today (Fort 1997: 447–8). Aeschylus too is a character in the play, positioned here as caretaker of the cemetery; in this guise he is situated firmly on the side of the oppressed, no longer the author of events but a retired playwright who now 'just takes notes on dying' (*ibid.*: 446). Cixous's depiction of Aeschylus might seem subversive, given that the conclusion of his *Eumenides* would seem to endorse the order and control of patriarchy: indeed, in 'Sorties' she depicted that play's blood-soaked trial scene as heralding the dawn of phallocentrism (Cixous 1986: 105). She argues in the interview with Fort, however, that Aeschylus does not side with Orestes in *The Eumenides*; rather he charts the trial and its outcome without backing this development. She claims that Aeschylus is 'loyal to each of his characters in turn', insisting further that he 'could not take sides with this or that character without betraying his mission as a playwright – which is to give equal opportunity to all of his characters' (Fort 1997: 446). We might fairly examine Cixous's own plays from this standpoint, therefore, to assess how far the playwright tells a story without partisanship, creating space instead for an audience to take sides. Like *The Eumenides*, *The Perjured City* centres upon a trial, but here of the very 'democracy' that the Greek play saw instated; in a sense, then, Cixous's play constitutes a fifth drama in the cycle of *Les Atrides*.

Translating *The Eumenides*, Cixous had been especially intrigued by the nature and function of the Chorus. In a short essay, included in the programme for *Les Atrides*, she plays upon the homophony of *chœur/cœur* (chorus/heart) to propose that we might regard the Chorus as the very centre and pulse of tragedy. The Chorus, she writes, is the body of ordinary people, is ourselves, 'overrun, trampled, criss-crossed by the racing assassins and victims'; the Chorus sees too much, 'knows' in advance, but is human, not prophetic and never in control of events. Her description of the Chorus casts it in a complex light: it is 'Powerless Witness', representing all who are deprived of 'the possibility of *acting*'; nevertheless, it 'resists, to the very end'. The Chorus embodies the human need to express pain, whilst recognising that doing so will not necessarily lead to its expulsion (Cixous 1999: 196–7). In *The Perjured City*, Cixous employs a Chorus that is composed of a variety of social outcasts: disenfranchised and marginalised, this Chorus has inhabited the 'bowels of the subway, the hideouts of the damned, the cardboard shacks' and now lives within the cemetery that forms the principal setting for the play (Cixous 2004: 103). Where Cixous's Furies desire revenge – preferably in as bloody a form as possible – her Chorus shift and vacillate: resolving in exhilaration at one moment to hold a retrial 'right here' of those who were too easily acquitted, they are overcome at the next by cynicism and a sense of their own weakness, and quickly abandon the idea (Cixous 2004: 104–6). This treatment of the Chorus is lightly parodic of its role within classical tragedy. As her analysis suggests, its members are witnesses, not truly *actors*; in one sense, they are 'all talk'. Her Chorus uses high-flown metaphors – 'Let's make the river flow uphill! Let's break open the doors of hell!' – but soon come back to earth: 'But, speaking concretely, what's to be done?' Later, disgusted by the refusal of those accused to admit responsibility for the children's deaths, the Chorus announces:

> One day I'll write a letter
> And address it to all the following popes:
> The royal pope, the presidential pope, the papal pope, the medical pope.
> My letter will read:
> Pope, what are you sowing on the surface of your State?
>
> (Cixous 2004: 160)

It is evident that this 'day' may never come: 'my feet are cold', the Chorus tells us, and '[w]hen my feet are cold, there is no more spring in them' (*ibid.*: 162–3). Cixous's Chorus suffers, aches and fears; self-deceiving, it hopes against hope. All the same, it knows outrage and desires justice. While its revolt is not active, the Chorus's resistant *potential* is clearly recognised by those in authority; for X1, one of two physicians implicated in the affair and subsequently captured by the Furies, its members are '[s]hadows, trash, refuse rebellious to reason and to law' (*ibid.*: 120). Any elements of mockery in the portrayal of the Chorus are gentle, therefore: these are 'the people', and Cixous's perception of their frailties remains compassionate.

There are comic touches in evidence throughout the play, a quality that in no way diminishes the gravity of the material treated; indeed, given the weight of the subject matter, Cixous's satirical notes are especially welcome. Frequently humour is derived from elements that appear anachronistic against the mythological frame. The Furies, fired by immemorial rage, none the less remark sardonically of the world to which they have been summoned: 'What's new here, / Except the telephone? I'd like to know' (*ibid.*: 110). Elsewhere such references – to the World Bank, or to international conferences – make it clear that the play is rooted in the contemporary moment: its language achieves a poetry in which the mythic and abstracted merge with the modern and mundane. Consider Scene 8, featuring the city's King and Queen, where the latter, Calphurnia-like, describes the portent of a dream:

> I was lost in the immense Parliament
> Teeming with people who were electing, or had just elected, whom?
> Leaning by chance against a newspaper rack
> Loaded with the day's newspapers, suddenly,
> I see a big black headline on the front page:
> 'Queen Dies at the Children's Cemetery.'
>
> (*Ibid.*: 121)

The King claims she is blowing 'out of proportion' what is in reality 'a petty medical affair' (*ibid.*: 122). In one of the play's many ironically self-referential moments, she and another Minister who admits to being troubled by nightmares are both recommended briskly by the monarch not to 'read any more Shakespeare or Aeschylus / If you have delicate little nerves' (*ibid.*: 126). Yet in the same scene the King is unnerved to be plunged into obscurity when the goddess Night abruptly 'puts out the candle'. An usher arrives with more candles: 'Candles?' asks his King, bewildered: 'Where is the electrician? Go get me Maintenance, right away.' The sequence captures the way in which *The Perjured City* depicts a modern world that here is not so much 'invaded' by ancient forces as persistently undermined by gestures, linguistic and physical, that underline the impermanence and inherent instabilities of the present state. This literal flickering between light and dark also speaks metaphorically of waning authority. When Maintenance finally arrives, he remarks that in the Palace '[t]he power has been going out every five minutes for the last three years'; the cause is a 'freezing up of energy' that requires more than an electrician to fix (*ibid.*: 127–8). The King insists, however, that he is 'neither blind nor ruthless', 'neither a monster nor a machine': he is simply a 'veteran of reality' (*ibid.*: 124). His words recall those of Anouilh's Creon; his will is for good, but his position requires that he dirty his hands from time to time. However he is fast losing the public vote and a rival waits in the wings. Senator Forzza is the fascistic leader of the republican opposition rejoicing in the present chaos. The negligence of the current government and magnitude of scandal hanging over them make his own party appear virtuous by contrast. That children are the plague's principal victims is as it were the icing on the cake: the Senator gloats that nothing can be counted upon to stir up popular feeling like the deaths of infants.

Both the King and Forzza are positioned at the margins of the drama. The people will decide the political fate of each effectively without him taking action: there is nothing the King will do to retrieve the situation and nothing Forzza need do but take advantage of this. The play's more extended scenes of argument and action are reserved to dramatise the Mother's campaign for justice. Having failed to find this in the official courts, she insists the accused doctors be brought to a second trial to be held within the cemetery itself: the very place of death. She is supported in this cause by Aeschylus – who here, since he is within the play and not its author, *can* 'take sides' – as well as by Night, a border-crossing goddess figure in the play who conjures characters and scenes without directly influencing the course these follow. While the Furies hunt down the doctors, two lawyers, Brackmann and Marguerre, pursue the Mother: they are ready with offers of 'compensation' but will, it is clear, adopt whatever means necessary to make her abandon the case. With Night's help, she is able to evade them until the trial itself – the central scene of the play – when they reappear in support of the accused. Aeschylus is invited to open the proceedings: 'I take the floor / And I yield it immediately to the mother', he announces, in words that seem a comment upon – perhaps even reparation for – the conclusion of *The Eumenides* (ibid.: 140). When she speaks, the Mother's demand is simple but absolute: the doctors must admit their guilt and ask for forgiveness. The Furies are appalled at this modesty, insisting that only 'bloody expiation' will serve. Words are too easy, they claim: 'Anyone / can pronounce them, those three syllables: "Fooor-giiiive-meee"!' (ibid.: 141). Yet Cixous shows words prove far from easy: they constitute the battleground itself. Marguerre prevaricates: 'These words, let's say we said them. / What then?' Despite the Mother's assurance that this would end the ordeal, the lawyers regard it as a 'diabolical trick', a 'woman's trap'. Convinced that her speech is untrustworthy, lawyers and defendants immediately reveal the slipperiness of their own. The doctors, X1 and X2, refuse to allow that they are criminals; they did not 'want to kill'. The Furies seize on the evasion: 'Wantokill, there's a strange word!'

> Your sentences start out straight and finish crooked,
> There is no rhyme.
> But you won't get away from me. Fine, I take back crime. But I
> keep kill.
> So, you have killed,
> Even if you did not wantokill [...]
> And not to kill is not not-to-kill,
> Not to kill is to do everything possible not to kill.
> Did you do everything possible not to kill?
> No. Did you *want not to* kill?
>
> (*Ibid*.: 142)

The Furies' speech exposes the doctors' manoeuvre to evade culpability. We witness a similar semantic struggle in a later scene in which members of the wider medical establishment discuss how best to preserve their reputation. Each representative in turn agrees that, at the time, he 'did not know' the blood they were selling was suspect; to support this, Dr Twin adds he distinctly recalls their 'not knowing' being widely reported in the newspapers. Only Madame Lion, perhaps significantly for Cixous the only woman in the group, refuses to add her name to the proposed 'philosophical, ethical and scientific letter' that will refute charges that they are in any way culpable.[6] She alone had tried, repeatedly, to sound the alarm: 'Ten times a day for ten days in a row I called the man in question and a hundred times he refused to answer me. [...] I did it a hundred times, and then I did it again, one last time. Without a single echo, ever. All my cries fell into the sea. My mouth filled with sand.' Lion has little faith that her moral stand will change anything; lies, she recognises, have a 'strange force' when the truth is so very unwelcome (*ibid.*: 154–5).

Through scene after scene exposing the failure of justice and the refusal in every quarter to accept responsibility for the deaths of so many, Cixous reveals a city hopelessly ensnared in its own lies. Of course, to perjure oneself is not only to lie but to lie after swearing to tell the truth: a double betrayal. The self-protecting strategies of deception practised by those implicated in the play's trials refer to and criticise the same mechanisms in the world outside. The 'Perjured City' promises integrity and transparency and then breaks its promise; this city has convinced itself that strategic dissimulation is a democratic building block. Beyond this, the 'false speech' of perjury suggests the duplicities of language itself and in certain respects this emphasis recalls the Cixous of the 1970s. 'The Laugh of the Medusa' denounced patriarchal language and its exclusions, insisting that an alternative feminine writing could and should put 'Woman' back into the text, into the world and into history; by contrast, Cixous's *Name of Oedipus* struck a somewhat pessimistic note – albeit a passionate one – that seemed to deny the possibility of overturning 'Jocasta's' tragedy. In *The Perjured City*, the manipulations of language are targeted in a more immediate, more overtly political and arguably more accessible way. The semantic manoeuvring of government ministers or the press, for instance, is all too familiar; and in the end, perhaps the deepest horror the play exposes is the corporate mentality that admits the existence of a crime but lifts from individuals any burden of guilt. In the 1970s essays and early plays Cixous's wordplay suggested a kind of exuberant abundance, an infinite fluidity and writerly playfulness; in *The Perjured City*, the crafting of language is integral to the political tale.

The Mother and her allies struggle in vain to awaken some stirrings of conscience in the establishment's representatives.

Even the Furies, although they do not surrender, acknowledge their ineffectuality in a complex new 'world [that] has become a clenched fist' (*ibid*.: 173). Their protest is represented as morally necessary but unable to 'put things right'. Not only is no justice achieved for the dead but the living are killed also when Forzza, newly elected to power, orders a flooding of the cemetery. This act is designed to purge the city of its 'insanitary' – for which read resistant – elements; the point is underlined when the Captain, Forzza's second-in-command, is murdered when finally he rebels. Cixous states that while writing the play she had not known how it would end but was always aware that she could not freely dictate the narrative outcome:

> When a world is rotten to the core, it is condemned to the flood [...] The mathematically elegant solution: you wipe everything out. After, we shall see. But it is terrible, cry the spectators. It is unbearable. Then God provides the spectators with an ark. But I am not God, and I was not able to save anyone. (Prenowitz ed. 2004: 34)

I have said that Cixous does not write the final scene until the last days of rehearsal, a policy that preserves a sense of liveness but which may also reflect her resistance to the idea of 'ending'. In 'Enter the Theatre', Cixous admits a distrust of conclusions but acknowledges the imperative of 'the last metro'; the audience's reality cannot be ignored (*ibid*.: 33). She proposed initially that the play ended with the flood, but no one involved in the production could accept this: the conclusion felt 'exceedingly cruel', Cixous explains, both to the audience and more importantly to the real-life victims and their families (Fort 1997: 450). They decided to follow the flood with an epilogue in which the dead children and otherworldly figures of Night and the Furies cast a net into the waters to haul up the bodies of the dead: lifted high above 'the Perjured City', the Mother, Aeschylus and the Chorus find safety in Night's 'immense City of black velvet' (Cixous 2004: 181). Dobson describes this ending as a breathtaking *coup de théâtre*: 'the main stage lights gradually dimmed to darkness only then to slowly reveal hundreds of tiny lights set into the ceiling of the Cartoucherie', creating the impression of a 'sudden celestial dawn' (Dobson 2002: 112). From this vantage point the Mother – relieved to be no longer 'main character in a ghastly drama' – tells the audience that the responsibility for action is now theirs: 'I'm going to put my words, my thoughts, my angers / Underground, beneath your feet [...] It is your turn to insist that what is just / Comes to pass justly' (Cixous 2004: 182–3). This epilogue divided audiences, welcomed by some as a vision of hope and consolation but rejected by others who either judged it not 'credible' or believed simply that this real tragedy should not be poetically alleviated. Critical analyses of the work have been similarly split. Martha Walker celebrated a play that closed with a 'rallying cry' to spectators and represented overall a 'manifesto for a return to politically-engaged theatre that confronts our contemporary crises'; for Dobson, however, the abstraction of the staged 'afterlife' made it too difficult to assimilate and the abrupt separation of public from protagonists lessened the capacity for politicised identification (Walker 2001: 500; Dobson 2002: 114). As with *The Name of Oedipus*, Cixous provided a conclusion that defied consensus.

The Perjured City has been challenged repeatedly on its mixing of myth and history and in the last section of this chapter I examine the implications of this. Like Dobson, David Bradby and Annie Sparks expressed concern that the play's gestures towards universalism, through the mythical dimension, correspondingly weakened its historical critique. While the layering of myth and reality produced potent and memorable images, there was 'a price to be paid for this mythologising approach: precise political points of reference [...] are effaced in favour of a vision that becomes progressively more generalised until the audience is left, at the end of the play, with a manichean-feminist view of a world forever divided between manipulative men and merciful mothers' (Bradby and Sparks 1997: 98). There is some justification for this criticism. Predominantly, female figures are identified on the side of resistance, or are sympathetic to this: the Mother, the Furies, the Queen, Madame Lion, Night herself. Furthermore, the male role of Aeschylus, who here supports the Mother's cause, was played by a woman in the Soleil's production; while cross-castings of this kind have regularly featured in the company's work, this choice will have contributed, for some, to this impression of gender polarisation. The actors themselves did not regard the piece in this light, however. Within her own more positive reading of the play, Walker quotes Juliana Carneiro de Cunha (Fury/Chorus/the Queen) and Renata Ramos Maza (the Mother), both of whom agree that, while the resistant impulse is chiefly located in women characters, metaphorically this should be taken to 'stand for' the possibilities of political action on the part of either sex (Walker 2001: 501–2). None the less, it is evident that audiences might not infer such expansion from the play as staged. For her part, Cixous has insisted she never sets out to privilege sexual politics in her plays – perhaps a softening of position since 'Aller à la mer' – but simply to listen to, illustrate and cherish the voices of women and through this to 'push the theatre [she has] inherited' (Fort 1997: 427). However, we have seen that in performance this aim risks translation into an idealised version of femininity and an unbalanced picture that some spectators, male and female, may find alienating rather than productively critical.

Yet while one might admit elements of romanticism in the play, highlighted, perhaps, by Mnouchkine's staging choices, does it follow that loss of political precision is the inevitable and overwhelming consequence of introducing myth? It might be argued conversely that only by expanding one's perspective beyond the immediate context can an event's larger significance be appreciated. Cixous recognised France's blood scandal as a grotesque atrocity, a betrayal of trust almost beyond comprehension and a continuing injustice. How can the impossible be understood if not through metaphor? Equally, while the play was inspired by one particular horror, its concerns extend to address wider issues of ethical responsibility, political disenfranchisement and societal apathy, emphasising the need to recognise and above all act upon a genuine moral emergency. To recast this real event through myth is to insist on the magnitude of the original affair and to expose its manifold implications. 'Mythologising' should not mean to abandon the specific for the general: on the contrary, while myth is by definition a form of abstraction, myths are resonant only in so far as they find echoes in our reception of them. Thus while *The Perjured City* has been criticised for using myth to step away from a specific contemporary crisis, I propose that ideally this element functions in the play to retain our sense of its true monstrosity; certainly, its language throughout – for example, the recurrent metaphors of blood – as well as the appeal made to the audience at the end constantly strives to retether the abstract with experience. Cixous's text suggests the simultaneous articulation of two realities: the society of today, abhorrent and familiar, corrupted values mercilessly laid bare; and a wider realm of myth, tragedy and human aspiration able to express a profound sense of pain and loss, as well as an abiding faith in the possibility of ethical recovery.

Notes

1 Von Kleist is a writer much admired by Cixous also. In 'Sorties' she states that from him she drew the 'will to live several lives. To be more than one feminine one or masculine one'. Cixous discusses in detail how Von Kleist's *Penthesilea* eloquently articulates a desire outside the law (Cixous 1986: 112–22 (112)).

2 Ovid recounts how Tiresias, coming upon a pair of copulating snakes in the forest, struck them with his staff; in punishment the gods changed him from a man into a woman, for seven years. Because he had experienced inhabiting both sexes, Jupiter calls on him to settle an argument with Juno whether the man or the woman enjoyed more pleasure in lovemaking; Tiresias endorses Jupiter's view that it is the woman (Ovid 1955: 89).

3 *The Perjured City* had its American premiere at Northwestern University in 1997 and its first US professional production in Chicago in a version by Streetsigns Theatre. In 2007 the play was staged in Melbourne by VCA Drama students, directed by Kirsten von Bibra.

4 The case is now well documented. Bernadette Fort describes the affair in some detail (Fort 1997); see also news reports such as this one: 'Europe Blood Scandal Ministers Walk Free', BBC News, 9 March 1999, http://news.bbc.co.uk/1/hi/world/europe/293367.stm. Accessed 14 December 2009.

5 In Cixous's play the children have several moving passages of speech; by contrast, in Mnouchkine's production the children were silent, represented by Bunraku-style puppets manipulated by the actors.

6 Fort notes in her translation that the play's 'Madame Lion' represents the real-life doctor Yvette Sultan, head of the haemophiliac ward at Hôpital Cochin in Paris, who was one of the first medical experts to testify at the appeals trial in 1993 (Cixous 2004: 188).

5

Sites of experience: myth re-vision at the end of the century

The two dramatists considered in this chapter each achieved critical prominence in her early twenties for plays staged in the last half-decade of the century. The late British playwright Sarah Kane and the Icelandic writer Hrafnhildur Hagalín are broadly contemporaries and internationally associated in so far as Hagalín has expressed admiration for Kane's work and translated the other's 1998 play *Crave* into Icelandic (her version broadcast by the country's national radio service, Ríkisútvarpith RUV, in 1999). Yet whilst Hagalín cites Kane as an influence, the aesthetic and thematic preoccupations of the two seem at first to have little in common. This difference in dramaturgical approach – above all, perhaps, the extent to which each directly implicates her audience – in part explains their converse treatment by critics. In a writing career unhappily cut short by suicide, Kane became notorious for plays characterised by scenes of brutal violence unflinchingly staged 'in the face' of spectators, metaphorically or actually; as a result she was immediately marked out as an *enfant terrible* of the new drama by the British press. By contrast, the poetic language, experimental structures and more obviously 'literary' character of Hagalín's theatre caused the author from the first to be hailed as a rising star and important new voice on the national playwriting scene. The reality is neither that Kane's plays lack poetry nor that Hagalín's material is non-confrontational. However, regardless of these commonalities the status and reputation of the dramatists today is quite different. Kane has become the theatrical equivalent of a household name: the hostility that initially surrounded her has very largely given way to praise; her plays are constantly staged in professional and amateur production throughout Europe and beyond; considerable critical space has been dedicated to analysis of her work and a 2008 conference in Cambridge devoted to the reassessment of her unique contribution (Saunders 2002 and 2009; De Vos and Saunders eds 2010).[1] Certainly, Hagalín is far less well known outside her native country, despite the fact that two of her plays have been widely translated and produced in and beyond Europe.[2] Her relative obscurity as a dramatist is explained both by the 'chamber' character of her early work (a quality that seems to invite studio rather than main house staging) and by the variety of genres in which she has worked: rather than concentrating exclusively on stage drama, Hagalín has produced numerous translations (including Icelandic versions of Arthur Miller's *All My Sons* and Harold Pinter's *Moonlight*) as well as writing for national radio and television.

The plays I examine here are Kane's *Phaedra's Love* (1996) and Hagalín's *Easy Now, Electra* (2000). As the titles suggest, each has as its centre a myth in which a maternal figure is effectively placed on trial. This shared characteristic invites analysis of gender concerns in a way that continues the discussions of previous chapters; it does not permit me to frame either playwright as a daughter of feminism. In interviews both Kane and Hagalín have resisted invitations even to comment on their work from this perspective. Kane insisted that the very term 'woman writer' was meaningless, stating simply: 'I am what I am'; in her view, exaggerated attention to sexual politics could serve only to distract attention from the larger *human* problems she aimed to address (Stephenson and Langridge 1997: 134). Elaine Aston has remarked on how little feminist interest Kane's drama has attracted to date, despite content – gendered conflicts, 'selves' deconstructed or remade – that would in principle lend itself to such analysis. Aston accounts for this reticence by pointing to the eagerness of contemporary commentators to include Kane as an honorary male amongst a number of 'angry young men' on the 1990s British playwriting scene, the result being that issues which would otherwise have been taken up by critics were rendered invisible or irrelevant (Aston 2003: 79).[3] Janelle Reinelt offers a different explanation: Kane's plays, especially the last, *4:48 Psychosis*, seem on the surface to reintroduce 'the very sort of self-loathing expressions second wave feminism tried to fight – preoccupation with the imperfect body, lack of self image or sense of self value, depression, guilt, masochism'. If not by her own definition a 'woman writer', Kane was nevertheless a woman writing and an extraordinary talent: and yet, as Reinelt explains, the nihilism many critics have found in her work – a perception arguably endorsed by the author's suicide – would trouble attempts to locate this within a feminist canon. However, for Reinelt the 'via negativa of [Kane's] example is a protest': whilst the plays may not display the explicit markers of feminist commitment, she proposes that the residue of this can none the less be traced in an unflinching ethical and political stance which demands 'audiences pay attention to real suffering, her own but also others' (Reinelt 2003).

Hagalín's *Easy Now, Electra* focuses intently on the attitudes and interrelationship of two female characters and the actresses who play them. The piece explores questions of the limits of freedom, particularly as these impact upon women, and investigates processes of identity construction asking how far these may be 'undone'. There would seem close correspondence here with feminism's theoretical concerns: but at the same time, and mirroring the enmity of Electra and Clytemnestra, the tone of the work is often bitter and the outcome signals no liberation. Hagalín has in any case rejected the suggestion that her work is informed by a feminist consciousness. She states that she would 'never consider [herself] a feminist' and, like Kane, finds sexual identity an inappropriate way to think about, let alone attempt to categorise, an author's work. In Hagalín's view, feminism as a term remains meaningful only in the context of countries where 'women have to fight for their rights where they are severely and really violated' (Hagalín 2006).

This explicit *dis*identification with feminism merits further reflection since I have chosen to include Hagalín and Kane rather than seek out playwrights whose example would more readily establish a continuity of purpose with authors featured previously. Plenty has been written over the last two decades, in the media and in academia, about the widespread reluctance of European women born after the 1960s to self-describe as feminists or even to recognise the movement's ambitions as still pertinent to their own experience. It is unnecessary to rehearse this debate in detail here, not least because to do so would inevitably involve engaging in the time-consuming and often depressing task of outlining, and then working to unpick, the partisan agendas that frequently underpin this discussion and the abundance of clichés encountered on the way. Briefly, popular explanations for the rejection of 'feminist' as a term include the argument that the word carries negative connotations of extremism and joylessness with which few women today – reasonably enough – would wish to be associated. Equally, it is regularly claimed, there is a prevailing assumption that equality of opportunity for men and women has been all but achieved, hence there is no longer the perceived need for feminism to exist. Both analyses contain elements of truth but are at the same time manifestly reductive; moreover, they do no favours to the intelligence of those whose attitudes they seek to elucidate. However, it is worth pausing to reconnect this second argument, of 'equality achieved', to Hagalín's remark. The playwright makes no such assertion but does find it important to distinguish her own relatively privileged position from that of women whose liberty is actively constrained. If feminism is understood as an urgent political cause, one might argue that the instinct of many so-called 'first world' women to distance themselves from this demonstrates an appropriate sense of perspective rather than blindness towards the persistence of inequities at home: in other words, the gesture acknowledges that all oppressions are not equal. From this position, to subscribe to feminism in respect of one's own circumstances might seem to debase the term itself.

Activism is only one face of feminism. In its diverse national manifestations, feminism has always also constituted itself as a way of thinking and being, of reflection on one's self and on the interface of self/other. Throughout the second wave of European women's movements, this gaze, both introspective and reflexive, increasingly established less commonality of experience than the reality of difference and the fluidity of identifications. Influenced by and intersecting with post-structuralist analysis, feminist theories of subjecthood problematised the category of 'woman' to the point where assumption of affiliation on the grounds of gender became unsustainable. Sarah Kane's 'I am what I am' might have been merely a curt response to inferred sexism (since male playwrights are not asked to comment on being a 'man writer'); alternatively, her words could signal recognition of the complexity of self-definition, or the refusal of some notional entitlement to represent women as a group. Kane and Hagalín are not atypical amongst their generation in refusing 'feminist' as a label, or in finding it unjustified, even insulting, to suppose the prefix 'woman' necessary to describe their profession. At the same time, in the work and attitudes of both writers one can clearly trace the residue of feminism, to borrow Reinelt's phrase, as well as the recognition of its tensions and limitations. Inclusion of their plays within this study reflects the complex relationship of these authors' generation with second-wave feminism and its legacies; their examples are not, however, intended to stand as any more than partially representative.

The analysis of previous chapters has demonstrated the diverse strategies employed by women playwrights of the 1960s, 1970s, 1980s and early 1990s in appropriating myths for artistic inspiration and as subjects of pressing critical or political attention. Their re-visions might not all have been written with Adrienne Rich's radical agenda in mind, but there has none the less been implicit consensus that myths constitute powerful ideological narratives that have both reflected and helped to structure gendered identities and experience. Pursuing alternative narrative paths, adoption of perspectives hitherto marginalised or repressed, transposition of action to a new cultural context, creation of rich visual and aural performance languages to offset an 'authorised' tale-telling: these and others have been the means whereby playwrights have worked to negotiate new meanings in and around inherited stories loaded with extraordinary cultural weight. Yet since Kane and Hagalín reject gendered identifications, it follows that their reasons for turning to myths in the first place will be different; we cannot suppose that myth remains for them a dramatic subject with especial potency, nor that they recognise in their own practice the tensions feminism has argued are inherent in working with such material. In the second part of this introduction, I discuss two ways – contrasting, yet not wholly unrelated – in which myths have continued to fuel work by younger writers. I consider first the extent to which classical myth serves Kane's particular brand of British 'in-yer-face theatre'; I then situate Hagalín's practice of myth re-vision within the context of contemporary 'postdramatic' performance.

The critic Aleks Sierz coined the now well-established term 'in-yer-face theatre' to describe a sensibility that emerged strongly in new, largely British, playwriting in the 1990s. As the phrase suggests, it stands for drama that is overtly provocative, brash, aggressive and invasive (this last, not least for the audience).

Plays by writers such as Mark Ravenhill, Anthony Neilson, Jez Butterworth, David Greig, Joe Penhall, Martin McDonagh, Philip Ridley and of course Sarah Kane forced audiences well beyond their comfort zones through the use of brutally explicit language and taboo-breaking enactments of sex, violence, humiliation and varieties of abuse. Alongside Ravenhill and Neilson, Kane is for Sierz one of in-yer-face's 'big three', but is not the only woman to make the long and predominantly male list: Judy Upton features, as does Rebecca Pritchard, and the two American writers Naomi Wallace and Phyllis Nagy.[4] These new playwrights' insistence that there was nothing that could not be staged and nothing that must not be said was demonstrated unmistakably and irreversibly through plays like Neilson's *Penetrator* (1993, at Edinburgh's Traverse Theatre), dealing with misogyny, sadism and homophobia; Upton's *Ashes and Sand* (1994, Royal Court Upstairs), centring on the violent rampage of a girl gang; Kane's *Blasted* (1995, Royal Court Upstairs), which I return to later; and Ravenhill's *Shopping and Fucking* (1996, the Royal Court at the Ambassador's), one of the defining plays of the decade and the Zeitgeist, which as its title implies exposes a culture in which consumerist values predominate to the point that all activity, including sex, has become transaction. As a body of work, in-yer-face theatre painted a profoundly bleak picture of society at the end of the century. But the counter-side to the combination of brutishness and cynicism that marked so many of these plays was the insistence that audiences should not so much watch as *experience* the drama. It has become a cliché to state that this theatre aimed to shock spectators into feeling, but this nevertheless accurately reflects the beliefs of many of its authors: the horrifyingly visceral encounters the plays offered were regularly defended as both challenge and antidote to a widespread and entrenched cultural insensitivity, heightened by increasing media overload.

It is not for this book to dwell on the appropriateness or otherwise of locating Kane beneath the in-yer-face umbrella. Graham Saunders has reservations about its suitability; Sierz continues to defend its application in Kane's case (Saunders 2009: 5; 127–8). Undoubtedly her first plays, especially, bear the hallmarks of this trend: *Blasted*, *Phaedra's Love* and her 1998 play *Cleansed* all present actions and images that continue to stun and appal audiences years after one might have supposed they would become inured. But while Kane's work might be indicative of a characteristically 1990s mindset – steeped in yet critical of consumerist culture, impatient with bourgeois complacency in all its forms, equally distrustful of the political left and right – it is also distinct from that of her peers in its bold reach and engagement with profound existential questions of love, faith and the possibility of redemption. Preoccupied with these larger concerns, Kane's plays do not limit their potential application by local or time-bound references. Recognition of this authorial ambition and of the underlying formal austerity in Kane's writing led Ravenhill to describe her, following her death, as 'a contemporary writer with a classical sensibility' (Ravenhill 1999). With this in mind, it becomes less surprising that Kane should have appropriated ancient myth for *Phaedra's Love*; indeed, such territory begins to appear a natural choice for a dramatist fundamentally concerned with the interplay of emotion and violence and wholly unafraid of epic extremes.

The myths that provide the narrative basis for classical tragedy typically deal with stark emotional conflicts and in the treatments of ancient dramatists the dilemmas they articulate are revealed as at once simple and infinitely complex. Kane recognised the potentially explosive effects of competing passions, above all on a personal level: 'My main source of thinking about how violence happens is myself, and in some ways all of my characters are me' (Stephenson and Langridge 1997: 133). The tale of Phaedra's forbidden desire for Hippolytus, his disgusted rejection and the horrors that result resists simplistic interpretation; further, as with myth narratives in general, critical rationalisation alone cannot sufficiently unpack its embedded meanings. Kane's writing is likewise driven by the conviction that spectators must feel as well as think and cannot expect simple answers. Classical tragedy is underpinned by the belief that people are ultimately powerless in the face of external forces, whether the gods or 'fate'; a corresponding impression of human vulnerability can be seen in Kane's plays, but accompanied by an insistence on the possibility of making ethical choices, however constrained the circumstances. Myth thus served Kane through the kinds of themes characteristically addressed, which spoke to her own acute sense of internal as well as wider human conflict; at the same time, its inherent abstractedness reflected her expansive dramaturgical vision. Finally, myth narratives deal not only with desire but with taboo. The notion of 'that which exists but cannot be acknowledged' was for Kane and many of her generation as a red rag to a bull. In interview she defended the most controversial scenes of *Blasted*, insisting that '[i]f you are saying you can't represent something, you are saying you can't talk about it, you are denying its existence, and that's an extraordinarily ignorant thing to do' (Bayley 1995). It is well known, however, that classical tragedies – or more precisely, those of the Greeks – did not represent violence onstage, essentially containing this element in language alone. Kane's contemporary drama obeys no such rules: in her work, the enactment of brutality forms part of her distinctive and resonant stage poetry. This conscious 'choice [...] to represent' proved one of the most controversial aspects of *Phaedra's Love* and is a theme I shall address in detail (Stephenson and Langridge 1997: 132).

Kane's last plays, *Crave* (1998) and *4.48 Psychosis* (first produced posthumously in 2000), contrast radically with her earlier work. They are more lyrical than plot-driven, dramaturgically highly fragmented; 'character' has become unfixed and unstable. These qualities have encouraged some critics to frame Kane's work within the quite different sensibility of contemporary postdramatic performance. In 1999, Hans-Thies Lehmann's now classic study of new forms in post-1960s theatre was published in Germany and has since been widely translated. For Lehmann, the descriptor 'postdramatic'

> denotes a theatre that feels bound to operate beyond drama, at a time 'after' the authority of the dramatic paradigm in theatre. What it does not mean is an abstract negation and mere looking away from the tradition of drama. 'After' drama means that it lives on as a structure – however weakened and exhausted – of the 'normal' theatre: as an expectation of large parts of its audience, as a foundation for many of its means of representation. (Lehmann 2006: 27)

Lehmann illustrates this trend with the examples of numerous directors, companies and dramatists, referring frequently to those whose practice crosses conventional dramaturgical dividers: thus director-dramatists such as Heiner Müller and the American artist Robert Wilson are discussed alongside the Polish director-designer Tadeusz Kantor and provocative experimental groups like Italy's Socìetas Raffaello Sanzio and Britain's Forced Entertainment.

Lehmann draws Kane into the frame, albeit briefly; David Barnett has since outlined her postdramatic credentials more fully (Lehmann 2006: 18; Barnett 2008).

Postdramatic theatre foregrounds the material situation of performance, the problems inherent in representation and the artificiality of composition, to the point where dramatic action, understood in conventional terms, is radically undermined if never quite eradicated. A postdramatic theatre work will obviously still remain time-bound, but two hours or so of performance may convey the impression of timelessness – or, perhaps, stasis – through establishing the dreamlike sense of a single instant expanded, or the reverse. Episodic and frequently alogical, the event of performance becomes something to experience more than to interpret. Whilst these qualities would not immediately seem to support the politicised practices of myth re-vision dealt with elsewhere, one can nevertheless find affinity with concepts fundamental to rewriting and restaging. I have argued that re-visions occupy an especially charged space, since, together with other forms of adaptation, they frequently (though not invariably) achieve impact through adherence to and departure from what has gone before. On the page and in the moment of performance this can create a peculiar kind of narrative accumulation. Readers and spectators are repeatedly made aware – whether or not attention is consciously drawn to this – of a larger architecture, composed of pre-existing or coexisting versions of a narrative, within and against which a new work attempts to assert its place. The plays examined in preceding chapters display varying degrees of self-consciousness in this respect. In Hrafnhildur Hagalín's *Easy Now, Electra*, however, this kind of reflexivity is intensified to the extent that it permeates, and ultimately becomes, the action 'proper'. Hagalín's piece requires two actresses, who also *play* actresses: these characters enact, abortively, fragments of a narrative that corresponds both to the myth behind the drama and to the lives of the characters themselves – or so we are told. The tension in the piece derives above all from a profound sense of entrapment, simultaneously manifest on multiple levels. The characters struggle to escape, or even subtly redirect, a narrative whose outcome appears unalterably determined. The performers are troubled by the limits of representation and their own failure, in exercises of 'improvisation', to find the thematic and theatrical liberty the method seems to promise. For spectators watching, it seems increasingly unclear that these figures – women, performers, characters – even desire the same end. As critical myth re-vision and as a text in the postdramatic tradition, *Easy Now, Electra* consciously operates 'beyond' classical tragedy yet, necessarily, in the midst of its remains.

On the surface, the two tendencies described – one cannot legiti-mately call them 'movements' – of in-yer-face and postdramatic theatre might seem antithetical. The former operates firmly within the dramatic paradigm: there are recognisable (if frequently alienating) characters and staged action is graphic, unapologetic and immersive. The postdramatic theatre event is far less heated – the implied quotation marks around all action, however upbeat or energetic, ensure this – though this does not make it cold. Yet the two practices, or attitudes, are connected by a strong underlying emphasis on audience *experience*. Each form, by different means and perhaps with varying degrees of insistence, draws spectators decisively into the present moment. Both perspectives deny audiences the security that accompanies distance: instead we are emotionally, intellectually and morally assaulted; or we are parodied, flattered, appealed to, implicated. Further, both forms are evidently preoccupied with the possibility of acting ethically – for the postdramatic theatre, 'acting' in both senses of the word – and with any degree of freedom. What follows in this chapter is an analysis of two dramatic texts, not an assessment of the relative qualities of in-yer-face and the postdramatic: nevertheless the discussion will show how Kane's and Hagalín's myth re-visions occupy, not always comfortably, these distinct yet curiously overlapping theatrical territories.

Shock treatment: Sarah Kane and *Phaedra's Love*

> Art isn't about the shock of something new. It's about arranging the old in such a way that you see it afresh. (Kane, in Saunders 2002: 28)

Sarah Kane (1971–1999) 'arrived' as a playwright at the age of twenty-four. *Blasted*, first presented at the Royal Court (Theatre Upstairs) in 1995, established her as a precocious new talent on the British theatre scene and a radically disruptive dramatic voice. The play's first half, set in a Leeds hotel room, stages an abusive encounter between a violent man and vulnerable younger woman. This world is shattered by the arrival of a soldier and explosion of a mortar bomb; the second half shows the original scene in tatters, a great hole blown in the wall and all covered in dust and rubble. The physical devastation is echoed in the fragmentation of the drama, in which language becomes increasingly sparse and action breaks down into a series of brief, chaotic images of human desperation and despair. *Blasted* was immediately and hugely controversial, in part for the liberties Kane took with dramatic structure, but overwhelmingly for the explicit and appalling acts of violence that permeated the play. It attracted reviews that, in some cases, were little more than catalogues of its supposed outrages against decency: masturbation, oral sex, multiple rape, urination, mutilation, defecation, cannibalism. Although Kane had her supporters from the beginning – among them Caryl Churchill – the notoriety of *Blasted* was such that it was a while before that furore died down sufficiently to allow a more measured assessment of her abilities (Saunders 2002: 25). For Kane herself it was ironic that representation of brutality onstage should, even momentarily, provoke greater anger and draw more extensive media coverage than the actuality of violence outside the theatre: 'While the corpse of Yugoslavia was rotting on our doorstep, the press chose to get angry, not about the corpse, but about the cultural event that drew attention to it' (Stephenson and Langridge 1997: 131). It is unsurprising the play produced this response, however. *Blasted* is genuinely shocking, sparking not prim affront but palpable horror and revulsion. Sierz has argued that the affective quality of Kane's work is a potential barrier to its appreciation: 'the power of her stage images tend[s] to detract from the depth of her writing' (Sierz 2001: 90). Yet to an extent Kane's drama exploits that very 'problem', forcing its audience into a feeling response rather than one of contemplation and judgement: part of *Blasted*'s impact is explained by how thoroughly it collapsed the distance between immediate domestic context and far-off 'foreign' war.

Given the storm that had surrounded *Blasted* in Britain, critics and theatregoing public alike were agog to see what Kane's next full-length play would look like. In 1996 she produced *Phaedra's Love*, described by the author as 'my comedy' and by Dan Rebellato as a 'riotously unblushing' reworking of Seneca (Saunders 2002: 78; Rebellato 1999: 280). Evidence suggests that Kane chose her subject somewhat arbitrarily and – in contrast with playwrights featured in precious chapters – with little sense of an ideological burden. Invited by London's Gate Theatre to contribute to a season of reinterpretations of ancient European myths and stories, she settled on Seneca's *Phaedra* only after her earlier suggestions of plays by Büchner and Brecht were rejected. Kane turned to Seneca after enjoying *Thyestes* in a new translation by Caryl Churchill, staged at the Theatre Upstairs in 1994 (Sierz 2001: 109). Kane's rewriting project did not grow through extensive research: she studied neither Euripides' *Hippolytus*, the more famous dramatic source for this story, nor Racine's *Phèdre* and read Seneca's play just once before starting work on her own (Saunders 2002: 72).[5]

Kane was attracted first by *Phaedra*'s theme of a sexually corrupt royal family, at the time eminently applicable to contemporary Britain. Scandalous revelations in the early 1990s of the extramarital affairs of both the Prince and Princess of Wales and of extravagant and 'inappropriate' behaviour by the Duchess of York had tainted public perception of the royals beyond recovery. While *Phaedra's Love* does not address the national context explicitly, it comments upon this indirectly. Kane was struck, too, by the play's depiction of Hippolytus. Certainly, Seneca makes him an extraordinarily dislikeable character (Stephenson and Langridge 1997: 131–2). Hippolytus's misogyny is apparent from the opening of the drama, long before Phaedra confesses her passion. Women are declared a 'damned race': 'I loathe them all, I dread, I shun, I curse them' (Seneca 1987: 77). Unappealing as he is, for centuries Hippolytus was widely regarded as the tragic hero.[6] In later versions, famously Racine's *Phèdre* (1677), sympathies shifted towards the heroine. This popular preference continued over time to the point where the British playwright Tony Harrison – offering his own *Phaedra Britannica*, in 1977 – could remark that the Phaedra role had come to dominate contemporary stagings. Harrison considered this a distortion, arguing that 'only when the characters around [Phaedra] are duly reinstated [can] the central figure [...] be seen in her true light' (Harrison 2002: 115). None the less, Harrison continues the modern trend by treating Phaedra as the protagonist; Kane diverges from it, returning Hippolytus to the centre of the drama. His absolutism is retained, but in place of sexual purity, to which the classical Hippolytus aspires, Kane substitutes uncompromising honesty. Relentless pursuit of that alternative virtue allows Kane's contemporary Hippolytus to become reluctantly likeable despite the abundance of unappealing qualities she heaps upon him and notwithstanding the destructive impact of his behaviour on other characters.

If Kane develops Hippolytus's role, she effectively reduces Phaedra's from its representation in Seneca. His *Phaedra* departs from Euripides' *Hippolytus* in numerous ways, but especially notable is Seneca's choice to prolong Phaedra's life until after Hippolytus dies, thereby granting her the opportunity to admit and take responsibility for the false accusation against her stepson.[7] However, Kane's Phaedra, as if reverting to the Euripidean model, kills herself just over half-way through, leaving the rape charge behind her to play out its catastrophic effects. Phaedra's motivation for the allegation remains largely unexplored in Kane's play. Of more interest to the author is its impact on Hippolytus; in tackling this myth, as in her writing more generally, Kane evidently felt no obligation to take the woman's side (Aston 2003: 80). Her fascination with the two central figures in the story derives from the dynamic between them, whereby obsessive love meets a blank wall of cynicism. Kane recognised the presence of both forces in her personality: writing the play, she became, she said, 'simultaneously Hippolytus and Phaedra' (Saunders 2002: 31). None the less, it is the presence of Hippolytus that dominates *Phaedra's Love*, in the text and onstage; beside him the other characters – perhaps especially the women, some have suggested – seem less developed (Stephenson and Langridge 1997: 134).

Kane did not seek to adapt Seneca's play in the conventional sense of the term. Her treatment is coolly disobedient, extracting from the source that which serves her purpose, discarding what does not, and throughout reinventing freely. As re-vision, *Phaedra's Love* is highly provocative; it is unsurprising therefore that amongst the mixed reviews it received many expressions of dissatisfaction were directed precisely at the relationship of the new work to the primary material. It is debatable how far 'respect' should be paid to a source text in any adaptive process; inevitably, however, awareness of literary ancestry will shape reception of the new work for at least some audience members. Reviewing the play for the *Guardian*, Michael Billington insisted that once you strip out the moral framework of the original – manifestly Kane's intention – 'you are left with a sensational melodrama'. His point was not that contemporary playwrights must retain this intact, rather that removal creates a gap of meaning: the shape of the action remains, but devoid of profound motivation. Billington argued that something must be found to fill or replace the ethical dimension of the original and questioned whether *Phaedra's Love* achieved this (Billington 1996). A harsher assessment came from the *Times Literary Supplement*. Edith Hall found Kane's retelling unenlightening and superficial. To support her argument, Hall singles out Strophe, an invented character introduced into the play as Phaedra's daughter and used by Kane to replace the Nurse/confidante figure in Seneca and Euripides. As Hall notes, the name 'Strophe' is drawn from the Greek term meaning one of a pair of stanzas in a dramatic chorus (the *strophe* and the *antistrophe*). To Hall, a classicist, what was frustrating was the apparent irrelevance of the appropriation: 'The gesture her name makes towards the drama's classical ancestry is indicative of the entire work; it is an attempt to disguise what is essentially inconsequential with a thin layer of allusive obscurantism' (Hall 1996). I return later to the figure of Strophe and the 'problem' of her name. It is useful to keep in mind, however, Hall's larger judgement that the play as re-vision is ill-informed and ultimately unproductive: that the classical text – indeed, like Kane's Strophe – is introduced superficially, brutally mistreated and ultimately trampled upon.[8] My own reading of *Phaedra's Love* prompts several responses to these criticisms: I explore that which the author substitutes for the narrative's traditional 'moral centre'; I argue that a comparison of Kane's play with Seneca's can be productive, regardless of Kane's authorial intentions; and I defend an approach to re-vision that is both highly partial and undeniably irreverent.

Kane's readiness to twist a narrative conventionally perceived as tragedy into a 'brutal black comedy' undoubtedly suggests an insubordinate relationship to the source (Gardner 2005). The mythic dimension of *Phaedra's Love* is not primarily included to stretch the play's dramatic horizons beyond the narrowly local, as in many re-visons; rather, Kane begins with the legendary and cuts this mercilessly down to size, denying its characters the magnitude traditionally claimed for them. I have remarked that *Phaedra's Love* is directly disrespectful: in the words of one reviewer, this rewriting 'brings the story kicking and screaming into the late twentieth century', a phrase that aptly conveys the ruthlessness with which Kane transplants mythic narrative to modern context (Tew 2004). The lengthy, wordless first scene of *Phaedra's Love* has a bored and bloated Hippolytus sprawled in front of a television set, mechanically eating junk food and periodically masturbating into discarded socks 'without a flicker of pleasure' (Kane 2001: 65). This opening inverts rather than abandons Seneca's text. *Phaedra* begins with a monody that establishes Hippolytus's energy and vitality, his self-conscious removal from all that adheres to the city and his dedication to Diana, goddess of nature and the hunt (Seneca 1987: 43–7). By contrast, Kane's reconfigured protagonist is passive and decadent, 'all muscle turned to fat', and joylessly promiscuous; anonymous sexual partners are brought in on demand, like the takeaway meals he ceaselessly consumes (Gardner 2005). The pretensions of classical tragedy are thus imposed with deliberate awkwardness on a stage world both thoroughly contemporary and alienated from itself.[9] Debasement of the male protagonist in this way suggests degradation of the myth: in Kane's sardonic reimagining the character, wholly emptied of 'nobility' or 'greatness', suggests only the grotesque image of exploitative, self-indulgent, undeserved privilege.

In Kane's re-vision, Phaedra too is unrecognisable from her Senecan model. The guilty acknowledgement of a desire 'joined to sin' and the self-condemnation with which Phaedra is typically identified are both entirely erased (Seneca 1987: 49). The secrecy and subsequent anguish of revelation are here concentrated into the sharpest of exchanges: when Strophe utters Hippolytus's name, Phaedra simply screams. To Strophe, Phaedra's love was in any case 'obvious'. She urges Phaedra not to indulge it:

STROPHE: Mother, this family –

PHAEDRA: Oh I know.

STROPHE: If anyone were to find out.

PHAEDRA: I know, I know.

STROPHE: It's the excuse they're all looking for.

(Kane 2001: 73)

Strophe's position is entirely pragmatic. The risk of discovery, heightened by the increasing vulnerability of the Royals to public perception, is simply too great; Phaedra should rejoin Theseus or simply 'fuck someone else, whatever it takes'. The moral abyss faced by the classical Phaedra is removed wholesale, replaced by nothing more profound than concern for preservation of image.

Kane's briskly parodic treatment of the forbidden desire and revelation motifs continues in the next scene where Phaedra avows her intention to 'get over him' but submits seconds later. She abases herself utterly: Hippolytus is coldly insulting even before she confesses and when she does he barely responds. Again, there is no hint here of the outrage emphasised by Seneca. In desperation, Kane's Phaedra kneels down and fellates her stepson. Passively permitting this, Hippolytus's only direct initiative is to grab hold of her head when she attempts to draw it away so that he can ejaculate in her mouth. Bizarrely, this action is a striking and very possibly coincidental echo of a parallel moment in Seneca when Phaedra, rejected by a furious Hippolytus, grovels at his feet:

HIPPOLYTUS: Remove your vile touch from my chaste body.

Away! What? She thrusts herself into my arms?

Out, sword, exact the fitting penalty.

Behold her twisted hair in my left hand,

Her vile head bent back.

(Seneca 1987: 87)

The shape of this image – Phaedra kneeling, her hair grasped aggressively – is almost identical in both texts. Some commentators on Seneca have even proposed that Hippolytus's drawing of his sword may be read as a phallic gesture, although admittedly 'of a ludicrous kind in the circumstances' (McCabe 1993: 94). The terrible, unspeakable quality of Phaedra's passion, highlighted by this gesture in Seneca's version, is summarily disposed of in Kane's. As Phaedra gets up, Hippolytus comments dryly: 'There. Mystery over' (Kane 2001: 81). No taboo has been broken, no secret pleasure released; for him she is just one more person who – inexplicably and despicably – will do anything to suck 'royal cock' (ibid.: 74). He gives her nothing in return but honesty. He does not desire her; does not like her; will not make her come. He tells her he has already had (better) sex with her daughter; more, that Strophe has also had sex with Theseus, Phaedra's husband. He is, as Phaedra says, a 'heartless bastard': and in that heartlessness, if not in much else, he recalls the classical Hippolytus of Seneca and Euripides (ibid.: 84).

As we have seen, the revelation of Phaedra's illicit love is not posed here as a moral problem. Equally, the play has no commentary to make upon incestuous relations *per se*. However, the motif of incest still functions crucially as metaphor to further the play's satirical attack on the nuclear family, the supposed cornerstone of society's ethical and moral values, and on that Family amongst families, the British monarchy. *Phaedra's Love* does not merely parody what was the increasingly erratic behaviour of the nation's royals, but attacks an institution: the tragic collapse of the house of Theseus is reinvented by her as triumphant destruction of an anachronistic and damaging hereditary system. With this in mind, and somewhat unusually amongst the re-visionings of classical myths discussed in this study, *Phaedra's Love* does not erase or pass over the elevated social status of its original protagonists: where for example Hagalín's Clytemnestra and Electra are reinvented as any (or every) mother and daughter, Kane's *dramatis personae* remain royal and are, at least in part, targeted as such. In harnessing Phaedra's desire to this cause, Kane participates in a longstanding dramatic tradition whereby perversions in the sexual politics of the home are made analogous for corruptions in the power politics of the state or church. As Richard McCabe argues, incest – and by extension, incest drama – calls into question 'the continued existence of families, nations and philosophies' since these 'largely [depend] upon maintaining "natural" relationships between their component elements' (McCabe 1993: 25). *Phaedra's Love* suggests less that the behaviour of Kane's royal family is corrupt than that the institution itself is a perversion within what purports to be a democratic society, a 'ludicrous repository for left-over notions of national glory' (Hemming 1996). Phaedra's eagerness to fellate her stepson and his passive agreement to serve as channel not only for her desire but for her daughter's (and, through both women, for his father's) suggest a family tree rotten from branch to root. The incestuous interrelationships of the characters signal a monarchy so inbred as to become self-consuming; moreover, Kane's decision to stage multiple promiscuities within the family circle makes mockery of the enduring 'myth', upheld by the British monarchy, that its line of succession is 'white and Christian and "pure-blooded"' (Phillips 2005).

The mood of pleasureless decadence and cold brutality established by these first scenes is disrupted by Phaedra's public accusation against Hippolytus. Again, Kane radically reworks one of the classical narrative's central motifs. In Seneca's *Phaedra* as in the more generic myth of the amorous stepmother the slanderous charge derives from the perceived necessity to 'rebound the guilt' – in the words of the Nurse – from the morally tarnished woman to the innocent man (Seneca 1987: 89).[10] Typically, the vengeful response brings down undeserved punishment on the victim and serves symbolically to expose the weaker character of the female sex, an inferiority already signalled through the evident susceptibility of the latter to base urges (Gérard 1993: 4). In *Phaedra's Love*, as we have seen, Hippolytus does not experience his stepmother's desire as a temptation, nor does he attempt to prevent her acting upon it; for all that, his rejection of her is as merciless as that in Seneca's *Phaedra*. The charge made against him is false in both plays. None the less, Kane invites us to recognise a kind of truth, albeit tentative and inadequate, in her Phaedra's act: 'what Hippolytus does to Phaedra is not rape – but the English language doesn't contain the words to describe the emotional decimation he inflicts. "Rape" is the best word Phaedra can find for it, so that's the word she uses' (Stephenson and Langridge 1997: 132). Although born of pain, Phaedra's accusation is more than revenge: it is, Kane emphasises, a gift. With the label of 'rapist' forced upon him – an identity that is at least dynamic, albeit abhorrent – Hippolytus finally shakes off the inertia that has swamped him thus far:

> HIPPOLYTUS: Not many people get a chance like this. This isn't tat. This isn't bric-a-brac.
>
> STROPHE: Deny it. There's a riot.
>
> HIPPOLYTUS: Life at last.
>
> (Kane 2001: 90)

As already noted, Seneca permits his heroine to confess the lie before she dies. By contrast, the prompt suicide of Kane's Phaedra ensures that her status as victim is preserved and Hippolytus's safety fatally undermined; the prince realises with gratitude that by her action he is 'Fucked. Finished' (*ibid.*: 91). In this way the play's incest theme receives an additional twist: where Phaedra's first attempt to 'fuck' her stepson leaves him unmoved, her second shatters his complacency and sets in motion a chain of events that brings the Royals down, one after another, like tumbling cards.

When Strophe warns her mother against a liaison with Hippolytus, she makes the seemingly throwaway remark that in the event of discovery the family would be 'torn apart on the streets' (*ibid*.: 73). In the final scenes of *Phaedra's Love* that prediction is literally fulfilled, the action escalating into what one reviewer termed an 'extravaganza of grisliness' (Bassett 1996). Theseus sets fire to Phaedra's corpse on its funeral pyre and then, disguised, enters a furious crowd composed of actors who – in the production at the Gate Theatre, directed by Kane – until this moment masqueraded as members of the audience. Spurred on by the King, the mob give free rein to resentment against the 'Royal raping bastard' and fall on Hippolytus, who willingly leaps into their midst. Hippolytus is strangled and castrated by the populace, then subsequently disembowelled by his father; Strophe draws the ire of the crowd for attempting to defend him and in punishment is brutally raped and killed by Theseus; finally, the king slits his own throat. In an interview, Kane joked that she had always found problematic the classical tradition of keeping violence off the stage: 'I mean, if you're not going to see what happens, why not stay at home? Why pay £10 *not* to see it?' (*ibid*.). In the tiny auditorium of the Gate, spectators were directly within the circle of action that takes an almost carnivalesque turn: Hippolytus's genitals are thrown to a dog, his bowels cast on to a barbecue. As vultures descend and begin to devour his body, he is able to smile and deliver, through a gurgle of blood, the play's sardonic last line: 'If there could have been more moments like this' (Kane 2001: 103).

For some critics, the 'casual atrocity' of the riot scenes reinforced the impression already gained from *Blasted* of the bleakness of Kane's vision. Driven by 'bloodthirsty nihilism', they suggested, a still immature playwright fails to 'tak[e] the hint' from the ancient dramatists that such matter is better left to the spectator's imagination (Spencer 1996; Hall 1996). Such commentaries scarcely admit possibility of critical intent behind Kane's dramaturgical choices; indeed, Charles Spencer of the *Telegraph* considered *Phaedra's Love* the product of 'a mind on the brink of breakdown' (Spencer 1996). To counter such dismissals, I offer two interdependent interpretations of the play's blood-spattered conclusion. First, we should note that the grotesquery of *Phaedra's Love* is rooted in Seneca and in more ways than one. Scenes are invoked in *Phaedra* that are exceptionally violent, even by the standards of ancient myth: the classical Hippolytus meets an appallingly grim end when his chariot, attacked by a monstrous bull that emerges from the ocean, is smashed to pieces against the rocks. Whilst that 'scene' is, unsurprisingly, described rather than shown, Seneca nevertheless flouts tradition by choosing to bring Hippolytus's mangled remains directly on to the stage. Moreover, when Phaedra recognises him she kills herself, once again in the presence of the audience.[11] In a macabre moment – one that seems to conflate the conclusion to Euripides' *Bacchae* with that of his *Hippolytus* – Seneca has Theseus struggle to reassemble the body for the funeral rites from its scattered parts:

> Be dry, cheeks, restrain these copious tears
> While a father counts out his own son's limbs
> And constructs his body. What's this ugly,
> Misshapen thing, torn with wounds on all sides?
> Which part I know not; but it's part of you.

(Seneca 1987: 125)

Coffey and Mayer describe this sequence as a *tour de force* 'intended as a deliberate shock, an example of enhanced horror'. Striking as it is, there is a potentially ludicrous dimension to this attempt to reconstruct Hippolytus from severed limbs and unidentifiable chunks of flesh; it is a quality that threatens to undermine classical conceptions of tragedy and indeed the scene has notoriously attracted ridicule from the playwright's detractors (Coffey and Mayer eds 1990: 17–18). But if Seneca's decision to dwell on Hippolytus's ruined body risks making the tragedy all too human, *Phaedra's Love* pursues this direction further, requiring that characters and audience alike face the physical reality – or at least, its vivid impression – of violence and bloodshed. Kane's dramaturgical strategy for these last scenes can thus be read, at one level, as extension of Seneca's rather than its antithesis. However, particular to Kane's refusal of the conventionally tragic is that, rather than strive to recompose a fragmented body, she has her rioters gleefully fling 'Royal' limbs and organs to all corners of the stage: purposeful *dis*integration is the order of the day.

If the violent ending of *Phaedra's Love* is viewed not from the perspective of re-vision but in context of Kane's other work, we can see consistency of authorial purpose. The emphasis on immediacy of experience in *Phaedra's Love* echoes the playwright's realisation that *Blasted* had to collapse the boundaries, conceptual and actual, that conveniently disconnected aggression at home from the atrocities of geographically remote conflicts (Saunders 2002: 38–9). Bringing (representation of) brutality literally up close removes the safeguard that accompanies distance. Some critics of *Phaedra's Love* judged Kane's methods too crude: Hall felt placed in 'embarrassingly close proximity' to the gory spectacle; Charles Spencer, whilst acknowledging an undeniably 'visceral impact', adds the qualification that 'it's hard not to shudder when a penis is being severed under your very nose' (Hall 1996; Spencer 1996). However, the implication that Kane is falling back on shock tactics can be decisively countered by comparison of this final sequence with her play's beginning. Initially, Hippolytus is passive consumer of a diet of violence served up by the mass media, his relationship to this essentially voyeuristic; he finishes an active participant, rediscovering intensity of sensation, pervasively and invasively. An existence that once consisted of 'Filling up time. Waiting' has become, for a brief moment, life truly 'happening' (Kane 2001: 79). This shift from detachment to intimacy, cold to hot, is mirrored in the structure of the play overall. Its first half is, as Kate Bassett notes, 'for [Kane], relatively restrained': like Hippolytus, the audience members are initially placed voyeuristically, observing staged acts of inhumanity and degradation within a contemporary scene pictured as morally bankrupt (Bassett 1996). The second half erases that distance, by disclosing actors in the audience's midst and allowing a farcical excess of horror to erupt 'under [the] very nose' of spectators.

The reviewer of a 2004 production of *Phaedra's Love* described it as parodic tragedy 'spliced with Tarantino', but Kane herself was adamantly resistant to the glamorising of violence (Tew 2004). An alternative comparison for her dramaturgy might be with Antonin Artaud, a link that has more than once been made (Smith 1999). Nils Talbert has termed Kane's approach 'Artaudian' in the appeal it makes to all the senses, resulting in a theatrical experience that is 'risky and exhausting [...] but at the same time very enriching' (Saunders 2002: 142). Certainly, Kane's directorial decisions for *Phaedra's Love* echo Artaud's call to break down spatial divisions between actor and spectator, replacing 'stage' and 'auditorium' with a single locale for all present that becomes 'the very scene of the action'. The fundamental purpose of overturning theatrical convention was for Artaud, famously, the creation of a 'theatre of cruelty' able to shatter the complacency of the 'present degenerative state' and awaken 'the mind through the body' (Artaud 1977: 74; 77). The climactic sequences of *Phaedra's Love* – repulsive, messy, 'embarrassing' and proximate – tend similarly, immersing even the most resistant of spectators in the liveness of the moment. If painfully confrontational, this is for Kane an ethical necessity:

> Sometimes we have to descend into hell imaginatively in order to avoid going there in reality. For me, it's crucial to commit to memory events we haven't experienced – in order to avoid them happening. I'd rather risk overdose in the theatre than in life. (Sierz 2001: 111)

For those who condemned Kane's methods, there were as many others who rather, like Hippolytus, yearned for *more* 'moments like this' in the contemporary theatre (Stratton 1996; Hemming 1996; Moseley 1996).

I have defended the conclusion of *Phaedra's Love* against the charge that it crudely seeks to shock but it would be disingenuous to dismiss the critics' resistance to these scenes wholesale. Edith Hall is particularly troubled by what she terms the 'singularly unmotivated' rape of Strophe: the sole purpose, she proposes, for which Kane introduces the character into the ancient story (Hall 1996). This charge merits more detailed consideration. Earlier in this chapter I noted Hall's objection to the invented name that was for her indicative of glibness in the entire treatment. I will address the lesser point first. 'Strophe' does jar, yet it is possible to offer a rationale. The play positions her as an outsider: as Hippolytus remarks, she is the 'one person in this family who has no claim to its history', a '[p]oor relation who wants to be what she never will' (Kane 2001: 88). With this in mind, it is apt that Kane's Strophe should be landed with a name that on the surface includes her in the royal family yet simultaneously brands her a fake.

Hall observes with justification that the assault on Strophe in the play's final scene is both unexpected and brutal in the extreme. I question, however, that Kane's purpose in this is merely to bolster up the theatrical mayhem (although it does do this). Strophe's rape and murder function further to expose perversion of values at the seat of power. It is significant that while the crowd as a whole turn against Strophe, it is Theseus who perpetrates the attack. In myth, Theseus is a consistently ambiguous figure: he is famously associated with order and justice, but equally notorious for ravishing innocent girls (Rippl 2004: 170). That he should rape Strophe, cut her throat and only then identify her '*with horror*' – 'I'm sorry. Didn't know it was you. God forgive me I didn't know' – mocks classical tradition. Theseus's shock and grief on belatedly discovering how unjustly he has used Hippolytus – the emphasis in Seneca and Euripides – is displaced by Kane on to a realisation of his treatment of Strophe. But in *Phaedra's Love*, Theseus identifies solely as victim of fatal misrecognition, evading moral responsibility for the acts themselves. His grief over Strophe's corpse is thus profoundly hypocritical, the satirical effect heightened by his dismissive glance at his son's body, and the offhand line: 'Hippolytus. Son. I never liked you' (2001: 102). Strophe is undeniably served harshly in *Phaedra's Love*, perhaps especially so since arguably she, of all the family, least merits the punishment the play deals out. In this sense she is 'used', but strategically so. Strophe's eventual death is not *for* the family, as she had predicted, but works critically against it by exposing its hypocrisies. That her death comes from Theseus's hands – and in turn prompts him to suicide – extends the incest motif, whereby the family destructively turns in upon itself.

My analysis reinterprets Kane's treatment of Strophe but does not remove the horror of its effect on the page or in performance. The very marginalisation of her death makes it arguably more disturbing than that of Hippolytus. Whilst Hippolytus as character is deliberately emptied of greatness by Kane at the play's beginning, he later regains something of that stature by electing to die as an honest sinner, refusing to 'cover [his] arse' in the hypocritical style of the priest who visits him in prison (Kane 2001: 96). Perversely, Hippolytus becomes in his embracing of death a kind of hero, or anti-hero, despite the indignity of the vengeance enacted upon him. The sacrifice of Strophe is given far less weight. She dies with the word 'Innocent' on her lips: the context implies this as a last attempt to clear Hippolytus, yet it is a word that might productively be directed back towards herself. Kane gave no interpretative guidance, emphasising: 'I really don't have any answers to any of the questions about violence, masculinity, morality, sexuality. What conclusions people draw are not my responsibility – I'm not in control of other people's minds and I don't want to be'

(Sierz 2001: 104–5). We should not be surprised, therefore, that in common with the rest of the plays Kane wrote before her death in 1999, *Phaedra's Love* does not explain and so cannot limit the disturbances it provokes.

'I've got the feeling we'll be eternal': Hrafnhildur Hagalín's *Easy Now, Electra*

> There is a way in which women inhabit the patriarchal symbolic order that separates them from one another, leaves them on their own, having snatched them away from a place of common belonging and of mutual signification. (Cavarero 1995: 66.)

> Before sisterhood, there was the knowledge – transitory, fragmented perhaps, but original and crucial – of mother-and-daughterhood [...] This cathexis between mother and daughter – essential, distorted, misused – is the great unwritten story. (Rich 1979: 225)

Like Sarah Kane, Hrafnhildur Hagalín Guthmundsdóttir made an immediate and powerful impression as a young playwright.[12] However, Hagalín's first play met with immediate acclaim: *I am the Maestro* (*Ég er meistarinn*), staged by the Reykjavik Theatre Company in 1990, won the Icelandic Critics' Award in 1991 and the Nordic Playwright's Prize the year after. *I am the Maestro* features two students of classical guitar and their music tutor and explores the complexities of the master–student relationship alongside the students' struggles to achieve artistic perfection. Thematically, the inspiration for the play came from Hagalín's own years of training as a classical guitarist. Formally it is a 'chamber' piece, as Alan Barr observes, intimate in scale and intense in focus (Barr ed. 2001: 561). The dramaturg and critic Hávar Sigurjónsson considered *I am the Maestro* an 'incredible debut' and 'remarkably mature'; for Sigurjónsson, this play and her next, *Easy Now, Electra* (*Hægan, Elektra*), in 2000, marked Hagalín as the strongest female voice in new Icelandic drama (Sigurjónsson 2001). The critic Leigh Woods goes further still: in a twenty-first century overview of Iceland's thriving contemporary theatrical scene, he names Hagalín as one of around half-a-dozen 'leading lights' from a list of directors, actors, designers and dramatists of both sexes (Woods 2001: 102). None the less, women have welcomed Hagalín's success especially warmly. The journalist and political activist Magdalena Schram emphasised the importance of *I am the Maestro* in an interview about the state of new drama in the country: 'it's about serious things, and it makes you think. People are looking for more things like this' (Woods and Gunnarsdóttir 1997: 52) In another interview conducted as part of the same research, the stage director Hlín Agnarsdóttir similarly drew attention to the stir Hagalín had caused: 'It's exciting that such a young woman has succeeded as a playwright, because this hasn't happened in Iceland in the last ten years' (*ibid*.: 36). Of course, women playwrights in almost every country have historically numbered fewer than male, or at least have found it more difficult to gain recognition. The significance of Hagalín's achievement in particular can be better appreciated by situating this briefly within the wider context of Icelandic theatre.

Playwriting in Iceland is still comparatively young. The national drama is usually considered to have emerged at the *fin de siècle* with the founding of the Reykjavik Theatre Company in 1897, although there are a few examples of new plays being written for the stage prior to this. At first the repertory consisted principally of foreign works in translation, but soon included occasional plays by native writers; however, the two most regarded authors, Guthmundur Kamban and Jóhann Sigurjónsson, chose not to write in Icelandic, anticipating more likely success abroad as a result (Thorbergsson 2004). The inauguration of the National Theatre in 1950 gave further impetus to the development of playwriting in the country and marked the beginning of professional theatre activity. Despite the National's express intention of encouraging Icelandic talent, according to critic Magnús Thór Thorbergsson it was not until the appointment of a new director in 1972 that this objective was truly tackled. His view is borne out by Sigurdur Magnússon's 1973 edition of Icelandic plays, which, whilst finding several works to include, is not unreservedly enthusiastic about any of them. Magnússon comments:

> there is a lot of searching and groping and experimenting going on, and a number of authors are writing interesting plays, but by and large the Icelandic theatre depends on imported material, because native dramatic literature is just about coming of age and, to reach full maturity, needs considerably more time. (Magnússon ed. 1973: 20)

If challenging new works had numbered relatively few until this point, the 1970s witnessed in Thorbergsson's words a 'boom' in both playwriting and theatrical production. The conventional emphasis on historical or folkloric themes gave way to a new engagement with contemporary political and social issues, addressing more directly and critically than hitherto the tensions produced by Iceland's exceptionally rapid processes of modernisation.[13] Stylistically, realism dominated, a trend that largely continued through the 1980s, although by this time the content of the drama had shifted towards the family and personal experience (Thorbergsson 2004). Few women's names appear in accounts of authorship in these decades. In the introduction to his 1973 collection, Magnússon does make mention of 'two ladies', Nina Björk Árnadóttir and Svava Jakobsdóttir, whose plays (1969 and 1970 respectively) sound intriguing by their description but which, disappointingly, are not included in the selection (Magnússon ed. 1973: 13).[14] Hagalín's *I am the Maestro* stood out in 1990 as one of the earliest plays by a woman to make a real impact. Indeed, Thorbergsson uses Hagalín's first and second plays as markers to reflect the trajectory of Icelandic theatre in the last decade of the century, from an emphasis on realism and conventional dramatic construction towards greater stylistic experimentation and metatheatricality; the Danish critic Monna Dithmer similarly uses Hagalín's example to illustrate a metatheatrical or self-referential turn in Nordic theatre (Thorbergsson 2004; Dithmer 2001). Neither critic invokes Lehmann's 'postdramatic' explicitly, but for both the models of metatheatricality described gesture in this direction.

Between writing these first two plays Hagalín studied French and Theatre at the Sorbonne. By the time she began work on *Easy Now, Electra* she had read much more widely into European and American drama than before – the Absurdists, as well as several contemporary British playwrights including Sarah Kane and Mark Ravenhill, evidently caught her imagination – and had become increasingly fascinated with theatrical form (Hagalín 2006). Where music had provided the subject of her first play, it chiefly informed the structure of her second (Hagalín 2000). *Easy Now, Electra* is the more formally complex work: it introduces and plays upon themes, rather than building up a plot; dialogue is often repetitive, circling back on itself, or is profoundly fragmented. Hagalín states that she wanted to make the form adapt to the content, but not vice versa. It is a riskier method than I used in my first play. I often felt like I was throwing myself off a cliff without the slightest idea where I would land, or if I would land at all. But I feel this way is a lot more exciting and I think the outcome can also be, if it is a success. If not, the fall is even worse. I took that chance. (Hagalín 2000)

In Hagalín's play, two women assume the parts of actresses (and of course actually *are* actresses): in these roles, the Older Actress is also the mother of the Young Actress. The confrontation between these characters operates in two spheres simultaneously, with live interaction on stage 'as themselves' repeatedly intercut by a video recording of the same actors, more overtly 'in role', projected on to a screen the full width of the performance area. A young man plays the Stage Manager, standing at the edge of the acting area almost throughout; he observes the women and is observed by them, but does not speak. There is little conventional action onstage and even less explanation for the situation in which the characters are placed. Theirs is in a sense an abstract conflict, reminiscent of the theatres of Beckett or Ionesco, as well as the contemporary postdramatic stage: stripped of external distractions, Hagalín's play seems to answer Ionesco's call for a drama 'not symbolist, but symbolic; not allegorical, but mythical; that springs from our everlasting anguish; drama where the invisible becomes visible, where ideas are translated into concrete images, of reality, where the problem is expressed in flesh and blood' (Ionesco 1964: 237). In *Easy Now, Electra* the clash of Clytemnestra and Electra provides a mythic frame for the 'flesh and blood' struggle of mother and daughter, actor and role.

The play begins with the women's entrance, the Older Actress wordlessly sitting down on a chair, the Young Actress staring blankly into space. A long silence ensues. When speech finally comes, it is not from the characters onstage but from a projected image of the Older Actress onscreen, shown entering the playing area and welcoming the audience to a piece of 'experimental theatre' to be spontaneously improvised: a somewhat paradoxical claim, since what we are watching is evidently recorded. What gradually unfolds in this film, through a number of episodic scenes shown at intervals throughout, is a supposedly unrehearsed drama in which the Older Actress, playing a much younger woman, is flattered by an older man – the Young Actress, in drag – into accepting a ride in his car (mimed). The screen characters border on caricature: the Older Actress in a child's dress and absurdly high heels, hair plaited, a perverse Red Riding Hood; the Young Actress in pinstripes and trilby, a spiv's moustache drawn on her upper lip. Their appearances lend a grotesquely comic edge to the screen action, which both offsets and complicates the increasing impression of a game gone out of control.

The fast-paced film encounter contrasts with the sense of stalemate on stage. The performers do not acknowledge the audience's presence. We gather it is 'long after the show now', a show that, it turns out, has been left unfinished; none the less, they seem unable to leave the theatre space (Hagalín 2001: 570). The stage is bare but for a couple of chairs, a sparse scenic image reinforced by dialogue that at times suggests past provision – 'Maybe we shouldn't have let all our books go. There are times when I think it would be so good to just grab a book' – and elsewhere fantasises plenitude: 'If there had been a garden, we could have been pottering about in it right now' (*ibid.*: 566–7). The mother's gestures towards communication are mocked by her daughter or simply ignored, their familial relation seemingly as barren as their professional one. The Older Actresses professes maternal fondness, but without conviction:

> OLDER ACTRESS: You didn't need much sleep when you were a child, but nothing on earth could wake you up whenever you did sleep.
>
> YOUNG ACTRESS: How would you know? You never tried to wake me up. You were relieved when I was asleep.
>
> OLDER ACTRESS: I was happy to see you rest ... As mothers are. Happy to see their children rest. Mothers. To see their children rest. [*As if she were striving to remind herself, but the words sound odd to her as she speaks them.*] And I am your mother ...
>
> (*Ibid.*: 567)

The stream of chatter from the Older Actress – platitudes, nagging, pleas for attention, nostalgic accounts of theatrical triumphs and romantic conquests – does not disguise wariness of her daughter that becomes outright alarm at the other's announcement that she is 'expecting a visit'. Their exchange conveys powerfully the sense of something known but unspoken in their relations, past events of which the daughter is aware – 'Let's not wake up any of the old ghosts, mother' – but which the Older Actress has, or pretends to have, forgotten: 'I don't know what you're talking about [...] As if I'd committed a crime. I haven't committed any crime, as far as I know ...' (ibid.: 571). Tension increases with a story related by the Young Actress, of a young male transvestite who came to her dressing room, a man who resembled her and whom she had to hide for his own safety:

OLDER ACTRESS: [Sarcastically.] And he hasn't been seen since
...
YOUNG ACTRESS: He's coming. Wait, he said. Wait for me.
    Wait. Electra.
OLDER ACTRESS: Stop it now! Stop it! Once and for all!

(Ibid.: 589)

The title of the play and Electra's name, uttered just once, are the only direct references to the narrative that underpins the action.

Moved by the Electra story as a student, Hagalín logged this mentally as a means of exploring the dynamics of parent–daughter relations (Hagalín 2000). It is a narrative that psychology has drawn on for the same purpose. Jung originally proposed the name 'Electra complex' for Freud's concept of the 'Oedipal attitude' as manifest in girls. According to Freud, where the male child initially desires the mother but is driven to repress this through fear of castration, the female – supposedly suffering from 'penis envy' – desires her father and consequently seeks to eliminate the mother rival.[15] Jung broadly concurred with this view, adding that the Oedipus conflict

> takes on a more masculine and therefore more typical form in a son, whereas the daughter develops a specific liking for the father, with a corresponding jealous attitude towards the mother. We could call this the Electra complex. As everyone knows, Electra took vengeance on her mother Clytemnestra for murdering her husband Agamemnon and thus robbing her – Electra – of her beloved father.
> (Jung 1961: 154)

Jung posited an Electra complex in part to counterbalance Freud's privileging of male experience and over-reliance on the Oedipus myth; none the less, Jung's contribution here arguably serves to complement and expand upon Freud's proposals rather than challenge their underlying assumptions.[16]

Feminist thinkers from various disciplines have returned to the Electra story, typically using Aeschylus's Oresteian trilogy, its first representation in drama, as a starting point. For some commentators the *Oresteia* has proved a valuable key to understanding the historic vulnerability of women's position through the development of western culture. Within this project the treatment of Clytemnestra in particular has come under scrutiny. Vellacott remarks that it 'would be possible to collect, from a score of scholarly books and articles, enough vituperation of Clytemnestra to fill a chapter'; Bell agrees that she is most often viewed 'as a cold-blooded murderess and unfaithful wife to one of the glorious heroes of the great Trojan War' (Vellacott 1984: 63; Bell 1991: 133). Far from 'cold-blooded', Clytemnestra in the *Agamemnon* fiercely defends the murder of her husband as just return for his sacrifice of Iphigenia – 'his child, and my own darling, whom my pain brought forth' – to ensure that the goddess Artemis would speed his army's journey during the Trojan War (Aeschylus 1959: 92). In *The Libation Bearers*, Orestes avenges his father's death, urged on by Electra, by slaughtering his mother: his act is condemned in the play as the most heinous of crimes, reflecting the fact that matricide in ancient Greece was considered wholly repugnant and 'worse than mere homicide or incest' (Smith 1992: 76). Yet in the *Eumenides*, the conclusion to the trilogy, the 'trial' of Orestes results in his exoneration on the grounds that motherhood is not true parenthood:

> APOLLO: The mother is not the true parent of the child
>   Which is called hers. She is a nurse who tends the growth
>   Of young seed planted by its true parent, the male.
>
> (Aeschylus 1959: 169)

This account is endorsed by Athena, significantly the Zeus-born goddess with no female parent, and Orestes' crime is ultimately judged less serious than Clytemnestra's.[17] Thus the innocent Iphigenia is sacrificed and her disquieting mother eliminated, whilst their killers are cleared of guilt for both offences. That the trilogy concludes with this ruling, with the vengeful Furies – who until this point have hounded Orestes for his matricide – finally transformed into the more benign Eumenides or Kindly Ones, has encouraged feminist interpretation of the narrative as one of systematic suppression of the matriarchal principle (see also Cixous's 're-awakening' of the Furies in *The Perjured City*, discussed in the previous chapter). In a work titled *Reclaiming Klytemnestra*, Kathleen Komar asserts that the eponymous protagonist 'represents the feminist cause par excellence. Her story is really *the* story of the struggle of female blood right against the founding of male, rational law and the establishment of patriarchy' (2003: 26). Similarly, Cavarero sees in the story a calculated underrating of motherhood that persists for centuries thereafter, at both symbolic and actual levels, leading her to propose that the whole history of western philosophy and culture could be readable as a 'complex form of compensation' for the fact that we are all born of woman (Cavarero 1995: xvi).[18]

Predating these readings from Komar and Cavarero, Cixous in 'Sorties' offers a perspective on this myth not dissimilar as part of a longer essay on 'The Dawn of Phallocentrism'. Cixous's special concern is with Electra, who fascinates her as a figure caught between old ways and new: if Clytemnestra adheres to a prior tradition of mother right, and Orestes is projected forward into an (Apollonian) future, 'only sister Electra orests' (Cixous 1986: 105). Cixous proposes that whilst Electra's championing of her brother and tireless call for the murder of her mother apparently 'lights the path, makes way for the patriarchy', the sheer strength and persistence of Electra's rage marks her out as a source of radically disruptive energy that ultimately resists domestication:

> Electra is a mixed-up, hesitant place: active and passive forces, the forces of life and death, still confront each other there without being absolutely attributable to sexual difference, but their values become more and more emphasised until, in a last electric discharge, what is Orestes wins everything. (*Ibid.*: 109)

Cixous argues that even though Electra is displaced by Orestes in *The Libation Bearers* (she disappears from the play approximately four hundred lines before the end) and is forcibly married off (twice) in Euripides' version, her 'electric' presence unsettles the putting-in-place of patriarchy, exposing the tensions that its imposed structures cannot wholly disguise. In her analysis Cixous is less concerned to 'reclaim' Clytemnestra as a feminist heroine – and certainly makes no attempt to assert this for Clytemnestra's daughter – than to undermine the narrative to reveal its internal contradictions.

Hagalín's primary focus in *Easy Now, Electra* is on the dynamic of mother–daughter relations, and thus it is Clytemnestra and Electra with whom she is chiefly engaged. The characters appear together in three Greek tragedies, initially in *The Libation Bearers* and subsequently in the *Electra* plays of Euripides and Sophocles.[19] Charles Keene distinguished the three treatments by proposing that Aeschylus articulated great principles, Sophocles depicted great characters and Euripides showed vacillating figures whose fluctuations of feeling added up to a representation that was the least conventionally tragic of the three (Keene 1893: xii). Although Hagalín's re-visioning is informed by knowledge of all these versions – as well as by Eugene O'Neill's *Mourning Becomes Electra* (1931), an adaptation that grounds the characters' motivations in psychological theory – her work seems more closely aligned to the two later classical plays, both of which centre on the mother's 'trial' before her virgin daughter. In *The Libation Bearers*, by contrast, Clytemnestra and Electra share the stage for barely fifty lines and do not enter into dialogue; equally, Hagalín's mother figure reveals little of the self-command, steely resolve and free acceptance of responsibility that characterises Aeschylus's Clytemnestra. In Hagalín's version, the sparks of resentment and bitterness and failures of communication above all recall the deeply polarised mother–daughter relations of Sophocles' *Electra*. Nevertheless, scattered hints that the bond of feeling between Hagalín's women has not been wholly severed recall the somewhat more ambiguous characterisations of Euripides' drama.[20] Unconcerned to play out the narrative of the myth in its entirety, *Easy Now, Electra* concentrates attention on the interaction of the women leading up to a 'matricide' that is threatened yet never realised. Hagalín's characters are far less articulate than the protagonists of Sophocles or Euripides, who staunchly assert mutually irreconcilable positions: her Older Actress lacks self-knowledge and appears confused by her daughter's animosity; the Young Actress in her turn shies away from making outright accusations. Hagalín's contemporary re-vision does not, then, conceive of Clytemnestra as determined avenger of her daughter's death, exponent of mother-right, nor does the play obviously endorse Cixous's perception of Electra as force of resistant energy. Instead we are given a complex, multilayered exploration of gendered identities and familial relations that exposes the inadequacy of dominant discourses of maternity.

Easy Now, Electra is a re-vision that wears a notoriously heavy myth lightly, an attitude underlined by the economy of its reference points. Motifs from the classical narrative are subtly reworked in the contemporary action: an absent father; the mother's swings of mood between defiance and anxiety; the unkempt, wilfully neglected appearance of the daughter; the assurances of the onscreen stranger that he will treat the Older Actress 'like a queen' (Hagalín 2001: 573). Such moments could be read as a delicate teasing of the audience, playful gesturing by Hagalín towards an older story of which this is manifestly *not* a re-enactment: for every connection that is drawn, the attached implication of textual repetition is elsewhere refused or undermined. This subversion of a narrative upon which the new work simultaneously depends is achieved by two principal and interrelated strategies. First, running through the whole is a thread of meta-commentary on mythmaking generally and this myth in particular; second, an intricate theatrical structure serves to problematise identification of actor with character, or character with any single 'archetypal' counterpart.

Hagalín's play remains highly ambiguous about the extent to which it is possible to 'rewrite' a narrative so embedded in cultural consciousness. Onscreen, the Older Actress assures the audience that 'Nothing is predetermined in the performance you're about to witness [...] – what we're talking about here is the art of the moment, where everything is possible and anything can happen' (Hagalín 2001: 563). The performers claim the right to direct their drama any way they choose. Yet this promise is cast into doubt first by the medium of communication – pre-recorded film footage – and subsequently by the admission of the Older Actress, onstage, that past experiments in improvisation have not brought freedom: 'We tried it so many times. First with characters written by other authors and then we tried to build our own, but the result was always the same. Don't you understand, you can't just step out of the character you're playing, it's not possible! We've already proven that!' (*ibid.*: 574). The 'spontaneous' encounter on film seems likewise driven by compulsive momentum towards a matricide traceable to the myth, yet grotesquely distorted. Both performers articulate their roles as if within quotation marks.

Thus the Older Actress, Hagalín's reinvented Clytemnestra, on screen plays a much younger girl, but through a ludicrous visual masquerade that intentionally leaves that illusion incomplete. Mother and daughter, 'experience' and 'innocence', sit awkwardly together within a single figure. It is as if the older woman seeks to construct a fantasised self from some prior, guiltless moment of her history. None the less, onscreen as onstage, she is unable to sustain the role of the ingénue. Her feigned artlessness does not disguise the apprehension that this irresistible stranger – a figure anonymous yet curiously familiar – will prove her nemesis. Equally the Young Actress, in onscreen role as the Man, is no heroic Orestes. His barely concealed intention to punish the 'guilty' woman seems inspired by the logic of the rapist and adopts the same repellent language:

> YOUNG ACTRESS: I've got the feeling there's more to you than meets the eye.
>
> OLDER ACTRESS: You've got the feeling? Since when do men have feelings!
>
> YOUNG ACTRESS: And yet you climb into the car of a total stranger with no feelings? There's something daring about you, isn't there? Something recklessly daring. Girls like you like to take risks. Girls like you long for adventure.
>
> (*Ibid.*: 575)

The car, driven by the man, hurtles towards a conclusion that seems to presage the death of *both* parties, as if implying that this avenger, visually an uneasy amalgam of Orestes and Electra, already acknowledges s/he is not without guilt. At the last second, he skids to a halt. Appalled at this attempt to kill her off – at the very least, as character – the Older Actress drops hastily out of role. The screen action is thus officially left open-ended, although the Older Actress, onstage, remarks bitterly that had they completed the scene she would now be 'six feet under!' Surprisingly, it is the Young Actress who, despite her seeming enslavement to a matricidal text, still cherishes the possibility of a more radical rewriting: of 'how it might have been after the show, had the show been different' (*ibid.*: 572).

The Young Actress's desire for an alternative 'show' is reflected throughout the play in the perpetual struggles of bodies to escape the narratives that threaten to consume them. The Older Actress cannot accept the reality of ageing, fishing for compliments from the younger woman on her complexion and figure (*ibid.*: 588). That she boasts the body of a thirty-year-old signals something more than orthodox femininity's characteristic valorisation of appearances. Ironically, the appeal *to* her daughter simultaneously *denies* her daughter, since it demonstrates reluctance to accept her maternal status – even whilst that status is elsewhere insisted upon:

> OLDER ACTRESS: I know you. You're a good girl. You're a good girl.
>
> YOUNG ACTRESS: [*Turning to face her mother, quietly, through clenched teeth*] Girl. Girl! What are you talking about?! I-am-not-a girl!!
>
> OLDER ACTRESS: Nonsense! Enough of that nonsense now! Course you're a girl. You're my girl ... I ought to know. I brought you up. Squeezed you out of my very own womb. I'm your mother.
>
> (*Ibid.*: 573)

As illustrated, the Young Actress similarly recoils at the actuality of their familial relations. Her distaste for the term 'girl' suggests not her insistence on a more mature 'womanliness' but rather contestation of the category of the feminine: a resistance made overtly manifest, in the original production, through the character's costume and mannerisms.[21] However, this theme is most provocatively explored through the daughter's fantasies of release from the constraints of gendered identity.

For the Young Actress, resentment of her mother is inextricably entwined with longing for an absent man: one who seems at times to be her father and elsewhere a brother or lover. Her description of the transvestite she claims visited her – and for whose return she still waits – sketches a figure that is in crucial respects her own mirror image. Their resemblance is literal and physical: like their classical counterparts, these symbolic siblings discover they have the '[s]ame hair. Same hands. Same size of shoes' (*ibid.*: 571; Aeschylus 1959: 112; Euripides 1963: 122–3). The stories of their lives, too, uncannily intersect. The Young Actress is fatherless; the young man's mother 'died. Years ago, when I was small' (Hagalín 2001: 576). The girl blames the mother for her father's absence while the boy cherishes his widowed parent, yet both children incline toward the gendered influence they have lost:

the Young Actress, by rejection of that which outwardly pertains
to the feminine; the transvestite, by adoption of the same. In
each case, physical display is thoroughly bound up in a complex
desire for mother *and* father. Hence the Young Actress onscreen
assumes the guise of an older man so that she may court her
mother, while onstage as 'herself' provokes her parent with lines
that issue strangely from a daughter's mouth: 'A woman of your
age. Unbelievable. You're not a bad piece of crumpet' (*ibid.*: 579).
Equally, the transvestite, it is implied, assumes feminine drag in
submission to his father's obsession with a film star:

> YOUNG ACTRESS: Night after night. One movie a night with
> Ginger Rogers. And he was happy ... in love ... a young man
> again ... [*Pause. Switches tone.*] And then, after a while ...
> something happened, I said. Didn't it? After a while, it wouldn't
> do anymore, am I right? It wasn't enough for him just to see her
> in movies anymore, was it?
>
> (*Ibid.*: 583)[22]

This tale of the young man, like many threads woven into Hagalín's
play, is abruptly broken off. Yet, in this case, lack of conclusion
is used not simply to deny an audience the comfort of narrative
cohesion but to reinforce the idea of an Orestes who may or may
not return to break the stultifying impasse of the women's mutual
antagonism.

The Young Actress appears initially to seek her mother's erasure,
both 'in character' as daughter and by implication through relating
the transvestite's tale. Hostility towards the mother provokes an
attempt to 'kill' her, onscreen and onstage; the Young Actress's
narration describes a familial scene from which the maternal
figure has already been eliminated. To this extent, the play's action
seems at first to endorse the Freudian assessment that both male
and female child must, for different reasons, necessarily sever
the originary maternal bond in order to achieve maturation as
social subject. That reading is arguably strengthened by an image
of seeming infantile regression, near the play's end: following
the arrested movement towards matricide, the daughter staggers
awkwardly towards the Older Actress, to the latter's applause,
finally to topple weakly into her outstretched arms. It might seem
then that Hagalín's reworking of the Electra myth presents two,
terrifyingly polarised choices: between a symbolic mother-murder

which in Freudian psychoanalysis opens the way towards mature selfhood; or, alternatively, a dangerous engulfment and implosion of identity which results when the 'natural' matricidal impulse is blocked or refused. However, this apparent deadlock is unsettled when the play's complex layering is taken into account. Rather than simply enacting the 'necessary rejection' of the mother, or suffering from the failure to achieve this, the behaviours of both Young Actress and fictional transvestite reveal deep dissatisfaction with the limits of these discourses. The daughter recognises that to attack or reject her mother is in effect to direct that same destructive drive against herself. The son's transvestism becomes a complex gesture of nostalgia for the lost maternal body of which he was once a part, as well as an expression of love for the bereft father. From this perspective, Hagalín's play serves to dramatise the younger woman's effort to come to terms with the feminine maternal, through her own confrontation with the mother and through her invention of an imagined brother/double.

The struggle to comprehend relations with the maternal is channelled through the medium of heavily stylised and self-referential performance. Transvestism and role-play provide the means by which imposed identities may be refused or subverted, gender variants constructed, the 'unity' of the subject overtly broken down. The complex metatheatrical devices employed consistently expose the materiality of the body on display; the construction is parodic rather than artfully disguised, as when the Older Actress assumes her screen role as ingénue. Crucially, this parody does not assume an original, for the elaborate enactments of gender implicitly reveal, in Judith Butler's terms, *'the imitative structure of gender itself – as well as its contingency'*, whereby femininity and masculinity are exposed as a set of codes that may be transcribed upon any body, regardless of sex (Butler 1990: 137). In this way, *Easy Now, Electra* complicates still further representation of the intra-familial conflict: the Young Actress performs father/lover and son/brother, as well as daughter; the Older Actress plays child to the Young Actress: 'you could easily have carried me around the stage in those arms of yours' (Hagalín 2001: 579). But whilst this structure of fluid performativities could open the way towards a liberating redefinition of roles, and hence an unfixing of relationships, the notion that improvisation successfully dislodges regulatory mechanisms has already been explicitly undermined.

Images, mythic or otherwise, may be destabilised, but Hagalín's theatre is far from offering a free space for re-vision.

Hagalín's deployment of the Electra myth in this play does not attribute any essential or unchanging character to what Adrienne Rich termed the mother–daughter 'cathexis' (1977: 225). Hagalín remarks that many women do experience difficulties negotiating their changing relatedness to the maternal parent, endeavouring to balance likeness to their mothers with the need to assert independence from them (Hagalín 2006). Her application of myth, layered together with more contemporary popular cultural narratives, implies chiefly that motherhood has become burdened by an 'overabundance of discourse' from which it is difficult if not impossible for women to extricate themselves. Mother and daughter seem permanently divided as the onstage action draws to its end. The Young Actress does not speak and the Older Actress's claim that at last 'we're... together' rings hollow as she gropes in vain for her daughter's hand; the light that has been steadily sinking throughout is now extinguished altogether. Convention would signal this moment as the end, yet this is not the final scene of Hagalín's play. Lights are brought up sharply by the Stage Manager and the actresses 'step [...] out of character': at least, they let the polarised images of their characters fall away. Until this point we have been tricked into taking their bleak onstage encounter effectively at face value, but a further layer of metatheatricality reveals this, too, as an improvised performance by those same characters. At the close of *Easy Now, Electra* we are left with two women playing actresses who are mother and daughter, but with a new dynamic exposed that is gentler and more mutually tolerant. The Stage Manager ceases to be a threat:

OLDER ACTRESS: [*To the* STAGE MANAGER.] Thank you for your help.

[*The* STAGE MANAGER *bows.*]

OLDER ACTRESS: Will you turn the lights off for us?

STAGE MANAGER: Will do... [*Exits.*]

[*Pause.*]

YOUNG ACTRESS: Well then ... What did you think?

[*The* OLDER ACTRESS *sighs, gives off a faint laugh, and shrugs her shoulders. They embrace.*]

(Hagalín 2001: 591)

The women's embrace is the sole physical exchange in the play, live or recorded, that is reciprocal. Their extended 'rehearsal' has not resolved anything, but nor have they abandoned exploration in the way their improvisation had invited the audience to suppose. Older woman and younger, mother and daughter, Clytemnestra and Electra, hold hands and for the first time address spectators directly. Each speaks one word: 'Theatre.' They thank the audience and exit the stage. The play's final moments are thus directly self-referential; we are left not with a drama of characters but with the problems and opportunities of performative representation. The simple address to 'Theatre' simultaneously invokes a past history of drama and the stage and acknowledges a diversity of potential futures. As a concluding gesture, it marks out Hagalín's theatre as a space for play in both senses of the word: in which roles are assumed, subverted, dropped, picked up again; where stories are made, temporarily discarded, then remade. Hers is a stage on which narratives of all kinds accumulate perpetually and at times threaten to engulf the players: it would be bleak were it not also a space of invention and improvisation in which all 'rules' can be negotiated.

Notes

1 'Sarah Kane: Reassessments' was held at the University of Cambridge on 16 February 2008.
2 A production of *Hægan, Elektra* based on a French translation was staged at the Théâtre de l'Est Parisien and the Théâtre Varia in Brussels (*Doucement, Electre*, 2004). Hagalín's first play, *Ég er meistarinn* (I am the maestro), has been translated into twelve languages and has had productions within and beyond Europe, including stagings in Minnesota, Gdansk and Genoa.
3 The male playwrights Aston refers to here include Mark Ravenhill, Jez Butterworth, David Eldridge and Patrick Marber. Aston counters dominant readings of Kane's drama by offering a feminist perspective on *Blasted* that represents Kane as critiquing, rather than being a part of, a 1990s playwriting 'cult of the masculine' (Aston 2003: 77–97).
4 See Aleks Sierz's online guide to in-yer-face theatre at http://www.inyerface-theatre.com/main.html. Accessed 10 August 2009.
5 Euripides treated this myth in two plays, of which only the second survives intact. In ancient times these were distinguished

as *Hippolytos Kalyptomenos* (Hippolytus who covered his head), assumed to have been written in the mid-thirties of the fifth century BCE and *Hippolytos Stephanephoros* (Hippolytus who offers a garland), 428 BCE. It is thought that the earlier, lost play was not well received, considered by some morally objectionable in showing an impassioned Phaedra attempting to lead the chaste Hippolytus astray (Coffey and Mayer eds 1990: 5–6).

6 Vellacott claims that Euripides' version represents Hippolytus ironically and that the playwright actually regards Phaedra with considerable sympathy. According to Vellacott, Euripides would have had to keep such attitudes largely implicit: the view that Phaedra might not have been 'a whore deserving the abuse Hippolytus hurled at her' was not one he could have pursued with the Athenian public (Vellacott 1975: 235).

7 Seneca's characterisation of Phaedra differs from that of Euripides in several ways. In the earlier play, Phaedra's love for Hippolytus is visited on her by Aphrodite as punishment against the latter for his refusal to honour her; in Seneca, this desire is explained by the history of 'unnatural' alliances that has marked Phaedra's family for generations. Second, Euripides has the Nurse tell Hippolytus of her mistress's desire (against Phaedra's will); by contrast, Seneca's Phaedra confronts him directly. Finally, Euripides' Phaedra kills herself and leaves the accusation of rape behind her, whilst as mentioned Seneca brings her back onstage to tell Theseus the truth before committing suicide. There is no critical consensus on the implications of these changes: Albert Gérard finds the Latin Phaedra 'thoroughly evil' in knowingly giving in to her desire, for instance, while for Hanna Roisman Seneca's heroine is an essentially good wife who becomes the victim of passion and is arguably less 'manipulative' than her Euripidean counterpart (Gérard 1993: 124; Roisman 2000).

8 Hall's challenge is in no way a conservative resistance towards rewriting *per se*; indeed, she praises Tony Harrison's *Phaedra Britannica* (1977) as one radical retelling that elucidates both archetype and modernity.

9 The silent scene has overtones of the 'reality television' show *Big Brother* (1999–), for which the webcam continually records and makes public the trivial and hitherto private; such shows makes 'celebrities' of all participants, in the process draining this idea of meaning.

10 The motif of the amorous older woman – actual stepmother, or stepmother equivalent – whose love is spurned by a young man is very common, famously illustrated in the Biblical example of Joseph

and Potiphar's wife. Patricia Watson analyses this theme as part of her wider study of the stepmother figure as social 'scapegoat' (Watson 1995).

11 There has been much debate about whether Seneca's drama was originally intended for stage performance. This question was first raised by nineteenth-century commentators, who might, however, been prompted by their distaste for qualities in the plays that did not fit Romantic criteria (Fitch 2000: 1). It is not known whether Seneca's plays were presented on stage during his lifetime but, as Boyle emphasises, 'it is certainly the case that they were and are performable: they have been and are performed' (Boyle ed. 1997: 11).

12 Hrafnhildur Hagalín Guthmundsdóttir is unusual amongst Icelanders in choosing to be referred to professionally by her surname, Hagalín, since it is customary in the country to use the first name both in person and in print.

13 Iceland, for centuries a traditional agricultural society, was modernised with extraordinary speed. The subsistence economy that had previously operated was replaced by an exchange economy, fostered through growing urbanisation and other features of industrialisation. Hávar Sigurjónsson considers that the rapidity of change, and the tension between old and new ways, proved the main source of inspiration for the country's writers (Turner and Nordquist 1982: 102–6; Sigurjónsson 2001).

14 Árnadóttir, a poet, wrote two one-act plays in 1969 that were surreal in content and somewhat experimental in structure. By contrast, *What Is in the Lead Tube?* (1970) by Jakobsdóttir, better known for her novels and short stories, is a more realistic representation of the role and position of women in modern society (Magnússon 1973: 19–20).

15 Freud's position on female sexual development has since been widely criticised, and Freud himself more than once acknowledged that less was known of this than of development in the male. In 1905, he wrote that the sexual life of little girls was 'still veiled in an impenetrable obscurity', and as late as 1926 believed that there remained far less certainty about this: 'But we need not feel ashamed of this distinction; after all, the sexual life of adult women is a "dark continent" for psychology' (Freud 1953: 151; and 1961: 212).

16 Mary Jacobus comments that later twentieth-century psychoanalytic or psychotherapeutic considerations of the so-called Electra complex have tended to fall into two camps: those who have pursued the idea in order to correct Freud's 'lop-sided masculinist account'; and those who have regarded Electra in the light of incest or abuse survivor

(drawing on her treatment by Clytemnestra and Aegisthus) (Jacobus 2002).

17 It will be apparent that the killing of Iphigenia carries little or no weight in this pronouncement. Cassandra, Agamemnon's 'prize' from the Trojan War and an eventual victim of Clytemnestra, is another female casualty of the narrative; her murder passes unmourned, paling into insignificance beside the killing of Agamemnon.

18 In presenting this argument, Cavarero acknowledges her debt to Adrienne Rich's *Of Woman Born* (1977). Rich's work has had very significant impact on Italian feminist thinking, as Braidotti notes in Cavarero 1995: xvi.

19 Aeschylus's *Oresteia* dates from 458 BCE. Euripides' *Electra* is generally dated 422–417 BCE, and it is likely (but remains unproved) that it preceded Sophocles' *Electra*, the latter thought to have been written in the 410s BCE. See Lloyd 2005: 31; Vellacott 1984: 151.

20 Sophocles' Clytemnestra is exceptionally harsh and critical of her daughter, lending credence to Electra's claim that she herself has become an 'alien slave', her mother a 'serpent sucking out my heart's red wine'. The Clytemnestra of Euripides seems to retain some mother instinct, as Electra predicts coming quickly to visit her estranged daughter at the (false) news that Electra has born a child. After the murder, Electra – speaking for herself and Orestes – admits: 'We love you, though we hated you' (Sophocles 1953: 74, 91; Euripides 1963: 148).

21 Steinunn Ólina Thorsteindsdóttir as the Young Actress wore no make-up, and had messy hair roughly pulled back. Her clothes were loose and plain: a man's shirt and trousers, heavy boots. This somewhat masculine appearance signalled her affiliation with the third actor of the play, the Stage Manager; in this role, Atli Rafn Sigurtharson was similarly dressed in casual men's clothes, but with a hint of gender ambiguity introduced by long hair tied back, like hers, into a ponytail. Femininity was more stereotypically displayed by Edda Heithrún Backman as the Older Actress, her hair luxuriantly curled, eyes and lips heavily painted, with open-necked dress and high-heeled shoes.

22 Hagalín notes that the father's strange obsession was not her own invention, but a true story: 'This man really watched all [Ginger Rogers's] films and knew everything about her and loved her so profoundly I was told. I found the story irresistible and therefore decided to use it' (Hagalín 2006).

Many Medeas:
women alone

In 2006, the University of Bristol held a three-day international, interdisciplinary conference titled 'Medea: Mutations and
Permutations of a Myth'. The event sought to reassess theories of
myth and myth-making and to examine transmission, reception
and appropriation of the Medea myth from antiquity to the
present day. The response to the call for papers was overwhelming,
especially, though by no means exclusively, from women academics
and artists; many more offers were made than the sixty-odd
contributions eventually selected.[1] The quantity and range of
material proposed testified to the subject's continuing critical
currency; and whilst the figure of Medea can always be counted
upon to attract particular interest – indeed, major publications
periodically appear on this theme – evidence suggests that classical
myth more generally remains a vibrant focus for feminist analysis
as well as for women's artistic creativity (see for example Clauss
and Johnston eds 1997; Doherty 2001; Garber and Vickers eds
2003; Hall, Macintosh and Taplin eds 2000; Sellers 2001; Zajko
and Leonard eds 2006).[2]

   Re-visions of myth in the contemporary theatre now assume
an extraordinary range of forms and test the boundaries of
performance as forcefully as they interrogate the myths themselves.
Confining the focus of this book more or less exclusively to the
work of playwrights has correspondingly meant marginalising the
great quantity of activity in the field that falls outside that frame.
Re-vision of myth in forms other than scripted drama, staged in
contexts beyond theatre venues, is by no means new – even if late
twentieth- and twenty-first century developments in site-specific
performance, installation, live art and more have shaped source
materials in increasingly startling and unpredictable ways.[3] A

study that sought to address such practices might include, for example, the Croatian-born artist Lena Simic's intimate solo piece *Medea/Mothers' Clothes* (2004), a performance-plus-installation that interrogates motherhood and foreignness by juxtaposing the archetype of an 'anti-mother' against recorded contributions from Liverpool mothers who attended the same local toddler groups as the artist herself.[4] At the other end of the scale, such a study might address the work of the Scottish director, writer and performer Fiona Templeton, whose multilayered poetic epic *The Medead* (2001–6) consists of six parts, presented variously in Lancaster, Cornwall, London, Glasgow and New York, examining the less familiar versions of and episodes in Medea's history; the project as a whole explores different stages of Medea's life, from a child to an elderly woman, with the protagonist's role performed by eight actresses.[5] Broadening its remit beyond practices instigated primarily by women artists, the proposed study might cover *Hotel Medea* (2009), result of a creative collaboration between the Anglo-Brazilian theatre collective Zecora Ura and East London performance lab The Urban Dolls Project. *Hotel Medea* is a visceral, immersive performance trilogy that runs unbroken from dusk for six hours through to dawn; audiences at the British premiere departed on a boat from London's Trinity Buoy Wharf, then to spend a disorientating night at the Arcola Theatre ending with a shared breakfast at 5.30 the next morning. Through this structure, *Hotel Medea* seeks to harness the distinctively compelling qualities of nocturnal experience: night would seem to suit a figure traditionally associated with witchery; but more than this, the night-long frame requires spectators to let go of normal patterns and expectations, leading them instead into a dreamlike state in which they, along with the actors, might come to feel 'together against the rest of the sleeping world' (Field 2009).[6] Such projects variously reframe relations between myth and contemporary experience, above all by exploiting the possibilities implied by different audience positions, whether these be emotional, intellectual, cultural or directly physical: sometimes, as with *Hotel Medea*, the extreme dynamics embedded in myth narratives find correspondence or are even to an extent displaced on to the formal conditions that the performance deliberately creates.

The study outlined above is another book altogether: but as a coda to this one, I want to describe a bridge that could begin to connect myth re-vision in drama with these wider-ranging, formally challenging developments in experimental and alternative performance. To do this I draw on one further Medea and through its example consider opportunities for myth re-vision peculiar to self-authored and especially solo artistic practice.

July 2005, Aberystwyth. The German writer-actress Gilla Cremer presents *m.e.d.e.a.*, the last part in her trilogy of solo shows reflecting on continuities and ruptures in German social history through the last century.[7] The first and second are set in 1938 and 1968 respectively, a thirty-year gap repeated with *m.e.d.e.a.*, located at the end of the millennium. Its protagonist Renate, a polished, highly educated woman in her late forties, or perhaps early fifties, learns from the man she has lived with unwed for twenty years – and with whom she has two sons – that he has been having a longstanding affair and is now leaving her to marry the 'other woman'. Swept away at a stroke are the values she had thought they still shared. Ostensibly liberated by the sexual revolution, the couple had embarked upon a 'lasting sexual relationship' intended to stand as a consensual, mutually pleasurable tie resolvedly unlike the restricting legal 'bond' their parents' generation firmly endorsed (Reich 1969: 119; Herzog 2005: 118). The union of Renate and her partner, without religious or legal sanction, is made broadly analogous to the illegitimate, unrecognised 'marriage' of Jason and Medea. Just as Jason seeks to consolidate his legacy through an authorised alliance, Cremer's modern counterpart reasserts his virility through a liaison with a younger woman and simultaneously 'plays it safe' by framing their relations with a conservative wedding: his choice accurately reflects the millennial climate in Germany, which was marked by a revived desire for traditional marriages and families (Cremer 2005a; Purvis 2006).[8] He is, he says, still 'very fond' of Renate. He hopes that they will arrive at a constructive solution for the future, for the sake of the children: 'maybe like Thomas and Barbara, or like John and Kathy, or Tina and Frederik ...', the comically lengthening list demonstrating that in their circle, as for Euripides' Medea, 'the thing is common' (Euripides 1963: 22). Renate's world is in pieces: yet she must cope with it since anything other than coping is considered 'uncivilised'. Cremer's *m.e.d.e.a.* appropriates a figure from myth as the channel through which her protagonist is able to give vent to emotions whose expression is otherwise disallowed: explosive rage; unattractive self-pity; and profound anxiety at the prospect of growing old alone. The prohibition against inhabiting these feelings directly – perhaps additionally, the very difficulty of doing so – is underlined by the opening sequence of the piece, which begins with weeping that implicitly references the misery which leaves Euripides' Medea 'collapsed in agony, / Dissolving the long hours in tears' (Euripides 1963: 18). Here, however, the protagonist's mounting sobs are undercut by her own dispassionate commentary:

> When I have to cry, it usually starts with a tickling behind my nose and in the back of my throat. Then I feel a pressure behind my eyes. My lips start to quiver. The breath goes deeper. My eyebrows lower. My face becomes a grimace. The voice goes with the breath. My stomach contracts, relaxes, contracts. The voice gets louder. The shoulders start shaking, the whole body starts shaking ... yes, something like that. (Cremer 2000)

Through face and body Cremer accurately mimics the phases she describes and in between each returns to an actorly 'neutral state'. Control and loss of control are juxtaposed, to comic effect; this in turn jars sharply with the emotional experience directly described. The fragmented and ironic mode of playing typifies the piece as a whole and signals that, despite its title, spectators will be offered the Medea archetype strictly in quotation marks.

For today's audiences, the (post)dramatic language *m.e.d.e.a.* employs may seem one that has become increasingly recognisable: parodic, knowing and coolly disruptive of conventional expectations. But, at the same time, the now familiar 'aesthetics of detachment' is itself brought under scrutiny. The impression of alienation established by these first moments is exaggerated to the point that spectators are forced to ask what it is in 'Medea' that 'Renate' should withstand so determinedly and what such resistance might signal about the contemporary culture that formed her. Contrast this with Franca Rame's explosive and passionate Medea, born in the midst of mid-1970s feminist protest, begged by a comically conformist and increasingly nervous Chorus to 'calm down' in fear of the consequences if she does not; at the century's end, Cremer's reimagined heroine appears emotionally numb, ineffectual in and strangely distanced from her life's crisis. Cremer's title for the piece likewise speaks of rupture and disengagement, drawing attention to gaps between ancient myth and classical drama, and modern perceptions of these. The lower case 'm' undercuts tragic status: it is precisely an acknowledgement and acceptance of littleness. The inserted full stops carve the name into fragments, metaphorically suggesting the way in which myths today are filtered, dispersed and transformed through a plurality of texts and practices. That quality of diffusion is very evident in *m.e.d.e.a.*, a self-consciously intertextual work which articulates a complex and troubled relationship to an archetype through a quantity of borrowings from drama, poetry and prose, social history, psychology and the contemporary German press.[9] Through these diverse routes 'Medea' forces herself/selves in, to disturb but not actively direct present experience. This kind of structure for myth rewriting, one that collates multiple narratives – disconnected, partial, frequently in tension with one another – through which the writer/performer negotiates what is, in part, a personal journey, has been variously encountered in this book, perhaps most explicitly in the exploratory methods of Serena Sartori and Renata Coluccini. All projects of adaptation embody a layering of sorts, but I have argued that the reworking of myth narratives in contemporary theatre carries with it a unique weight and order of textual baggage. The title of *m.e.d.e.a.* crystallises the complexities inherent in this practice for its creators and for spectators also: our remoteness, in more than one sense of the word; a distinctive variety of awkwardness in approaching narratives whose extremes can simultaneously excite and embarrass; the apprehension that accompanies the attempt to claim space in already densely populated territory.

Cremer's *m.e.d.e.a.* is also, as emphasised, a solo work. The decision to perform alone manifestly shapes articulation of the material in significant ways, as must be true for all solo theatre. When making a piece for just one actor, much of that which is usually associated with the theatrical event must be discarded or at least modified. This in turn makes space, potentially, for dramaturgical experimentation and innovation. The specific possibilities that solo performance suggests for myth re-vision are intriguing and exciting, not least in that deciding what *not* to include when recasting a subject can in itself be an expression of resistance. I have touched on solo stagings in Chapter 2 through analysis of *The Same Old Story* and *Medea*, but otherwise the one-woman theatres of Rame and Cremer have little in common. The monologues of Fo and Rame exploit the latter's ability to switch, with great skill, between one sharply defined role and another. Their *Medea* has a single protagonist, with oppositional Chorus members sketched in as satirical cameos; the struggle the piece dramatises is on the surface relatively unambiguous, yet the representation of all roles through the medium of one performer permits the more complex interpretation that progressive and conservative forces may be located within one 'self'. In stylistic contrast, *m.e.d.e.a.* frequently leaves its spectators unsure whom exactly they are watching. At any given moment, the middle-aged woman before us could 'stand for' Renate, Medea, Cremer or all three: it is a constructive uncertainty that encourages reverberation of echoes whilst evading the rigidity of 'parallels'. We interpret Cremer, on stage, above all as an actress doing a job of work. Her relationship to the playing space reinforces that perception: she moves the furniture, operates her own lights; her actions are charged at times with the emotional energy of a scene but elsewhere seem essentially to be the fulfilment of necessary tasks. Solo presentation automatically directs an audience's attention to the larger job of performance and the entirety of an actor's work. Since *m.e.d.e.a.* demands complex stage management, the effort involved becomes particularly conspicuous. We recognise the sheer labour required to produce this artwork. This in consequence has the unexpected effect of lending new poignancy to the theme of the woman who finds herself unexpectedly alone.

It might be considered on one level perverse to connect the archetypal figure of the abandoned female with the form of one-woman theatre. Women's solo performance is usually received, justifiably, as a positive and self-empowering practice signalling the confidence, and indeed the right, to occupy centre stage unsupported: 'abandoned', then, only in the sense of acting without constraints. In *m.e.d.e.a.*, however, the operation of one-woman theatre becomes distinctly double-edged. The dramatic content is both powerful and playful, fundamentally 'liberating' by implication and in effect. On the other hand, the physical job of performance partly undercuts this. When Cremer manoeuvres her set, this comes to appear at times too laborious, as if the table were too heavy or the scene changes too frequent: 'managing' by herself begins to look a little like drudgery. In correspondence, Cremer explains that she generally makes solo work: 'I must, because I need to keep all the profits! I have to support my children' (Cremer 2005a). Through the matter and the medium, *m.e.d.e.a.* provokes spectators to reflect upon the distinctive tensions of 'aloneness', both voluntary and enforced. It is ironic perhaps that a re-vision of the Medea narrative, a myth widely interpreted as an attack on 'family values', should be so decisively structured by the sense of maternal responsibility.

Traditional theatre does not usually encourage audiences to speculate on correspondences between the performer 'herself' – in the sense of an existence beyond and apart from the theatre – and the role she represents. The solo form substantially blurs this distinction, whether or not the material of the piece is framed as autobiographical. Where the performer is also the writer, boundaries may be disturbed still further. Cremer's *m.e.d.e.a.* is part-scripted, part-improvised, part-devised, part-borrowed: the artist is conduit for multiple voices in this piece as much as she is its author and consciously exploits the narrative and performative instabilities that result. I have argued throughout this book that practices of myth re-vision require playwrights and theatre-makers to look in many directions at once: towards present experience, directly personal or of the culture, to find the resonances that would make a narrative worth retelling now; and away from the immediate, in a gesture that refuses the narrowness of the purely local or time-bound and looks instead for comparison and connection. This distinctive dynamic of inward/outward is strikingly exposed by self-authored solo performance and in turn makes the form highly productive as a vehicle for the interrogation and reassessment of myth narratives from diverse, yet evidently interdependent, perspectives.

Cremer's example highlights the way in which numerous and frequently competing threads may be interwoven in performance: socio-cultural, political, psychological, mythical, economic, theatrical. In common with very many contemporary theatre-makers, Cremer constructs and describes her artistic practice in plural: she is a writer, performer, director, her own stage manager and technician, as well as, not inconsequentially, a mother. Self-supporting, integrated or multilayered practices of this kind have become widespread, prompted partly by financial pressures but also by the desire to challenge traditional hierarchies of creative production; hence in *m.e.d.e.a.* the laborious activity of scene shifting becomes at times the primary focus of an audience's attention. Equally, such plurality can be a way of underlining interconnectedness between the various spheres of daily life. I have mentioned Simic's *Medea/Mothers' Clothes*, which found the material for performance through the experience of Simic (necessarily) attending toddler groups. Simic continues to make work as a solo artist but also in association with her husband, the filmmaker Gary Anderson. In 2010 Simic's website lists, amongst other projects, 'The Institute for the Art and Practice of Dissent at Home', an 'artist-activist initiative' run jointly with Anderson 'from the spare bedroom of our council house in Everton, Liverpool'. Together the couple seek to interrogate and unsettle naturalised conceptions of the family, with the self-conscious (but also unavoidable) participation of their three children: not as source for a work of art but *already as* creative practice. In very different ways, the examples of Cremer and Simic illustrate how women artists are critically rethinking cultural spaces of all kinds, observing the frayed edges between them as closely as the activities at the centre. Myths and myth narratives continue to run through such work. Sometimes Medea comes with a capital M; elsewhere, a little m; or no m at all.

Notes

1 See the conference website, at www.bristol.ac.uk/arts/birtha/themes/ medea_conference.html. Accessed 3 March 2008.

2 The intersection of myth and gender continues to be a popular conference focus. 'American Women and Classical Myths' was held at the University of Maryland in 1999; 'Myths and Mythmaking' was the topic of the Women in German Studies (WIGS) Millennium Conference in 2000.

3 The first issue of *The Open Page*, journal of the international women's theatre network Magdalena, was exclusively devoted to interrelationships between women, theatre and myth. Many contributors were practitioners – Gerd Christiansen, Geddy Aniksdal and Cristina Castrillo among others - writing about their own performance re-visions and creative processes of the 1980s and 1990s; all are artists operating outside traditions of dramatic theatre. *Theatre, Women, Myth. The Open Page*, 1. January 1996. Cardiff: The Magdalena Project.

4 For more information about this project, see www.lenasimic.org/index.html. Accessed September 7 2010.

5 For a fuller description of Templeton's *The Medead*, see www.fionatempleton.org. Accessed 7 September 2010.

6 For more information about this piece, see www.medea.tv/. Accessed 7 September 2010.

7 Gilla Cremer is a writer, actress and producer who works primarily as solo artist with her company Theater Unikate (Unique Theatre). The performance I describe was presented at the 2005 conference 'The Articulate Practitioner: Articulating Practice', at Aberystwyth University. Cremer's *m.e.d.e.a.* was first staged in 2000 at the Kammerspiele in Hamburg and has since toured extensively at home and overseas. The trilogy begins with *The Bitch of Buchenwald* (1995), set in 1938; the play is a study of Ilse Köhler, the woman who became the wife of the Nazi concentration camp commander Karl Koch and became notorious in her own right for sadistic treatment of prisoners. Cremer followed this with *Morrison Hotel* (1997), located amidst the turmoil of the 1968 student protests and New Left uprising, documenting the radical and excessive lives, and eventual suicides, of two men: Jim Morrison, lead singer of the legendary rock band The Doors, and Cremer's own older brother, Tom Cremer. *m.e.d.e.a.* is unpublished; the piece was originally written and performed in German and quotations included in this book are from Cremer's own English translation, which she was kind enough to give me.

8 Cremer explained to me that *m.e.d.e.a.* had been a way to explore matters with which she had become increasingly preoccupied: 'Do we go back to the values of our parents? Why do people, who swore in the 60s "to never ever marry", marry nowadays? And even in white dresses? These were part of my questions. What happened to our dreams, our ideals from the 60s?' (Cremer 2005a).

9 The play uses material from Euripides' *Medea*, Hans Henny Jahnn's *Medea* (1926) and Heiner Müller's *Medeamaterial* (1981). In addition, Cremer's piece quotes from numerous texts tangentially related to the Medea narrative, including Sylvia Plath's *Three Women: A Monologue for Three Voices*, a radio work set in a maternity ward (written and broadcast in 1962), Françoise Chandernagor's novel *La Première épouse* ('The First Wife', 1998) and Michel Houellebecq's *Les particules élémentaires* ('The Elementary Particles', also 1998). Cremer's trilogy is situated within a framework of dramatically changing cultural values: *m.e.d.e.a.* employs selections that range historically from Horst Becker's profoundly conservative tract *Die Familie* (1935), through Wilhelm Reich's radical critique of marriage

in *Die sexuelle Revolution* (published originally in the mid-1930s, but widely circulated in Germany in the late 1960s), to a 2000 edition of the German newspaper *Die Zeit* bemoaning the increasing numbers of women choosing 'selfishly' to remain childless.

References

Aercke, Kristiaan ed. (1994) *Women Writing in Dutch*. New York and London: Garland Publishing.

Aeschylus (1959) *The Oresteian Trilogy*. Ed. and trans. Philip Vellacott. Harmondsworth: Penguin.

Allen, Sue and Harne, Lynne (1988) 'Lesbian Mothers: The Fight for Child Custody.' Eds Bob Cant and Susan Hemmings *Radical Records: Thirty Years of Lesbian and Gay History, 1957–1987*. London: Routledge. 181–94.

Anderlini-D'Onofrio, Serena (2000) 'From *The Lady Is to Be Disposed Of* to *An Open Couple*: Franca Rame and Dario Fo's Theater Partnership.' Ed. Valeri. 183–204.

Anderson, Bonnie and Zinsser, Judith (1990) *A History of Their Own: Women in Europe from Prehistory to the Present*. Vol. 2. London: Penguin.

Aneja, Anu (1999) 'The Medusa's Slip: Hélène Cixous and the Underpinnings of *Écriture Féminine*.' Eds Lee Jacobus and Regina Barreca (1999) *Hélène Cixous: Critical Impressions*. Amsterdam: Overseas Publishers Association: Gordon and Breach. 57–74.

Anouilh, Jean (1997) *Plays: Vol. 2*. Trans. Jeremy Sams and Peter Meyer. London: Methuen.

Anouilh, Jean (1960) *Antigone*. Trans. Lewis Galantiere. London: Eyre Methuen.

Antonelli, Judith (1997) 'Beyond Nostalgia: Rethinking the Goddess.' *On the Issues: The Progressive Woman's Quarterly*. 6: 3. www.ontheis-suesmagazine.com/su97goddess.html.

Artaud, Antonin (1977) *The Theatre and Its Double*. London: John Calder.

Aston, Elaine (2003) *Feminist Views on the English Stage: Women Playwrights, 1990–2000*. Cambridge and New York: Cambridge University Press.

Aston, Elaine (1995) 'Daniels in the Lion's Den: Sarah Daniels and the British Backlash.' *Theatre Journal* 47. 393–403.

Atwood, Margaret (2005) *Curious Pursuits: Occasional Writing.* London: Virago.

Bachofen, John Jacob (1992) *Myth, Religion and Mother Right: Selected Writings by J. J. Bachofen.* Trans. Ralph Manheim. Princeton: Princeton University Press.

Bakhtin, Mikhail (1981) *The Dialogic Imagination: Four Essays.* Ed. Michael Holquist. Trans. Caryl Emerson and Michael Holquist. Austin, Texas: University of Texas Press.

Bakhtin, Mikhail (1968) *Rabelais and His world.* Trans. Helene Iswolsky. Cambridge Massachusatts, and London: MIT Press.

Barber, John (1986) 'Lacking a Certain Courage.' Review of *Neaptide. Daily Telegraph*, 3 July.

Barbin, Herculine (1980) *Herculine Barbin: Being the Recently Discovered Memoirs of a Nineteenth Century French Hermaphrodite.* Trans. Richard McDougall. Intro. Michel Foucault. Brighton: Harvester Press.

Barnett, David (2008) 'When is a Play Not a Drama? Two Examples of Postdramatic Theatre Texts.' *New Theatre Quarterly* 24: 1. 14–23.

Barr, Alan ed. (2001) *Modern Women Playwrights of Europe.* Oxford and New York: Oxford University Press.

Barthes, Roland (1977) *Image Music Text.* London: Fontana.

Barthes, Roland (1973) *Mythologies.* London: Paladin.

Barton, Alana (2005) *Fragile Moralities and Dangerous Sexualities: Two Centuries of Semi-Penal Institutionalisation for Women.* Aldershot: Aldgate

Bascom, William (1965) 'The Forms of Folklore: Prose Narratives.' Ed. Alan Dundes (1984) *Sacred Narrative: Readings in the Theory of Myth.* Berkeley: University of California Press. 5–29.

Bassett, Kate (2004) Review of *By the Bog of Cats. The Independent*, 5 December.

Bassett, Kate (1996) 'Bloodbath at the Court of Copulation.' *The Times*, 22 May.

Bassnett, Susan (1992) *Magdalena: Women's International Experimental Theatre.* Oxford: Berg.

Bassnett, Susan (1986) *Feminist Experiences: The Women's Movement in Four Cultures.* London: Allen and Unwin.

Bayley, Clare (1995) 'A Very Angry Young Woman.' Interview with Sarah Kane. *The Independent*, 23 January.

Beccalli, Bianca (1994) 'The Modern Women's Movement in Italy.' *New Left Review* 204. 86–112.

Bell, Robert (1991) *Women of Classical Mythology.* Oxford: Oxford University Press.

Bell, Vikki (1999) *Feminist Imagination: Genealogies in Feminist Theory.* London: Sage.

Belli, Angela (1969) *Ancient Greek Myths and Modern Drama*. New York: New York University Press.

Billington, Michael (2004) 'The Horror, the Horror.' *The Guardian*, 22 December.

Billington, Michael (1996) 'Classic Case of Love and Guts.' Review of *Phaedra's Love*. *The Guardian*, 21 May.

Billington, Michael (1986) Review of *Neaptide*. *The Guardian*, 5 July.

Binchy, Maeve, Bannister, Ivy *et al*. (1992) *Ride On, Rapunzel: Fairy Tales for Feminists*. Dublin: Attic Press.

Blom, J.C.H. (1995) 'Suffering as a Warning: The Netherlands and the Legacy of War.' *Canadian Journal of Netherlandic Studies* 16: 2. 64–8.

Bly, Robert (1992) *Iron John*. London: Vintage.

Blyth, Ian and Sellers, Susan (2004) *Hélène Cixous: Live Theory*. New York and London: Continuum.

Bode, Christoph (1999) '"Variety of image, variety of language, variety of viewpoint": An Interview with Maureen Duffy.' Eds Rudolf Freiburg and Jan Schnitker. *'Do you consider yourself a postmodern author?' Interviews with Contemporary English Writers*. Münster: LIT Verlag. 89–100.

Bono, Paola and Kemp, Sandra eds (1991) *Italian Feminist Thought: A Reader*. London: Basil Blackwell.

Bowie, Malcolm (1991) *Lacan*. London: Fontana.

Boyle, A.J. (1997) *Tragic Seneca: An Essay in the Theatrical Tradition*. London and New York: Routledge.

Bradby, David and Sparks, Annie (1997) *Mise en Scène: French Theatre Now*. London: Methuen.

Brater, Enoch ed. (1989) *Feminine Focus: The New Women Playwrights*. New York: Oxford University Press.

Breedt Bruyn, Martje (1992) 'Confrontation with the Naked Self: Interviews with Hella Haasse and Monika Van Paemel.' Trans. Greta Kilburn. Ed. Lucie Vermij. *Women Writers from the Netherlands and Flanders*. Amsterdam: International Feminist Book Fair Press. 10–14.

Brown, Sarah Annes (2005) *Ovid: Myth and Metamorphosis*. London: Bristol Classical Press.

Bryant-Bertail, Sarah (1999) '*Écriture Corporelle* and the Body Politic: *Les Atrides*.' Ed. David Williams. *Collaborative Theatre: The Théâtre du Soleil Sourcebook*. London and New York: Routledge. 179–85.

Butler, Judith (1990) *Gender Trouble: Feminism and the Subversion of Identity*. New York: Routledge.

Campbell, Joseph (1991) *Creative Mythology: The Masks of God*. Harmondsworth: Arkana.

Canning, Charlotte (1999) 'The Critic as Playwright: Performing Hélène Cixous' *Le Nom d'Oedipe*.' Eds Lee Jacobus and Regina Barreca.

Hélène Cixous: Critical Impressions. Amsterdam: Gordon and Breach. 305–25.

Carlson, Marvin (2001) *The Haunted Stage: The Theatre as Memory Machine*. Ann Arbor: University of Michigan Press.

Carlson, Susan (1993) 'Issues of Identity, Nationality, and Performance: The Reception of Two Plays by Timberlake Wertenbaker.' *New Theatre Quarterly* 35. 269–74.

Carr, Marina (1999) *Plays: One*. London: Faber and Faber.

Carter, Angela (1998) *Shaking a Leg: Collected Journalism and Writings*. London: Vintage.

Carter, Angela ed. (1991) *The Virago Book of Fairy Tales*. London: Virago.

Case, Sue-Ellen (1988) *Feminism and Theatre*. London: Macmillan.

Cavallaro, Daniela (2002) 'Penelope: Variations on a Theme.' *Italian Quarterly* 39: 153–4. 31–8.

Cavarero, Adriana (1995) *In Spite of Plato: A Feminist Rewriting of Ancient Philosophy*. Trans. Serena Anderlini-D'Onofrio and Áine O'Healy. Cambridge and Oxford: Polity Press.

Cavarero, Adriana (1993) 'Towards a Theory of Sexual Difference.' Trans. Giuliana de Novellis. Eds Kemp and Bono. 189–221.

Cavarero, Adriana (1986) 'The Need for a Sexed Thought.' Eds Bono and Kemp (1991). 181–5.

Chesler, Phyllis (1997) *Women and Madness*. New York and London: Four Walls Eight Windows.

Churchill, Caryl and Lan, David (1986) *A Mouthful of Birds*. London: Methuen.

Cixous, Hélène (2004) *The Perjured City, or The Awakening of the Furies*. Trans. Bernadette Fort. Ed. Eric Prenowitz. *Selected Plays of Hélène Cixous*. London and New York: Routledge. 89–190.

Cixous, Hélène (1999) 'The Communion of Suffering.' Ed. David Williams. *Collaborative Theatre: The Théâtre du Soleil Sourcebook*. London and New York: Routledge. 195–8.

Cixous, Hélène (1995a) 'The Place of Crime, the Place of Pardon.' Trans. Eric Prenowitz. Ed. Richard Drain. *Twentieth Century Theatre: A Sourcebook*. London: Routledge. 340–4.

Cixous, Hélène (1995b) 'Aller à la mer.' Trans. Eric Prenowitz. Ed. Richard Drain. *Twentieth Century Theatre: A Sourcebook*. London: Routledge. 133–5.

Cixous, Hélène (1994) *The Name of Oedipus: Song of the Forbidden Body*. Trans. and eds Christine Makward and Judith Miller. *Plays by French and Francophone Women*. Ann Arbor: University of Michigan Press. 253–326.

Cixous, Hélène (1986) 'Sorties: Out and Out: Attacks/Ways Out/Forays.' Hélène Cixous and Catherine Clément. *The Newly Born Woman*. Trans. Betsy Wing. Manchester: Manchester University Press. 63–134.

Cixous, Hélène (1976) 'The Laugh of the Medusa.' Trans. Keith Cohen and Paula Cohen. *Signs* 1: 4. 875–93.

Cixous, Hélène (1974) 'The Character of "Character."' Trans. Keith Cohen. *New Literary History* 5: 2. 383–402.

Clarke, Simon (1972) *Foundations of Structuralism: A Critique of Lévi-Strauss and the Structuralist Movement*. Brighton: Harvester.

Clauss, James J. and Johnston, Sarah Iles eds (1997) *Medea: Essays on Medea in Myth, Literature, Philosophy and Art*. Princeton: Princeton University Press.

Coffey, Michael and Mayer, Roland eds (1990) *Phaedra*. Cambridge: Cambridge University Press.

Coluccini, Renata (2006) Personal correspondence with the author. 20 November.

Cottino-Jones, Marga (2000) 'The Transgressive Voice of a *Resisting Woman*.' Ed. Valeri. 8–56.

Coupe, Laurence (1997) *Myth*. London: Routledge.

Cousin, Geraldine (1988) 'The Common Imagination and the Individual Voice'. Interview with Caryl Churchill. *New Theatre Quarterly* 4: 13. 3–16.

Coveney, Michael (1986) Review of *Neaptide*. *The Financial Times*, 3 July.

Cremer, Gilla (2005a) Personal correspondence with the author. 3 December.

Cremer, Gilla (2005b) *m.e.d.e.a.* publicity leaflet. Cremer and Theater Unikate.

Cremer, Gilla (2000) *m.e.d.e.a.* Unpublished manuscript.

Csapo, Eric (2005) *Theories of Mythology*. Oxford: Blackwell.

Cutter, Martha J. (2000) 'Philomela Speaks: Alice Walker's Revisioning of Rape Archetypes in *The Color Purple*. *MELUS* 25: 3–4. 161–80.

Daly, Mary (1991) *Gyn/Ecology*. London: The Women's Press.

Daly, Mary and Caputi, Jane (1988) *Websters' First New Intergalactic Wickedary of the English Language*. London: The Women's Press.

Daniels, Sarah (1991) *Plays One*. London: Methuen.

D'Arcangeli, Luciana (2000) 'Franca Rame "Giullaressa"'. Ed. Valeri. 157–74.

Davis, Jill ed. (1987) *Lesbian Plays*. London: Methuen.

De Beauvoir, Simone (1960) *The Second Sex*. Trans. H.M. Parshley. London: Four Square.

De Gay, Jane (2003) 'Seizing Speech and Playing with Fire: Greek Mythological Heroines and International Women's Performance.' Eds Goodman and De Gay (2003). 11–36.

De Jongh, Nicholas (2004) Review of *By the Bog of Cats*. *The Evening Standard*, 2 December.

De Jongh, Nicholas (1989) Review of *The Love of the Nightingale*. *The Guardian*, 23 August.

Deleuze, Gilles and Guattari, Félix (1984) *Anti-Oedipus: Capitalism and Schizophrenia*. Trans. Robert Hurley, Mark Seem and Helen Lane. London: Athlone Press.

Déprats, Jean-Michel (1999) 'Shakespeare Is Not Our Contemporary: An Interview with Ariane Mnouchkine.' Ed. David Williams (1999) *Collaborative Theatre: The Théâtre du Soleil Sourcebook*. London and New York: Routledge. 93–8.

Diamond, Elin (1992) '(In)Visible Bodies in Churchill's Theater.' Ed. Lynda Hart. *Making a Spectacle: Feminist Essays on Contemporary Women's Theatre*. Ann Arbor: University of Michigan Press. 259–81.

Diamond, Irene and Orenstein, Gloria Feman eds (1990) *Reweaving the World: The Emergence of Ecofeminism*. San Francisco: Sierra Club Books.

Dickinson, Hugh (1969) *Myth on the Modern Stage*. Urbana: University of Illinois Press.

Dithmer, Monna (2001) 'New Nordic Drama – On Its Way Out of the Drawing Room?' Transcript of the first address to the *Scandinavia On Stage* conference, New York 19 April 2001. www.nytheatre-wire.com/dithmer.htm. Accessed 13 November 2009.

Dobson, Julia (2002) *Hélène Cixous and the Theatre: The Scene of Writing*. Oxford: Peter Lang.

Doherty, Lillian E. (2001) *Gender and the Interpretation of Classical Myth*. London: Duckworth.

Doniger, Wendy (1998) *The Implied Spider: Politics and Theology in Myth*. New York: Columbia University Press.

Downing, Christine ed. (1994) *The Long Journey Home: Re-Visioning the Myth of Demeter and Persephone for Our Time*. Boston: Shambhala.

Duffy, Maureen (2001) *England: The Making of a Myth from Stonehenge to Albert Square*. London: Fourth Estate.

Duffy, Maureen (1969) *Rites*. Ed. Michelene Wandor. *Plays by Women: Vol. 2*. London: Methuen. 11–28.

Dundes, Alan ed. (1984) *Sacred Narrative: Readings in the Theory of Myth*. Berkeley: University of California Press.

Dymkowksi, Christine (1997) 'Breaking the Rules: The Plays of Sarah Daniels.' Eds Wolfgang Lippke and Nicole Boireau. *Beyond Taboos: Contemporary Theatre Review* 5: 1. 63–75.

Eliade, Mircea (1976) 'Myths and Mythical Thought.' Ed. Alexander Eliot (1990) *The Universal Myths*. New York and London: Meridian. 14–40.

Eliot, Alexander (1990) *The Universal Myths*. New York and London: Meridian.

Engel, Stephen (2001) *The Unfinished Revolution: Social Movement Theory and the Gay and Lesbian Movement*. Cambridge: Cambridge University Press.

Ettore, E.M. (1980) *Lesbians, Women and Society*. London: Routledge and Kegan Paul.

Euripides (1998) *Plays: One*. Ed. and trans. J. Michael Walton. London: Methuen.

Euripides (1981) *Ten Plays by Euripides*. Trans. Moses Hadas and John McLean. Toronto and New York: Bantam.

Euripides (1974a) *Hippolytus*. Trans. Robert Bagg. London: Oxford University Press.

Euripides (1974b) *Alcestis and Other Plays*. Trans. Philip Vellacott. London: Penguin.

Euripides (1963) *Medea and Other Plays*. Trans. Philip Vellacott. London: Penguin.

Euripides (1954) *The Bacchae and Other Plays*. Trans. and ed. Philip Vellacott. Harmondsworth: Penguin.

Farrell, Joseph (2001) *Dario Fo & Franca Rame: Harlequins of the Revolution*. London: Methuen.

Farrell, Joseph (2000) 'Franca Rame's Nose, or What if They Had Never Met?' Ed. Valeri. 205–19.

Felski, Rita (2003) *Literature after Feminism*. Chicago and London: Chicago University Press.

Field, Andy (2009) 'Up all night: the intimacy of *Hotel Medea*.' *Guardian* Theatre Blog. 6 February. www.guardian.co.uk/stage/theatreblog/2009/feb/06/zecora-ura-hotel-medea-arcola. Accessed 10 September 2010.

Fitch, John (2000) 'Playing Seneca?'. Ed. George Harrison. *Seneca in Performance*. London: Duckworth. 1–12.

Foley, Helen (2004) 'Bad Women: Gender Politics in Late Twentieth-Century Performance and Revision of Greek Tragedy.' Eds Edith Hall, Fiona Macintosh and Amanda Wrigley. 77–111.

Fort, Bernadette (1997) 'Theater, History, Ethics: An Interview with Hélène Cixous on *The Perjured City, or the Awakening of the Furies*.' *New Literary History* 28: 3. 425–56.

Foucault, Michel (2001) *Fearless Speech*. Ed. Joseph Pearson. Los Angeles: Semiotext(e).

Frazer, James George (1922) *The Golden Bough: A Study in Magic and Religion*. Abridged edition. London: Macmillan.

Freeman, Sandra (1998) 'Bisexuality in Cixous's *Le Nom d'Oedipe*.' *Theatre Research International* 23: 3. 242–48.

Freeman, Sara (2008) 'Group Tragedy and Diaspora: New and Old Histories of Exile and Family in Timberlake Wertenbaker's *Hecuba* and *Credible Witness*.' Eds Sara Freeman and Maya Roth. *International Dramaturgy: Translation and Transformations in the Theatre of Timberlake Wertenbaker*. Brussels: Peter Lang. 61–76.

Freud, Sigmund (1964) *The Standard Edition of the Complete Psychological Works of Sigmund Freud*. Vol. 23 (1937–39). *Moses and*

Monotheism; An Outline of Psychoanalysis; and Other Works. Trans. and ed. James Strachey. London: Hogarth Press.

Freud, Sigmund (1961) *The Standard Edition of the Complete Psychological Works of Sigmund Freud. Vol. 19 (1923–25). The Ego and the Id; and Other Works.* Trans. and ed. James Strachey. London: Hogarth Press.

Freud, Sigmund (1959) *The Standard Edition of the Complete Psychological Works of Sigmund Freud. Vol. 20 (1925–26). An Autobiographical Study; Inhibitions, Symptoms and Anxiety; The Question of Lay Analysis; and Other Works.* Trans. and ed. James Strachey. London: Hogarth Press.

Freud, Sigmund (1958) *The Standard Edition of the Complete Psychological Works of Sigmund Freud. Vols. 4 and 5 (1900). The Interpretation of Dreams.* Trans. and ed. James Strachey. London: Hogarth Press.

Freud, Sigmund (1953) *The Standard Edition of the Complete Psychological Works of Sigmund Freud. Vol. 7 (1901–05). Three Essays on Sexuality and Other Writings.* Trans. and ed. James Strachey. London: Hogarth Press.

Friedan, Betty (1965) *The Feminine Mystique.* Harmondsworth: Penguin.

Furlong, Ray (2005) 'Tradition Frustrates German Women.' 11 November 2005. http://news.bbc.co.uk/1/hi/world/europe/4428800.stm. Accessed 16 November 2009.

Gadon, Elinor (1990) *The Once and Future Goddess.* New York: HarperCollins.

Gamble, Sarah ed. (2001) *The Routledge Companion to Feminism and Postfeminism.* London: Routledge.

Garber, Marjorie and Vickers, Nancy eds (2003) *The Medusa Reader.* London and New York: Routledge.

Gardner, Lyn (2005) Review of *Phaedra's Love* at Bristol Old Vic. *The Guardian*, 31 October.

Gash, Anthony (1993) 'Carnival and the Poetics of Reversal.' Ed. Julian Hilton. *New Directions in Theatre.* Basingstoke: Macmillan. 87–119.

Geertz, Clifford (1993) *The Interpretation of Cultures.* New York: Basic Books.

Gérard, Albert (1993) *The Phaedra Syndrome: Of Shame and Guilt in Drama.* Amsterdam: Rodopi.

Godiwala, Dimple (2003) *Breaking the Bounds: British Feminist Dramatists Writing in the Mainstream since c. 1980.* New York: Peter Lang.

Goodman, Lizbeth ed. (2000) *Mythic Women/Real Women: Plays and Performance Pieces by Women.* London: Faber and Faber.

Goodman, Lizbeth (1993) *Contemporary Feminist Theatres: To Each Her Own.* London: Routledge.

Goodman, Lizbeth and De Gay, Jane eds (2003) *Languages of Theatre Shaped by Women.* Bristol: Intellect.

Goodman, Lizbeth and De Gay, Jane eds (1996) *Feminist Stages: Interviews with Women in Contemporary British Theatre*. Amsterdam: Harwood Academic Publishers.

Gore, Keith (1989) Review of *The Love of the Nightingale*. *The Times Literary Supplement*, 18–24 November.

Göttner-Abendroth, Heide (1995) *The Goddess and Her Heros*. Trans. Carol Anthony. Stow, Massachusetts: Anthony Publishing.

Graves, Robert (1961a) *Greek Myths*. London: Cassell.

Graves, Robert (1961b) *The White Goddess: A Historical Grammar of Poetic Myth*. London: Faber.

Green, Amy S. (1994) *The Revisionist Stage: American Directors Reinvent the Classics*. Cambridge and New York: Cambridge University Press.

Griffin, Gabriele (2000) 'Violence, Abuse, and Gender Relations in the Plays of Sarah Daniels.' Eds Elaine Aston and Janelle Reinelt (2000) *The Cambridge Companion to Modern British Women Playwrights*. Cambridge: Cambridge University Press. 194–211.

Griffiths, Trevor (1993) 'Waving Not Drowning: The Mainstream, 1979–88.' Eds Trevor Griffiths and Margaret Llewellyn-Jones (1993) *British and Irish Women Dramatists Since 1958*. Buckingham: Open University Press. 47–76.

Grosz, Elizabeth (1990) *Jacques Lacan: A Feminist Introduction*. London and New York: Routledge.

Haasse, Hella (1997) *A Thread in the Dark*. Ed. Cheryl Robson. *A Touch of the Dutch: Plays by Women*. Amsterdam and London: Nederland Theater Institut and Aurora Metro Press. 95–150.

Hagalín, Hrafnhildur (2006) Personal correspondence with the author. 4 February 2006.

Hagalín, Hrafnhildur (2001) *Easy Now, Electra*. Trans. Brian FitzGibbon. Ed. Alan Barr. *Modern Women Playwrights of Europe*. Oxford and New York: Oxford University Press. 562–92.

Hagalín, Hrafnhildur (2000) Interview by Melkorka Tekla Ólafsdóttir. Programme for *Hægan, Elektra* at the National Theatre of Iceland (February 2000). Trans. Lovísa Árnadóttir.

Hall, Edith (1996) 'A Real Turn-Off, Strophe.' Review of *Phaedra's Love*. *The Times Literary Supplement*, 7 June.

Hall, Edith, Macintosh, Fiona and Wrigley, Amanda eds (2004) *Dionysus Since 1969*. Oxford: Oxford University Press.

Hall, Edith, Macintosh, Fiona and Taplin, Oliver eds (2000) *Medea in Performance: 1500–2000*. Oxford: Legenda.

Harrison, Tony (2002) *Plays: Two*. London: Faber and Faber.

Hart, Lynda ed. (1992) *Making a Spectacle: Feminist Essays on Contemporary Women's Theatre*. Ann Arbor: University of Michigan Press.

Hazel, Ruth (2000) 'Performing the Bacchae.' www2.open.ac.uk/Classical Studies/GreekPlays/GreekDramaVideoImages/HazelPPtalk.htm. Accessed 14 January 2010.

Heath, John (2005) *The Talking Greeks*. Cambridge: Cambridge University Press.

Hemming, Sarah (1996) 'The "Phaedra" Myth Updated.' Review of *Phaedra's Love. The Financial Times*, 23 May.

Hersh, Allison (1992) '"How Sweet the Kill": Orgiastic Female Violence in Contemporary Re-visions of Euripides' *The Bacchae.' Modern Drama* 35. 409–23.

Herzog, Dagmar (2005) *Sex after Fascism: Memory and Morality in Twentieth-Century Germany*. Princeton: Princeton University Press.

Hirst, David (1989) *Dario Fo and Franca Rame*. London: Macmillan.

Hodges, Andrew and Hutter, David (1974) 'With Downcast Gays.' Gay Liberation pamphlet. Http://www.outgay.co.uk/wdg3.html. Accessed 23 November 2009.

Honko, Lauri (1972) 'The Problem of Defining Myth.' Ed. Alan Dundes (1984) *Sacred Narrative: Readings in the Theory of Myth*. Berkeley: University of California Press. 41–52.

Hoyle, Martin (1989) Review of *The Love of the Nightingale. The Financial Times*, 24 August.

Hoyle, Martin (1986) Review of *A Mouthful of Birds. The Financial Times*, 3 September.

Ionesco, Eugène (1964) *Notes and Counter Notes*. Trans. Donald Watson. New York: Grove Press.

Irigaray, Luce (1993) *Je, tu, nous: Toward a Culture of Difference*. Trans. Alison Martin. London: Routledge.

Jacobus, Mary (2002) 'Complex Electra: Clytemnestra's Daughters.' *Didaskalia* 5: 3. www.didaskalia.net/issues/vol5no3/jacobus.html. Accessed 16 November 2009.

Jameson, Fredric (1983) 'Postmodernism and Consumer Society'. Ed. Hal Foster. *Postmodern Culture*. London: Pluto Press. 111–25.

Jefferson, Lara (1975) *These Are My Sisters: A Journal from the Inside of Insanity*. London: Victor Gollancz Ltd.

Jones, Ann Rosalind (1985) 'Writing the Body: Toward an Understanding of *l'Écriture féminine.'* Ed. Elaine Showalter (1986) *The New Feminist Criticism*. London: Virago. 361–77.

Jones, Kathy ed. (1996) *On Finding Treasure: Mystery Plays of the Goddess*. Glastonbury: Ariadne Publications.

Jung, Carl (1971) *The Collected Works of C.G. Jung. Vol. 6. Psychological Types*. Trans. R.F.C. Hull. London: Routledge and Kegan Paul.

Jung, Carl (1969) *The Collected Works of C.G. Jung. Vol. 8. The Structure and Dynamics of the Psyche*. Trans. R.F.C. Hull. London: Routledge and Kegan Paul.

Jung, Carl (1968) *The Collected Works of C.G. Jung. Vol. 9 Part 1. The Archetypes and the Collective Unconscious.* Trans. R.F.C. Hull. London: Routledge and Kegan Paul.

Jung, Carl (1961) *The Collected Works of C.G. Jung. Vol. 4. Freud and Psychoanalysis.* Trans. R.F.C. Hull. London: Routledge and Kegan Paul.

Jung, Carl (1959) *The Collected Works of C.G. Jung. Vol. 9 Part 2. Aion: Researches into the Phenomenology of the Self.* Trans. R.F.C. Hull. London: Routledge and Kegan Paul.

Jung, Carl (1953) *The Collected Works of C.G. Jung. Vol. 7. Two Essays on Analytical Psychology.* Trans. R.F.C. Hull. London: Routledge and Kegan Paul.

Jung, Carl and Kerényi, Carl (2002) *The Science of Mythology.* Trans. R.F.C. Hull. London and New York: Routledge.

Kane, Sarah (2001) *Complete Plays.* London: Methuen.

Keene, Charles Haine (1893) *The Electra of Euripides.* London: George Bell and Sons.

Kemp, Sandra and Bono, Paola (1993) *The Lonely Mirror: Italian Perspectives on Feminist Theory.* London: Routledge.

Kemp, Sandra and Squires, Judith eds (1997) *Feminisms.* Oxford and New York: Oxford University Press.

Knapp, Bettina (1989) *Women in Twentieth-Century Literature: A Jungian View.* University Park: Pennsylvania State University Press.

Komar, Kathleen (2003) *Reclaiming Klytemnestra: Revenge or Reconciliation.* Urbana: University of Illinois Press.

Lacan, Jacques (2001) *Écrits: A Selection.* London and New York: Routledge.

Lacan, Jacques (1997) *The Seminar of Jacques Lacan. Book 7: The Ethics of Psychoanalysis.* Ed. Jacques-Alain Miller. Trans. Dennis Porter. New York and London: Norton.

Lacan, Jacques (1981) *The Seminar of Jacques Lacan. Book 11: The Four Fundamental Concepts of Psychoanalysis.* Ed. Jacques-Alain Miller. Trans. Alan Sheridan. New York and London: Norton.

Lapointe, François and Lapointe, Claire (1977) *Claude Lévi-Strauss and His Critics.* New York: Garland.

Larrington, Carolyne ed. (1992) *The Feminist Companion to Mythology.* London: Pandora.

Lauter, Estella (1984) *Women as Mythmakers: Poetry and Visual Art by Twentieth-Century Women.* Bloomington: Indiana University Press.

Lawler, Steph (2000) *Mothering the Self: Mothers, Daughters, Subjects.* London and New York: Routledge.

Leeming, David Alan (1990) *The World of Myth.* New York: Oxford University Press.

Lehmann, Hans-Thies (2006) *Postdramatic Theatre.* Trans. Karen Jürs-Munby. London and New York: Routledge.

Leonard, Miriam (2006) 'Lacan, Irigaray, and Beyond: Antigones and the Politics of Psychoanalysis.' Eds Vanda Zajko and Miriam Leonard. 121–39.

Lévi-Strauss, Claude (1995) *Myth and Meaning.* New York: Schocken Books.

Lévi-Strauss, Claude (1985) *The View From Afar.* Trans. Joachim Heugroschel and Phoebe Hoss. Oxford: Blackwell.

Lévi-Strauss, Claude (1966) *The Savage Mind.* Trans. John and Doreen Weightman. London: George Weidenfeld and Nicolson Ltd.

Lévi-Strauss, Claude (1963) *Structural Anthropology.* Trans. Claire Jacobson and Brooke Grundfest Schoepf. London: Allen Lane Penguin Press.

Lewis, Ioan (1971) *Ecstatic Religion: an Anthropological Study of Spirit Possession and Shamanism.* Harmondsworth: Penguin.

Lipking, Lawrence (1988) *Abandoned Women and Poetic Tradition.* Chicago and London: University of Chicago Press.

Lloyd, Michael (2005) *Sophocles: Electra.* London: Duckworth.

Lonzi, Carla (1970) 'Let's Spit on Hegel.' Eds Paola Bono and Sandra Kemp. Trans. Veronica Newman (1991) *Italian Feminist Thought: A Reader.* Oxford and Cambridge, Massachusetts: Blackwell. 40–59.

Lorde, Audre (1984) *Sister Outsider: Essays and Speeches.* Berkeley: Crossing Press.

Magnússon, Sigurdur ed. (1973) *Modern Nordic Plays: Iceland.* New York: Twayne.

Marcuse, Herbert (1965) 'Repressive Tolerance.' Robert Wolff, Barrington Moore, Jr and Herbert Marcuse. *A Critique of Pure Tolerance.* Boston: Beacon Press. 81–123.

Marks, John (1998) *Gilles Deleuze: Vitalism and Multiplicity.* London: Pluto Press.

Mazor, Marya (2010) Personal correspondence with the author. 5 January.

McCabe, Richard (1993) *Incest, Drama and Nature's Law 1550–1700.* Cambridge: Cambridge University Press.

McDonald, Marianne (2003) *The Living Art of Greek Tragedy.* Bloomington: Indiana University Press.

Michielsen, John (1990) 'Hella S. Haasse (1918–).' *Canadian Journal of Netherlandic Studies* 11: 2: 'Women Writers in the Netherlands and Flanders.' 46–50.

Mitchell, Juliet and Rose, Jacqueline eds (1982) *Feminine Sexuality: Jacques Lacan and the École Freudienne.* London: Macmillan.

Mitchell, Tony ed. (1989) *File on Fo.* London: Methuen.

Moi, Toril (1985) *Sexual/Textual Politics.* London: Routledge

Moogk, Peter (1995) 'Nederland Ontwaak!: The Nazis' Failure to Win Over the Dutch During the Occupation.' *Canadian Journal of Netherlandic Studies* 16: 2. 42–9.

Morrissey, Belinda (2003) *When Women Kill: Questions of Agency and Subjectivity*. London and New York: Routledge.

Moseley, John (1996) Review of *Phaedra's Love*. *Camden New Journal*. June 6 1996.

Moss, Jane (1987) 'Women's Theatre in France.' *Signs* 12. 548–67.

Murray, Gilbert (1906) *Euripides: The Athenian Drama Vol. 3*. London: G. Allen.

Neumann, Erich (1955) *The Great Mother: An Analysis of the Archetype*. Trans. Ralph Manheim. New York: Pantheon Books.

O'Neill, Eugene (1966) *Mourning Becomes Electra*. London: Jonathan Cape.

Ostriker, Alicia (1986) 'The Thieves of Language: Women Poets and Revisionist Mythmaking.' Ed. Elaine Showalter. *The New Feminist Criticism*. London: Virago. 314–38.

Ovid (1955) *The Metamorphoses of Ovid*. Trans. Mary Innes. Harmondsworth: Penguin.

Pater, Walter (2002) 'The Bacchanals of Euripides.' *Greek Studies: A Series of Essays*. Honolulu, Hawaii: University Press of the Pacific. 49–79.

Patterson, Michael (2003) *Strategies of Political Theatre: Post-War British Playwrights*. Cambridge and New York: Cambridge University Press.

Pavlides, Merope (1986) 'Restructuring the Traditional: An Examination of Hélène Cixous' *Le Nom d'Oedipe*.' Ed. Karelisa Hartigan. *Within the Dramatic Spectrum*. Lanham Maryland and London: University Press of America. 151–9.

Phillips, Caryl (2005) 'No Thanks, Ma'am.' *The Guardian*, 15 June.

Picard, Anne-Marie (1999) '*Le Père de l'Écriture*: Writing Within the Secret Father.' Eds Lee Jacobus and Regina Barreca. *Hélène Cixous: Critical Impressions*. Amsterdam: Overseas Publishers Association: Gordon and Breach. 23–56.

Piccolo, Pina (2000) 'Rame, Fo and the Tragic Grotesque: the Politics of Women's Experience.' Ed. Valeri. 115–38.

Pinkola Estés, Clarissa (1992) *Women Who Run With the Wolves*. New York: Ballantine Books.

Poesio, Paolo Emilio (1979) Review of *Tutta casa, letto e chiesa*. *La Nazione*, 17 March. Http://www.archivio.francarame.it. Accessed 12 June 2006.

Pomeroy, Sarah (1994) *Goddesses, Whores, Wives, and Slaves: Women in Classical Antiquity*. London and Sydney: Random House.

Prenowitz, Eric ed. (2004) *Selected Plays of Hélène Cixous*. London and New York: Routledge.

Purkiss, Diane (1992) 'Women's Rewriting of Myth.' Ed. Carolyne Larrington. 441–57.

Purvis, Andrew (2006) 'Why Merkel Is Not Enough.' January 22 2006.

www.time.com/time/europe/html/060130/story.html.   Accessed   16 November 2009.

Rame, Franca (2004) 'I Am Ready.' Interview by Stefania Taviano. *The Open Page 9: Theatre, Women, Struggle.* Holstebro: Odin Teatret Forlag. 19–23.

Rame, Franca and Fo, Dario (1991) *A Woman Alone and Other Plays.* London: Methuen.

Rame, Franca and Fo, Dario (1989) *Venticinque monologhi per una donna.* Turin: Einaudi.

Ravenhill, Mark (1999) Obituary for Sarah Kane. *Independent,* 23 February.

Re, Lucia (2002) 'Diotima's Dilemmas: Authorship, Authority, Authoritarianism.' Eds Graziella Parati and Rebecca West. *Italian Feminist Theory and Practice.* Cranbury, New Jersey, Mississanga, Ontario and London: Associated University Presses. 50–74.

Rebellato, Dan (1999) 'Sarah Kane: An Appreciation.' *New Theatre Quarterly* 15: 3. 280–1.

Reich, Wilhelm (1969) *The Sexual Revolution: Toward a Self-Governing Character Structure.* Trans. Theodore Wolf. London: Vision.

Reinelt, Janelle (2003) 'States of Play: Feminism, Gender Studies and Performance.' *The Scholar and Feminist Online,* 2: 1, Summer 2003. http://www.barnard.edu/sfonline/ps/reinelt3.htm. Accessed 26 March 2008.

Reitz, Bernhard and Von Rothkirch, Alyce eds (2001) *Crossing Borders: Intercultural Drama and Theatre at the Turn of the Millennium.* Trier: WVT.

Remnant, Mary ed. (1988) *Plays by Women: Vol. 7.* London: Methuen.

Remnant, Mary ed. (1987) *Plays by Women: Vol. 6.* London: Methuen.

Reynolds, Margaret (2000) 'Performing Medea; or, Why Is Medea a Woman?' Eds Hall, Macintosh and Taplin. 119–43.

Rich, Adrienne (1979) *On Lies, Secrets, and Silence: Selected Prose 1966–1978.* New York: Norton.

Richardson, Diane (2000) *Rethinking Sexuality.* London: Sage.

Rippl, Gabriele (2004) 'Culture and Transgression: Phaedra's Illicit Love and Its Cultural Transformations.' *REAL (Research in English and American Literature)* 20. 165–82.

Rissik, Andrew (1986) Review of *A Mouthful of Birds. The Times,* 4 September.

Robson, Cheryl ed. (1997) *A Touch of the Dutch: Plays by Women.* Amsterdam and London: Nederland Theater Institut and Aurora Metro Press.

Rogerson, J.W. (1979) 'Slippery Words: Myth'. Ed. Alan Dundes (1984) *Sacred Narrative: Readings in the Theory of Myth.* Berkeley: University of California Press. 62–71.

Roisman, Hanna (2000) 'A New Look at Seneca's *Phaedra*'. Ed. George Harrison (2000) *Seneca in Performance*. London: Duckworth. 73–86.

Rubik, Margarete (1996) 'Fringe or Mainstream: What Is Marketable?' Ed. Peter Paul Schnierer. *Contemporary Drama in English, Vol. 4. Beyond the Mainstream*. Trier: WVT. 15–24.

Rumens, Carol (1986) 'Inquisitors versus Handmaidens.' *Times Literary Supplement*, 11 July.

Rushdie, Salman (1990) *Haroun and the Sea of Stories*. London: Granta Books.

Sajé, Natasha (1994) *Red Under the Skin*. Pittsburgh: University of Pittsburgh Press.

Saltzman, Pauline (1960) 'Ouija Board Messages for Ella Wheeler Wilcox.' *Fate Magazine* 13: 9. www.ellawheelerwilcox.org. Accessed 23 November 2009.

Sartori, Serena (2006) Personal correspondence with the author. 4 August.

Sartori, Serena and Coluccini, Renata (1995) *Demeter Beneath the Sand*. Trans. Susan Bassnett. *Contemporary Theatre Review* 2: 3. 114–27.

Saunders, Graham (2009) *About Kane: The Playwright and the Work*. London: Faber and Faber.

Saunders, Graham (2002) *'Love me or kill me': Sarah Kane and the Theatre of Extremes*. Manchester and New York: Manchester University Press.

Saunders, Graham and De Vos, Laurens eds (2010) *Sarah Kane in Context*. Manchester and New York: Manchester University Press.

Schechner, Richard (1994) *Environmental Theater*. New York: Applause.

Schmidt, Michael (1988) Review of *The Love of the Nightingale*. *The Daily Telegraph*, 15 November.

Segal, Lynne (1990) *Slow Motion: Changing Masculinities, Changing Men*. London: Virago.

Seidler, Victor (1989) *Rediscovering Masculinity*. London: Routledge.

Sellers, Susan (2001) *Myth and Fairy Tale in Contemporary Women's Fiction*. Basingstoke and New York: Palgrave.

Seneca (1987) *Phaedra*. Ed. and trans. A.J. Boyle. Liverpool: Francis Cairns.

Shiach, Morag (1991) *Hélène Cixous: A Politics of Writing*. London: Routledge.

Shorter, Eric (1986) Review of *A Mouthful of Birds*. *The Daily Telegraph*, 8 September.

Shulman, Milton (1986) 'Men – It's All Your Fault.' Review of *Neaptide*. *London Standard*, 3 July.

Sierz, Aleks (2001) *In-Yer-Face Theatre: British Drama Today*. London: Faber and Faber.

Sigurjónsson, Hávar (2001) 'Icelandic Theater, 1975–2000.' Transcript of a talk given at the *Scandinavia On Stage* conference, New York

19 April 2001. Http://www.nytheatre-wire.com/icelandictheater.htm. Accessed 13 November 2009.

Smith, Barbara (1992) 'Greece'. Ed. Carolyne Larrington. *The Feminist Companion to Mythology.* London, Pandora. 65–101.

Smith, Mal (1999) 'Sarah Kane: A Nineties "Take" on Cruelty'. *Antonin Artaud and His Legacy.* London: Theatre Museum Education Pack.

Sophocles (1984) *The Three Theban Plays.* Trans. Robert Fagles. Harmondsworth: Penguin.

Sophocles (1953) *Electra and Other Plays.* Trans. E.F. Watling. London: Penguin.

Sophocles (1912) *The Tragedies of Sophocles.* Trans. Richard Jebb. Cambridge: Cambridge University Press.

Spencer, Charles (2004) Review of *By the Bog of Cats. The Independent,* 2 December.

Spencer, Charles (1996) 'All Lust and Casual Atrocity.' Review of *Phaedra's Love. The Daily Telegraph,* 22 May.

Spencer, Charles (1989) Review of *The Love of the Nightingale. The Daily Telegraph,* 25 August.

Stallybrass, Peter and White, Allon (1986) *The Politics and Poetics of Transgression.* London: Methuen.

Stephenson, Heidi and Langridge, Natasha (1997) *Rage and Reason: Women Playwrights on Playwriting.* London: Methuen.

Stratton, Kate (1996) 'Grotesque Passions of the Royal Family.' Review of *Phaedra's Love. Evening Standard,* 21 May.

Sutton, Dana (1984) *The Lost Sophocles.* Lanham, New York, and London: University Press of America.

Taplin, Oliver (1985) *Greek Tragedy in Action.* London: Routledge.

Tatar, Maria (1992) *Off With Their Heads! Fairy Tales and the Culture of Childhood.* Princeton: Princeton University Press.

Tatar, Maria (1987) *The Hard Facts of the Grimms' Fairy Tales.* Princeton: Princeton University Press.

Taylor, Jolanda Vanderwal (1994) 'Hella S. Haasse.' Ed. Kristiaan Aercke (1994) *Women Writing in Dutch.* New York and London: Garland Publishing. 423–44.

Taylor, Paul (2004) Review of *By the Bog of Cats. The Independent,* 6 December.

Tennant, Emma (1975) 'Philomela.' Ed. Malcolm Bradbury (1987) *The Penguin Book of Modern Short Stories.* London: Penguin. 407–13.

Tew, George (2004) Review of *Phaedra's Love* at the Burton Taylor Theatre, Oxford. 26 May. www.dailyinfo.co.uk/reviews/theatre/phaedraslove.htm. Accessed 10 November 2005.

Thomas, Helen (1995) *Dance, Modernity and Culture.* London: Routledge.

Thorbergsson, Magnús Thór (2004) 'Second Fiddle.' *Nordic Literature*

2004. Http://www.nordic- literature.org/2004/english/articles/143.htm. Accessed 13 November 2009.

Thornber, Robin (1986) Review of *A Mouthful of Birds*. *The Guardian*, 4 September.

Tommasini, Anthony (1998) 'A Feminist Look at Sophocles.' Review of *Jocasta* by Vision and Voice at the Cornelia Connelly Center for Education, New York. 11 June. www.nytimes.com/1998/06/11/arts/opera-review-a-feminist-look-at-sophocles.html. Accessed 10 December 2009.

Turner, Barry and Nordquist, Gunilla (1982) *The Other European Community: Integration and Co-operation in Nordic Europe*. London: Weidenfeld and Nicolson.

Ucko, Peter (1968) *Anthropomorphic Figurines of Predynastic Egypt and Neolithic Crete*. London: Royal Anthropological Institute: A. Szmidla.

Uskalis, Ericks (2000) 'Contextualizing Myth in Postcolonial Novels: Figures of Dissent and Disruption.' *Jouvert: Journal of Postcolonial Studies* 5: 1. http://english.chass.ncsu.edu/jouvert/v5i1/uskal.htm. Accessed 11 January 2010.

Ussher, Jane (1997) *Fantasies of Femininity: Reframing the Boundaries of Sex*. London: Penguin.

Valeri, Walter ed. (2000) *Franca Rame: A Woman on Stage*. West Lafayette Indiana: Bordighera.

Van Buuren, Hannah (1986) 'Hella S. Haasse et le thème du labyrinthe.' *Septentrion* 15. 12–14.

Van Deursen, Jackelien and Eggermont, Pol *et al.* (1994) 'The Netherlands.' Ed. Don Rubin. *The World Encyclopaedia of Contemporary Theatre: Vol. 1. Europe*. London: Routledge. 596–615.

Varley, Julia ed. (1998) *The Open Page 3: Theatre – Women – Politics*. Holstebro: Odin Teatret Forlag.

Vellacott, Philip (1984) *The Logic of Tragedy*. Durham, North Carolina: Duke University Press.

Vellacott, Philip (1975) *Ironic Drama: A Study of Euripides' Method and Meaning*. Cambridge, London and New York: Cambridge University Press.

Vermij, Lucie ed. (1992) *Women Writers from the Netherlands and Flanders*. Trans. Greta Kilburn. Amsterdam: International Feminist Book Fair Press.

Volli, Ugo (1977) Review of *Tutta casa, letto e chiesa*. *La Repubblica*. 6 December.

Von Kleist, Heinrich (1988) *Penthesilea. Five Plays*. Trans. Martin Greenberg. New Haven and London: Yale University Press. 159–268.

Waelti-Walters, Jennifer (1982) *Fairy Tales and the Female Imagination*. Montreal: Eden Press.

Wagner, Jennifer (1995) 'Formal Parody and the Metamorphosis of the

Audience in Timberlake Wertenbaker's *The Love of the Nightingale*.' *Papers on Language and Literature* 31: 3. 227–54.

Walker, Barbara (1996) *Feminist Fairy Tales*. New York: HarperCollins.

Walker, Barbara (1995) *The Woman's Encyclopedia of Myths and Secrets*. London: Pandora.

Walker, Martha (2001) 'Rehabilitating Feminist Politics and Political Theatre: Hélène Cixous's *La Ville Parjure ou le réveil des Erinyes* at the Théâtre du Soleil.' *Modern and Contemporary France* 9: 4. 495–506.

Wandor, Michelene (1987) *Look Back in Gender*. London: Methuen.

Wardle, Irving (1986) 'Anger from the Head not the Gut.' Review of *Neaptide*. *The Times*, 3 July.

Warner, Marina (1994a) *From the Beast to the Blonde: On Fairytales and Their Tellers*. London: Chatto and Windus.

Warner, Marina (1994b) *Managing Monsters: Six Myths of Our Time (The Reith Lectures)*. London: Vintage.

Watson, Patricia (1995) *Ancient Stepmothers: Myth, Misogyny and Reality*. Leiden, New York and Cologne: E.J. Brill.

Wertenbaker, Timberlake (2004) 'The Voices We Hear.' Eds Hall, Macintosh and Wrigley. 361–8.

Wertenbaker, Timberlake (1989) *The Love of the Nightingale*. London: Faber and Faber.

Whitmont, Edward (1983) *Return of the Goddess: Femininity, Aggression and the Modern Grail Quest*. London: Routledge and Kegan Paul.

Wilcox, Ella Wheeler (1883a) 'Solitude.' www.ellawheelerwilcox.org. Accessed 23 November 2009.

Wilcox, Ella Wheeler (1883b) Letter to Lucy Larcom. 27 July. www.ellawheelerwilcox.org. Accessed 23 November 2009.

Winkler, Elizabeth Hale (1993) 'Three Recent Versions of *The Bacchae*.' Ed. James Redmond. *Themes in Drama Vol. 7: Drama, Sex and Politics*. Cambridge and New York: Cambridge University Press. 217–28.

Winston, Joe (1995) 'Re-Casting the Phaedra Syndrome: Myth and Morality in Timberlake Wertenbaker's *The Love of the Nightingale*.' *Modern Drama* 38: 4. 510–19.

Wolf, Matt (2004) Review of *By the Bog of Cats*. *Daily Variety*, 8 December.

Wood, Sharon (2000) '*Parliamo di donne*: Feminism and Politics in the Theater of Franca Rame.' Eds Joseph Farrell and Antonio Scuderi. *Dario Fo: Stage, Text, and Tradition*. Carbondale and Edwardsville: Southern Illinois University Press. 161–80.

Woods, Leigh (2001) 'Iceland: The Contemporary Theatre Scene.' *Western European Stages* 13: 1. Ed. Marvin Carlson. 99–102.

Woods, Leigh and Gunnarsdóttir, Ágústa (1997) *Public Selves Political Stages: Interviews with Icelandic Women in Government and Theatre*. Amsterdam: Harwood Academic Publishers.

Worth, Katharine (1989) 'Images of Women in Modern English Theater.' Ed. Brater. 3–24.

Yourcenar, Marguérite (1971) *Théâtre II*. Paris: Gallimard.

Yourcenar, Marguérite (1984) *Plays*. Trans. Dori Katz. New York: Performing Arts Journal Publications.

Zajko, Vanda and Leonard, Miriam eds (2006) *Laughing With Medusa: Classical Myth and Feminist Thought*. Oxford and New York: Oxford University Press.

Zipes, Jack (1994) *Fairy Tale as Myth: Myth as Fairy Tale*. Lexington, Kentucky: University Press of Kentucky.

Zipes, Jack ed. (1986) *Don't Bet on the Prince*. Aldershot: Gower.

Index

Aeschylus 8, 78, 175, 177, 179,
    216, 218, 228n.19
  Agamemnon 216
  Eumenides, The 8, 78, 175,
    176, 177–8, 181, 216
  Libation Bearers, The 216–18,
    221
Anouilh, Jean 4, 37, 39–40,
    180
Antigone, in myth 33, 153, 164
archetypes 15–16, 30, 49, 71, 85,
    88, 99, 140, 142, 146–62
    passim, 165, 231, 232–3
Ariadne, in myth 36–47 *passim*
Árnadóttir, Nina Björk 212,
    227n.14
Artaud, Antonin 207–8

Bakhtin, Mikhail 31, 136–7n.11
Barthes, Roland 19–21, 24, 51,
    59
Bascom, William 12
Beckett, Samuel 213
Brecht, Bertolt 4, 53, 55, 198
Butler, Judith 64, 223
Butterworth, Jez 192, 225n.3

carnival 100, 102, 132, 136n.11,
    205
Carr, Marina 1–4, 33
  By the Bog of Cats 1–4, 33,
    54

Carter, Angela 10, 12, 23
Cavarero, Adriana 25, 29–32, 37,
    38, 44, 46n.3, 46n.4, 69,
    71, 171–2, 174, 210, 217,
    228n.18
Churchill, Caryl 4, 98–103,
    111–24, 197, 198
  David Lan and 8, 95, 115, 132,
    135n.2, 140
  Mouthful of Birds, A 8, 95–6,
    99–103, 111–24, 126, 131–2,
    137n.13, 137n.15, 142
  Skriker, The 112
  Vinegar Tom 111–12
Cixous, Hélène 4, 6, 8, 15, 17,
    28–9, 36, 41, 62, 139–40,
    142–5, 162–86, 217, 218
  *Name of Oedipus: Song of
    the Forbidden Body,
    The* 8, 143–5, 162–74,
    182, 184
  *Perjured City, or The
    Awakening of the Furies,
    The* 8, 143–5, 162, 163,
    174–86, 217
  Portrait of Dora 162
  *Terrible but Unfinished Story
    of Norodom Sihanouk,
    King of Cambodia* 162
Clytemnestra, in myth 33, 97,
    150–1, 158, 189, 213,
    215–19

Cocteau, Jean 4
Coluccini, Renata 6, 8, 142,
    146–62, 233
    Demeter Beneath the Sand 6,
    7, 8, 35, 142–62
    Teatro Cooperative del Sole 8,
    35, 142, 146–7, 154
Cremer, Gilla 6, 7, 231–8
    m.e.d.e.a. 7, 231–8

Daly, Mary 26–8
Daniels, Sarah 7, 48, 51–3,
    73–91
    Masterpieces 73–4, 76
    Neaptide 7, 48, 51–4, 73–92,
    93
De Beauvoir, Simone 15, 21, 22
Deleuze, Gilles 118–19, 123
Demeter, in myth 30, 35, 46n.4,
    51, 52–3, 77–8, 80–5, 87–8,
    148, 151–2, 158
Dionysos, in myth 39, 93–6, 99,
    104, 110, 120, 122, 131–2,
    136n.8
Diotima group 32
Diotima, in myth 30, 46n.4
Doniger, Wendy 18–19, 20
Duffy, Maureen 8, 94–111, 132,
    136n.10, 137n.14, 140
    Rites 8, 94–5, 98–111, 112,
    126, 131, 132, 137n.12
Dworkin, Andrea 27

écriture féminine 28–9, 143,
    165–6, 172
Electra, in myth 33, 125, 164,
    189, 213, 215–19
Eliade, Mircea 11
Eliot, Alexander 12
Eliot, T.S. 4, 102, 135n.3
essentialism 27, 32, 141
Euripides 1, 2, 8, 34, 46–7n.6,
    54, 67, 93–124 *passim*, 128,
    175, 198, 199, 200, 218

Bacchae, The 8, 93–6, 98,
    103–24 *passim*, 133, 135n.1,
    140, 206
Electra 217–18, 221, 228n.19,
    228n.20
Hippolytus 124, 128, 198, 199,
    202, 209, 225–6n.5, 226n.6,
    226n.7
Iphigenia in Aulis 175
Medea 2, 33, 34, 54, 67, 231,
    232, 237n.9
Trojan Women, The 124

Forced Entertainment 194
Foucault, Michel 120–1, 124,
    130
Frazer, James 12–14, 15, 17, 18,
    25, 46n.1
Freud, Sigmund 14–16, 17, 18, 20,
    25, 140–3, 166–7, 215, 222,
    223, 227n.15, 227–8n.16
    Oedipus the King, interpre-
    tation of 14–15, 215

Gadon, Elinor 25–6
Giradoux, Jean 37
Greenham Common peace
    protests 114
Greig, David 192
Grimm, Jakob and Wilhelm 11
Guattari, Félix *see* Deleuze,
    Gilles

Haasse, Hella 6, 7, 37–46, 47n.10,
    49, 52, 54, 69
    Thread in the Dark, A 6, 7,
    32, 37–46, 47n.8, 47n.9, 52,
    54, 69
Hagalín, Hrafnhildur 6, 8,
    187–96, 203, 210–28
    Easy Now, Electra 6, 8, 188,
    189, 195, 203, 210–28
    I am the Maestro 210–12,
    225n.2

Harrison, Tony 198, 226n.8
Homer 30, 47n.7, 102, 157
Hunter, Holly 1–3, 33

improvisation 16, 57, 112, 146,
    154–5, 159, 195, 213, 219,
    223–5
in-yer-face theatre 9, 187, 191–4,
    196
Ionesco, Eugène 213

Jakobsdóttir, Svava 212,
    227n.14
Jameson, Fredric 116–18,
    137n.16
Jefferson, Lara 82
Jung, Carl 15–17, 140–2, 146,
    148, 150, 151, 157–60, 215

Kamban, Guthmundur 211
Kane, Sarah 4, 8, 187–210, 212,
    225n.1, 225n.3
    4:48 Psychosis 188, 194
    Blasted 192, 196–7, 205, 207,
        225n.3
    Cleansed 192
    Crave 187, 194
    Phaedra's Love 8, 188, 192–4,
        196–210
Kantor, Tadeusz 194

Lacan, Jacques 20, 28, 116,
    141–3, 166–8
Lévi-Strauss, Claude 17–19,
    46n.1
Lorde, Audre 27

McDonagh, Martin 192
Magdalena Project 6, 236n.3
Mazor, Marya 173–4
Medea, in myth 1, 2, 4, 9n.1,
    33, 36, 49, 66–72 passim,
    93, 97, 125, 133, 150, 151,
    158–9, 229–36 passim

Miller, Arthur 188
Mnouchkine, Ariane 4, 143,
    162, 174–8 passim, 185,
    186n.5
Müller, Heiner 4, 194, 237n.9

Nagy, Phyllis 192
Neilson, Anthony 192

O'Neill, Eugene 4, 218
Ovid 38–9, 47n.7, 96, 98, 125–6,
    127, 134, 135n.1, 135n.4,
    138n.23, 141, 186n.2

parrhesia 124, 130–2
Penelope, in myth 30–1, 36, 37,
    46n.4, 172
Penhall, Joe 192
Penthesilea, in myth 148, 150,
    151, 155–8
Phaedra, in myth 33, 97, 128,
    137n.20, 148, 150, 151,
    158, 193, 197–210 passim,
    225–6n.5, 226n.6, 226n.7
Philomela, in myth 35, 96–8,
    125–38 passim
Pinter, Harold 188
postdramatic theatre 8, 9, 191,
    194–6, 212, 213, 232
Pritchard, Rebecca 192
Purkiss, Diane 17, 21, 24, 33

Rame, Franca 6, 7, 34, 46n.6,
    48, 50–73, 87, 90n.6, 93,
    232
    Dario Fo and 7, 48, 50–1,
        56–8, 72, 90n.3, 91n.12,
        146, 234
    Medea 7, 34, 46–7n.6, 48,
        50–4, 59, 65–72, 90n.2,
        91n.11, 93, 232–4
    Same Old Story, The 7, 48,
        50–4, 59–65, 66, 68, 72, 87,
        90n.2, 90n.4, 233

Ravenhill, Mark 192, 193, 212,
    225n.3
reflectionist and interventionist
    models 53–6
Rich, Adrienne 22–3, 191, 210,
    224, 228n.18
Ridley, Philip 192

Sartori, Serena *see* Coluccini,
    Renata
Sartre, Jean-Paul 4, 37
Schechner, Richard
    Dionysos in 69 94
Seneca 197–209 *passim*, 226n.7,
    227n.11
    Phaedra 197–202, 204,
        205–6, 209, 226n.7,
        227n.11
    Thyestes 198
Serban, Andrei 4
Sigurjónsson, Jóhan 211
Simic, Lena
    Medea/Mothers' Clothes 230,
        236, 237n.4
Socìetas Raffaello Sanzio 194
solo performance 7, 64, 146, 230,
    231, 233–6, 237n.7
Sophocles 124, 126, 137–8n.21,
    164, 167, 168, 169, 172, 218,
    228n.19, 228n.20
    Antigone 33, 164
    Electra 33, 103, 218, 228n.19,
        228n.20

Oedipus Rex 14–15, 125, 141,
    166–9, 172, 215
Tereus 126
Soyinka, Wole 94

Templeton, Fiona
    Medead, The 230, 237n.5

Upton, Judy 192

Von Kleist, Heinrich 146, 151,
    157, 186n.1

Wallace, Naomi 192
Warner, Marina 21, 23
Wertenbaker, Timberlake 4, 8, 35,
    96–8, 100–3, 124–38, 140
    Credible Witness 124
    Deianeira 124
    Hecuba 124
    Love of the Nightingale, The 8,
        35–6, 96–103, 124–38
    Our Country's Good 96
Wilcox, Ella Wheeler 83, 91n.19,
    91n.20
Wilson, Robert 4, 194

Yourcenar, Marguerite 37, 47n.7,
    146

Zecora Ura
    Hotel Medea 230
Zipes, Jack 11, 22–3